2006

THE ETHICAL DIMENSIONS OF SCHOOL LEADERSHIP

STUDIES IN EDUCATIONAL LEADERSHIP

VOLUME 1

SCOPE OF THE SERIES

Leadership we know makes all the difference in success or failures of organizations. This series will bring together in a highly readable way the most recent insights in successful leadership. Emphasis will be placed on research focused on pre-collegiate educational organizations. Volumes should address issues related to leadership at all levels of the educational system and be written in a style accessible to scholars, educational practitioners and policy makers throughout the world.

The volumes – monographs and edited volumes – should represent work from different parts in the world.

THE ETHICAL DIMENSIONS OF SCHOOL LEADERSHIP

Edited by

PAUL T. BEGLEY

The Ontario Institute for Studies in Education,
University of Toronto, Ontario, Canada

and

OLOF JOHANSSON

Department of Political Science,
University of Umea, Sweden

KLUWER ACADEMIC PUBLISHERS
DORDRECHT / BOSTON / LONDON

A C.I.P. Catalogue record for this book is available from the Library of Congress.

ISBN 1-4020-1159-8 (HB)
ISBN 1-4020-1160-1 (PB)

Published by Kluwer Academic Publishers,
P.O. Box 17, 3300 AA Dordrecht, The Netherlands.

Sold and distributed in North, Central and South America
by Kluwer Academic Publishers,
101 Philip Drive, Norwell, MA 02061, U.S.A.

In all other countries, sold and distributed
by Kluwer Academic Publishers,
P.O. Box 322, 3300 AH Dordrecht, The Netherlands.

Printed on acid-free paper

Printed in the Netherlands.

In Memory of Donald J. Willower

TABLE OF CONTENTS

PART 3: CROSS-CULTURAL PERSPECTIVES ON EDUCATIONAL COMMUNITIES

LIST OF CONTRIBUTORS

Paul T. Begley is Professor and Head of the Centre for the Study of Values and Leadership in the Department of Theory and Policy Studies at the Ontario Institute for Studies in Education of the University of Toronto, Ontario, Canada.

Elizabeth Campbell is Associate Professor in the Department of Theory and Policy Studies at the Ontario Institute for Studies in Education at the University of Toronto, Ontario, Canada.

John L. Collard is Senior Lecturer in the Division of Communication and Education at the University of Canberra, ACT, Australia.

Cyril P. Coombs is Research Associate of the Centre for the Study of Values and Leadership in the Department of Theory and Policy Studies at the Ontario Institute for Studies in Education of the University of Toronto, Ontario, Canada.

Isaac A. Friedman is Director of the Henrietta Szold Institute at the National Institute for Research in the Behavioural Sciences, Jerusalem, Israel.

Christopher Hodgkinson is Professor Emeritus at the Faculty of Education, University of Victoria, British Columbia, Canada.

Olof Johansson is Associate Professor and Head of the Centre for Principal Development at Umeå University, Sweden.

Lawrence J. Leonard is Associate Professor in the Department of Education at the Louisiana Technological University, Ruston, Louisiana, USA.

Pauline E. Leonard is Assistant Professor in the Department of Education at the Louisiana Technological University, Ruston, Louisiana, USA.

Joan Poliner Shapiro is Professor in the Department of Educational Leadership and Policy Studies of the College of Education of Temple University, Philadephia, Pennsylvania, USA.

Malcolm Richmon is Research Associate of the Centre for the Study of Values and Leadership in the Department of Theory and Policy Studies at the Ontario Institute for Studies in Education of the University of Toronto, Ontario, Canada.

Robert J. Starratt is Professor in the School of Graduate Studies in Education at Boston College, Chesnut Hill, Massachusetts, USA.

Jacqueline Stefkovich is Professor in the Department of Educational Policy and Theory at Pennsylvania State University, University Park, Pennsylvania, USA.

Kenneth Strike is Professor and Chair of the Department of Education, Policy, Planning and Administration at the University of Maryland, College Park, Maryland, USA.

Allan D. Walker is Associate Professor in the Department of Educational Administration and Policy of the Chinese University of Hong Kong, Shatin, Hong Kong, SAR, China.

ACKNOWLEDGEMENTS

We are grateful to Tamara Welschot and Esther de Jong at Kluwer Academic Publishers for their patience and steadfast support throughout the preparation of this book. Thanks also to our associates at the Centre for the Study of Values and Leadership (OISE/UT), its affiliate the UCEA Center for the Study of Leadership and Ethics (University of Virginia), and the various manuscript reviewers for their support and helpful comments. With your advice we have produced a better book. In particular, we would like to acknowledge the contribution of Vashty Hawkins and Catherine Hands to the formatting, editing and proofreading of the manuscript.

Chapter 1: In Pursuit of Authentic School Leadership Practices by Paul Begley is a revised and updated version of a paper originally presented at the 2000 Conference of the UCEA Center for the Study of Values and Leadership, Bridgetown, Barbados. It has also been previously published as an article in a special issue (Vol. 4, No. 4, 353-365) of the *International Journal of Leadership in Education* (2001).

Chapter 2: Democratic Leadership Theory in Late Modernity: Oxymoron or Ironic Possibility? by Robert Jerome Starratt is a revised and updated version of a paper originally presented at the 2000 Conference of the UCEA Center for the Study of Values and Leadership, Bridgetown, Barbados. It has also been previously published as an article in a special issue (Vol. 4, No. 4, 333-352) of the *International Journal of Leadership in Education* (2001).

Chapter 3: Let Right Be Done: Trying to Put Ethical Standards into Practice by Elizabeth Campbell was published originally in the *Journal of Education Policy*, and appears with the permission of Taylor and Francis Ltd.

Chapter 8: Valuing Schools as Professional Communities: Assessing the Collaborative Prescription by Lawrence and Pauline Leonard is a revised and updated version of a paper previously published as an article in a special issue (Vol. 4, No. 4, 353-365) of the *International Journal of Leadership in Education* (2001).

Chapter 13: Tomorrow, and Tomorrow, and Tomorrow: A Post-postmodern Purview by Christopher Hodgkinson is a revised and updated version of a paper originally presented at the 2000 Conference of the UCEA Center for the Study of Values and Leadership, Bridgetown, Barbados. It has also been previously published as an article in a special issue (Vol. 4, No. 4, 297-307) of the *International Journal of Leadership in Education* (2001).

EDWARD HICKCOX

FOREWORD

Among the many significant features of this volume is the dedication to the late Don Willower, Professor of Education at Pennsylvania State University. It is significant in light of Willower's long record of major contributions to the empirical literature in Educational Administration and his mentorship of many students steeped in the tradition of the so-called science of administration. These include scholars like Wayne Hoy and Peter Cistone who readily acknowledge their personal and intellectual debt to Willower.

How is it, then, that Willower, a colleague of the giants of Educational Administration in the 60s and 70s, people such as Dan Griffiths, Jack Culbertson, and Roald Campbell, to name just a few, came to associate himself with this relatively upstart group of academics and practitioners interested in values, of all things? As an inheritor of the mantle thrown down by Getzels and Guba all those years ago, it might seem strange to see Willower consorting with people who argue about the distinction between fact and value.

It is true, of course, that Willower majored in philosophy at the State University of New York at Buffalo as an undergraduate. So the language and the ways of thinking among many of those interested in values and ethics were not all that foreign to him. He could certainly hold his own in debate with his friend, Chris Hodgkinson, the foremost philosopher of Educational Administration in the field today, and a contributor to this volume.

But Willower's interest in this thrust, and in the particular group represented by the authors of these papers, was more than simply a connection to his very early undergraduate studies or his ongoing joy in engaging in academic debate of any kind. Rather it had to do, I think, with a recognition on his part that the work of the members of the UCEA Values Centre at Virgina and at OISE represented an important beginning thrust at conceptualizing a new central focus for educational administration, or educational leadership as we now tend to call it.   Perhaps he imagined that over time this thrust would become a defining set of ideas informing research and practice in our field, even as notions of the science of administration had informed activity beginning in the 60s.

Paul Begley, the head of the Values Centre at OISE/UT and the organizer of the conference at which these papers were presented (in Barbados of all places), has an apt phrase in his introduction to the volume. He says that the field of leadership studies should be "a working of the edge of administrative practice..." And that is what I see in this book, efforts to define, to take a creative look at what we do in organizational leadership, to grope here and there for some new synthesis, to thrust up and down, to see what is there.

There are a number of important aspects to the volume. For one thing, there is a kind of global perspective, bursting out, in a sense, from the strictures of strictly western notions of values and their relationship to leadership. The emphasis on community and community values is crucial in this respect. The difficult notions about democracy and values in organization are treated. And there is a lot about self awareness. In a sense, the writers here, and in the previous volumes in this series, are pushing the envelope. But they are pushing it overall in the same direction.

And there is a need. Our field is in a pretty sorry state, in my view. The journals are full of articles unrelated to any central theme or way of thinking. Doctoral students write theses in isolation, seldom linking with any programmatic research program. There is diminishing interest in educational organizations or educational administrators, especially school principals and superintendents. In Canada and the United States, at least, there are fewer and fewer Departments of Educational Administration or Leadership. Instead we have Departments of Policy Studies, a name so general that anything is possible, any study approved, any grant acceptable no matter what the topic. There is no common frame of reference any longer. As a result, the responsibility for the training and nurture of administrators and for the development of knowledge about organizations is falling to government agencies, professional organizations and other disciplines.

William Butler Yeats had it right in his poem *The Second Coming*: "Things fall apart; the centre cannot hold." And he wrote in 1921, before postmodernism. But Yeats also spoke of a new unity emerging, in some form we might not recognize but nevertheless a form which could inform and guide.

What I see in these chapters, but more, in the small group of able and inquisitive investigators who write them, who attend the yearly meetings, who talk and argue in a refreshingly focused manner about interesting and important issues, is the start of some creative ways of thinking about organizations. Maybe, just maybe, these efforts eventually will rescue our field and make it once again relevant to the practice of administration in educational organizations.

I have no way of knowing but I would like to think that Don Willower saw something in this group of scholars that gave him hope for a future that he would not see but which his students and their students would inherit.

Edward Hickcox
Winnipeg, Manitoba
October, 2002

PAUL T. BEGLEY AND OLOF JOHANSSON

INTRODUCTION

NEW EXPECTATIONS FOR DEMOCRATIC SCHOOL LEADERSHIP IN A GLOBAL COMMUNITY

This book is very much a product of our times. Not so long ago school communities in Canada, Sweden, the United States, and the United Kingdom reflected the relatively stable cultural homogeneity of the communities they served. Administrators managed schools through a fairly limited repertoire of managerial processes. There was seldom much need to reflect on the suitability of established practices as guides to action, although, as Coombs argues in Chapter 4, such reflection has always been the mark of a wise leader. Management was largely a function of comfortable, well-worn, and proven procedures. As Johansson points out in Chapter 12, schools were traditionally an arena for professional activity, the community stayed at a comfortable distance, and professional expertise seemed a sufficient warrant to earn the trust of the community.

Those days now seem to be pretty much gone and have been replaced by a much more complex set of social circumstances. Societies have become more pluralistic in make-up and the demands and needs of communities more diversified and insistent. On the surface, these circumstances would seem to signal the onset of a golden age for nations and communities with democratic forms of governance; however, as Starratt (Chapter 2) and Johansson (Chapter 12) explain, democratic leadership theory is as much strained as vindicated by current social circumstances. Consequently the nature of school administration has altered dramatically. One very obvious outcome is the increase in the frequency of value conflicts in school environments. Campbell (Chapter 3) discusses the extent to which putting ethical standards into practice can be extremely challenging as administrators strive to "let right be done." Begley (Chapter 1) argues that school administrators must strive for authenticity in their leadership practices. Johansson (Chapter 12) suggests that administrators conceptualize their work context in terms of arenas of influence in order to lead schools effectively.

Fortunately, there have been a number of encouraging trends. During 1996, two research centres were established in North America, both devoted to the study of values. One is the OISE (University of Toronto) Centre for the Study of Values and Leadership. The other is it's University Council for Educational Administration (UCEA) affiliate based at the University of Virginia (Charlottetown), the Center for the Study Leadership and Ethics. Annually, since that year, an important gathering of the minds has occurred at the Values and Educational Leadership Conference held alternately in Toronto and Charlottesville, Virginia. In 2000 this pattern deviated with a decision to hold the conference in an international setting, Bridgetown, Barbados.   Philosophers, theorists, and researchers in the values field assemble for three days annually at this conference to engage in what has since become a sustained dialogue. Many outstanding papers have been delivered at the five annual conferences held to date. The best papers of the year 2000 conference in Barbados have been edited, updated, and brought together in this book. We have also included invited chapters by three additional scholars who did not attend the conference - Richmon (Chapter 3), Walker (Chapter 9), and Collard (Chapter 11).

Of course, value conflicts have always been present in educational administration to some extent, if only as a result of the generation gap between adult faculty and youthful students. However, value conflicts now seem to have become a defining characteristic of the school leadership role. The work of educational leaders has become more complex, much less predictable, less structured, and more conflict-laden. For example, in many sectors of the world there is considerable social pressure for greater stakeholder involvement in significant decision making within school organizations. There is also a heightened sensitivity to matters relating to racial, ethnic and gender equity. This implies the acquisition of new skills by school administrators who must now lead and manage outside the immediate and traditional professional context of the school. Several contributors to this book explore these important issues and concepts. Notions of community and collaboration are defined by Strike in Chapter 5. Two further chapters (Chapter 6 by Stefkovich and Shapiro, and Chapter 8 by Leonard and Leonard) deepen our understandings of community and collaboration in the applied setting of education. Walker (Chapter 9) advocates for the adoption of a cross-cultural perspective to replace the Western dominated notions of culture that dominate the English language leadership literature. Finally, Collard (Chapter 11) focuses specifically on gender as a context variable that influences leadership practices.

What has made these new demands on the school leadership role profoundly more challenging is that the achievement of consensus on educational issues among even the traditional educational stakeholders has become more difficult. School administrators increasingly encounter value conflict situations where consensus cannot be achieved, rendering obsolete the traditional rational notions of problem *solving*. Administrators must now often be satisfied with responding to a situation since there may be no solution possible that will satisfy all. As Begley (Chapter 1) and Johansson (Chapter 12) discuss in their chapter contributions to this book, such value dilemmas can occur within a single arena of administration or among two or more arenas. For example, conflict can reside within the mind of the individual when the relatively unnegotiable personal core values of the individual compete with each other or run counter to professional or organizational expectations. Value conflicts may also be the outcomes of interactions among two or more individuals. Finally, value conflicts may be outcomes of an incongruence or incompatibility among one or more of several value arenas; that is, conflicts occurring among the domains of personal values, professional values, and/or organizational values. Richmon (Chapter 3) also addresses these persistent difficulties by critically examining existing values theory.

More than ever before, administrators recognize that the values manifested by individuals, groups, and organizations have an impact on what happens in schools, chiefly by influencing the screening of information or definition of alternatives. The more reflective life-long learners among administrators have also become more conscious of how their own personal values may blind or illuminate the assessment of situations. This capacity is one of the marks of what Begley theorizes in Chapter 1 as an 'authentic leader'. Friedman (Chapter 10) presents a research-based demonstration of how the clear articulation of organizational values can be used in a strategic way to motivate personnel.

Some respected scholars of school leadership working in the empiricist tradition still dismiss values and ethics as concepts too abstract and resistant to inquiry to be of any practical use to school administrators. Indeed, the need to clarify values only becomes important when one needs to know about intents and purposes, or when difficulty is encountered attempting to establish consensus within a given population. As previously suggested, school leaders in many sectors of the world are clearly encountering such situations these days. This is definitely the current situation in Ontario, Canada where several years of unrelenting educational chaos has resulted from the reform policies of a government with a ruthless commitment to an economic agenda. Similarly, principals from Petrozavodsk, Karelia in the former USSR and in Belarus report similar conditions of social turmoil associated with the collapse of their political systems. Recent visits to Hong Kong also produced observations of much the same circumstances. School administrators there are still struggling to understand the full implications of the 1997 reunification of Hong Kong with China. School administrators from these radically different contexts have intuitively developed an appreciation of the relevance of values to administrative practice. As the traditional managerial strategies of school leadership fail, administrators confront a challenge to respond creatively with new forms of leadership. One approach that is attracting increased attention within the scholarly community is the notion of cross-cultural perspectives, as presented by Walker in Chapter 9.

As tempting as it might be to use the theory and research findings presented in this book as a basis for developing a prescriptive guide to ethical or value-added leadership, this not possible. Attempting to catalogue the correct values which school administrators ought to adopt without reference to context is not possible. The processes of valuation in school leadership situations are much too context-bound to permit this quick fix. Furthermore, although something is known about the problems currently confronting schools, nobody can predict with any degree of certainty the nature of future school leadership beyond the certainty that there will be more problems to solve and new dilemmas to confront. As a result, it is not enough for school leaders to merely emulate the values of other principals viewed as experts. Leaders of future schools must become both reflective practitioners and life-long learners that understand the importance of the intellectual aspects of leadership, and authentic in their leadership practices in the sense that many scholars have advocated for some time. The first step towards achieving this state is, predictably enough, to engage in personal reflection - familiar advice to anyone who has kept up with the leadership literature. However, the adoption of a values perspective on school leadership can transform this sometimes vague advice into something specific enough for school administrators to act upon. Once a degree of improved self-knowledge has been achieved through personal reflection, administrators must then take the next step towards authentic leadership. That step is to strive to develop sensitivity to the values orientations of others in order to give meaning to the actions of the students, teachers, parents and community members with which they interact. The payoff to this authentic form of leadership occurs when understanding the value orientations of others, and the political culture of schools, provide leaders with information on how they might best influence the practices of others towards the achievement of broadly justifiable social objectives.

The concluding chapter of this book is a classic piece by the best known and most respected philosopher of educational administration, Christopher Hodgkinson. It briefly summarizes our modernist past and examines our future prospects, using a tongue-in-cheek Post Post-modern non-structure to make the argument one last time for the adoption of an axiological perspective on educational administration. This is the essence of the message intended by this book. The traditional parameters of managerial and procedural responses to administrative situations must now be augmented with more creative approaches to leadership - a working of the edges of common administrative practice, perhaps even extending to artistry. The traditional notion of administrative knowledge based on the experience of many instances is superceded by a superior class of knowledge based on the form, essence, or idea, underlying each instance. Such knowledge can develop only as an outcome of reflection, cognitive flexibility, and sophistication - which leads to a key proposition introduced in chapter one: Acquiring administrative sophistication is a function of understanding the influence of personal values and collective valuation processes. It is values awareness that provides the links between theory and practice and generates praxis.

PART 1:

EXPLAINING THE ETHICAL DIMENSIONS OF SCHOOL LEADERSHIP

PAUL T. BEGLEY

IN PURSUIT OF AUTHENTIC SCHOOL LEADERSHIP PRACTICES[1]

Abstract. A practice-grounded and research-validated reinterpretation is presented of the ways in which values and ethics influence administrative practices in schools. The basic proposition is that acquiring administrative sophistication is a function of understanding the influence of personal values on the actions of individuals and the influence of values on organizational and social practices. A values perspective is used to link theory and practice with the objective of promoting authentic leadership and democracy in schools. The perennial challenges of leadership are discussed together with the special circumstances of our times. The following are then proposed: the pursuit of personal sophistication, sensitivity to others, and the promotion of reflective professional practice. Examples of findings from recent research that demonstrate the utility and relevance of values and valuation processes as guides to educational leadership are presented. These findings are used to reinterpret key values theories in ways that increase their relevance to school leadership practices. Specifically, the values typology of Hodgkinson is reconceptualized and informed by the accumulated findings of research on administrative valuation processes in schools conducted since 1988. This reconceptualization of theory also reflects efforts to integrate cognitive theory perspectives, together with experiences working with groups of school administrators in Canada, Barbados, Sweden, Australia, and Russia.

Authentic leadership may be thought of as a metaphor for professionally effective, ethically sound, and consciously reflective practices in educational administration. This is leadership that is knowledge- based, values informed, and skillfully executed. With these notions in mind, values are formally defined and proposed as an influence on the actions of individuals as well as on administrative practice. A syntax of values terminology is then developed and grounded within the context of a single individual living among many in a social environment. Several persistent conceptual issues are given brief discussion. Finally, the seven arenas of administration are identified and their relevance to authentic leadership practice is discussed.

An Initial Conceptual Image of Authentic Leadership

Appreciating the nature of authentic leadership begins with a thoughtful and rigorous analysis of leadership activity. This can occur through formal research, through personal reflection, but preferably both. Leadership by definition refers to practices that extend beyond the usual procedural context of organizational management. Authentic leadership implies a genuine kind of leadership --a hopeful, open-ended, visionary and creative response to social circumstances, as opposed to the more traditional dualistic portrayal of management and leadership practices characteristic of now obsolete and superceded research literature on effective principal practices (e.g., Leithwood & Montgomery, 1986). Traditionally management was viewed as mechanistic, short-sighted, precedent focussed and context constrained practices. An image of leadership and management that is more in keeping with current times is a values informed leadership -- a sophisticated, knowledge-based, and skilful approach to leadership. It is also a

1

P.T. Begley and O. Johansson (eds.), The Ethical Dimensions of School Leadership, 1–12.

form of leadership that acknowledges and accommodates in an integrative way the legitimate needs of individuals, groups, organizations, communities and cultures -- not just the organizational perspectives that are the usual preoccupation of much of the leadership literature. The innovative dimension being proposed here is the adoption and application of a values and valuation process perspective to educational administration makes the objectives of leadership more understandable, compelling and achievable.

The Nature of Values

There is much inclination in recent years for educators, politicians and other publicly accountable individuals to speak in terms of lost values or declining social values rather than a perception of any sort of improvement in social values. Within our recent social history, many traditional values seem to have become threatened or at least fragile. To suggest that one does not have values implies a rejection of the formative experiences of family, community and society. Possessing values is generally viewed as a good thing, although a person could just as easily be imagined to hold bad values as good values. The real issue is who gets to decide which values are good and bad. Administrators, for their part, readily acknowledge the importance of values to leadership situations in organizations. It is their role to act as agents for the values of their society, and research suggests they usually employ such values most consciously when they are encountering ambiguous, unprecedented, or time constrained problem situations, or when consensus is impossible to establish (Leithwood & Steinbach, 1995).

Other basic characteristics of values can be identified. Pirsig's more recent novel *Lila* (1991) incorporates a conception of the dynamic and static nature of values which is instructive. Using the example of an individual who hears a piece of music and likes it increasingly from day to day, Pirsig illustrates the dynamic nature of a value. In time, the dynamic value of the musical piece increases to the point that the individual must buy the recording so they can hear it as often as they want. As time passes though, the dynamic value of the music declines through familiarity and frequent play, and the piece of music assumes a more subdued, but enduring static value. The dynamic value is gone or reduced. Yet, the dynamic value may experience a resurgence when, for example, a friend drops by who has not heard the tune and the owner of the recording vicariously experiences it anew by playing it for the friend.

Where values come from is also a matter subject to debate. Are we born with some values 'hard-wired' as part of our nature, or are they all socially acquired? Conventional wisdom has it that most values are socially acquired. However, empiricist scholars like Edward Wilson, author of *Consilience* (1998), attribute human predispositions to things such as a fear of snakes to mankind's evolutionary past. It is not that difficult to imagine how such instinctual values could persist as a biologically fixed human condition. Other similar biologically fixed human values might include the instinct to survive, a fear of death, and the drive to reproduce. On the other hand, it is also clear that lots of values are socially acquired. Many values are formatively accumulated, and an apparent, objectively shared meaning can often be assigned to such values. By this, is meant that people appear to share the same values even though the acquisition of those shared values may have occurred in radically different ways from person to person. Nevertheless, the opposite, more existentialist perspective is also possible. It is likely that individuals may also possess at least a few distinctly personal values. Some values have a rational, consensual or factual basis, but there is evidence to also support the existence of non-rational and transcendental values. The nature of God is an example that has meaning for many people.

These are complex matters to ponder, and language can be a significant barrier to dialogue on these issues. Accordingly, a critical first step towards exploring these matters more fully is being clear about what the term 'values' means and adopting a suitably comprehensive working definition.

A Working Definition of Values

> Values are a conception, explicit or implicit, distinctive of an individual or characteristic of a group, of the desirable which influences the selection from available modes, means, and ends of action. (Parsons & Shils, 1962, p. 395)

Conceptualizing values in this manner highlights their function in making choices. In administration, the making of choices is usually termed decision-making, problem solving or dilemma solving: activities familiar to most administrators. Willower puts it this way:

> Because a significant portion of the practice in educational administration requires rejecting some courses of action in favour of a preferred one, values are generally acknowledged to be central to the field. (1992, p. 369)

The Parsons and Shils definition expands the scope of the term *value* beyond the relatively narrow philosophical domain of the meta-physical (the study of first principles) to several other types of values relevant to educational administration. It includes: social ethics (e.g., Beck, 1990, 1993, 1999; Cohen, 1982; Frankena, 1973); transrational values (Hodgkinson, 1996), the rational moral domain of administrative decision making (Shapiro & Stefkovich, 2000; Strike, 1990, 1999; Willower, 1994, 1999); plus the realm of self-interest and personal preference (Begley & Johansson, 1998; Evers & Lakomski, 1996; Hodgkinson, 1996).

So, values are essentially a conception of the desirable with motivating force. However, further explication is required. Within the administrative context, it is possible, even necessary, to distinguish the values manifested by individuals from the more collective social values of a group, profession, society or organization. Doing so highlights the interactive relationship between the formation of personal values and social values, implying an answer to the question about which comes first. Values appear to be derived from both within the individual's psychology as well as from the individual's interaction with collective groups, organizations and societies. For this reason, it is important to establish a balanced appreciation of the relationships among personal values, professional values, organizational values, and social values. The bulk of the literature of leadership and management has not been helpful in this regard, as it reflects a predominantly organizational perspective, to the extent that individual and professional values are often ignored, assumed to be the same as, or fully subordinated to an organizational imperative. The current interest of many educators in 'organizational learning' stands as a shining example of this pathology. In the literature on this subject, the importance of the individual to the leadership process is usually acknowledged on the first page and henceforth lost to an unremitting collective perspective. During a time of heightened social awareness and environmental activism, it is easier to see why a profit-oriented corporate sector might not be allowed to dominate or to remain unaccountable to the broader interests of community and society. The same can be said of educational organizations and organized religion. Sophisticated administrators are wise to consciously distinguish among the arenas of personal, professional, organizational, and social values of their environments. A further discussion of these inter-related arenas of administration occurs later in this chapter.

Other semantic difficulties. There are other semantic difficulties that need to be acknowledged. Certain commonly used synonyms and closely related values terminology must be distinguished from one another for the sake of clear communications. Words like *morals, values, quality* and *ethics* are often used interchangeably in school leadership literature. Is there one overarching term within which the other terms can be subsumed? It can be illuminating to substitute one term for the other in a sentence or phrase. For example, substituting the word 'value' for 'quality' in the ubiquitous phrase, 'total quality leadership', produces 'total value leadership' or 'value added leadership.' These alternatives sound plausible, and the substitution actually works reasonably well in application. However, several troublesome questions may also be triggered. If one espouses 'total *value* leadership', one may then reasonably ask *which values*, and *who decides* which values? The procedurally preoccupied proponents of the 'total quality' movement may not examine such questions too deeply.

In the school leadership literature, and particularly among North American scholars of educational administration, there is a pronounced tendency to adopt the word *ethics* or *moral* as an umbrella term for anything values-related (e.g., Grogan & Smith, 1999; Sergiovanni, 1992). In contrast, other scholars, notably several Canadians (i.e., Begley, 2000; Campbell-Evans, 1991; Leonard, 1999), follow Hodgkinson's lead (1996). They reserve the term *ethic* or principles for a particular and very special category of transrational values and employ the word *values* as a generic umbrella term for all forms of 'conceptions of the desirable.' Ethics represent a particular category of social/collective values of a transrational nature and research (Begley & Johansson, 1998) suggests they are employed under quite particular circumstances by educational administrators. For example, most administrators appear to avoid using ethics as guides to practice when they can (Begley & Johansson, 1998). This is not so much due to a character deficiency on their part or a lack of moral integrity; rather, it is a natural outcome of the particular accountability patterns associated with school leadership. Ethics are often culturally exclusive and they therefore can be a very troublesome category of values to employ as guides to action in our increasingly diverse societies. As a practical consequence, administrators naturally tend to opt for employing rational consequences and consensus grounded values as guides to action and decision making whenever that is possible.

A syntax of values terminology. It is now appropriate to conceptually situate values within the broader context of one person's being. Basic questions might include the following: Where do values fit in as a component of human nature? What is their relationship to the other dimensions of an individual's or a group's identity? What is the relationship of actions, speech, and attitudes to values? What is the relationship of values to psychological motivations? One of the simplest ways to illustrate the relationships among these terms is through the use of an onion figure which illustrates a syntax of values terminology. Figure 1 is an adaptation of a graphic found in several of Hodgkinson's books (e.g., 1991; see also Chapter 13). When considering the figure, it is important to keep in mind that one person is portrayed; one individual, not a group or organization or collective social context.

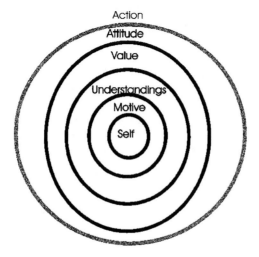

Figure 1. Values Syntax.

Beginning from the outside, the first ring represents the observable actions and speech of the individual. This is the way by which one makes empirical attributions about the value orientations of any other person. Observed actions and speech are also the source of data used to generate research findings. There is nothing else that is empirically discernible. Accordingly, most people intuitively rely on the clues provided by the actions and attitudes of others to make predictive insights into the nature of values held by other people. This is a generally sound strategy, but it has the same limits to its reliability in day-to-day life as it does in a research context. As political leaders, principals, teachers, parents and children regularly demonstrate through their speech and actions, the observable actions they manifest may or may not be accurate indicators of the person's underlying values, particularly when individuals articulate or posture certain values while actually being committed to quite different values. This implies the significant limitations associated with the reliability and validity of conventional research as a source of information about anything, as well as a cautionary note to us as we interpret day to day events.

The next ring or layer of the figure represents attitudes. Attitudes can be thought of as the thin membrane between values and the observable actions or speech of an individual, or the permeable boundary of personality that acts as the interface between the psychological and the physical world. Attitudes can be formally defined as the predisposition to act specifically as a result of values or value systems acquired previously and elsewhere. To elabourate, consider how the values acquired in one personal or social context can have a general influence on the relatively specific attitudes, and potentially the actions, of the same individual or collective group operating in another context. For example, school principals might discover that their attitudes towards children in the school change when they become parents and have young children of their own. Similarly, a person's values as a teacher and principal might spill over into other social roles he or she carries out; army reserve officer, scout or guide leader, municipal politician and so on. The strength of this extended influence can be residual in nature, a significant spillover of effect, or intrude to such an extent that it overrides or neutralizes the influence of the second value or value system. Moreover, attitudes may be reflected in the body language of posture, gait, or unconscious muscular tensions. They are outward and visible signs of inward and invisible inclinations.

The next layer represents a domain, or conceptual placeholder, for the actual values held or manifested by an individual. For example, an individual might value chocolate over Australian red wines, a chat at the pub over reading, working independently over working with others, a monarchial system of government over a republican system. In the case of an educator, the individual might value phonics over the 'whole language' approach, relatively controlled approaches to delegating authority over more laissez-faire styles of distributed leadership, computer mediated instruction over workbook exercises, or doing what's best for kids as opposed to a teacher-centered curriculum. In fact, with a modest amount of cooperation from a subject, it is relatively easily to catalogue a person's values. However, it is important to emphasize that identifying these values is one thing, while knowing why they are held is quite another. This is because any specific value can be held in response to one or more in a range of potential motivations. For example, a person could subscribe to honesty as a value to avoid the pain of sanction for dishonesty, or manifest honesty because this is a shared professional or community orientation, or because the consequences of widespread dishonesty is social chaos, or because it is the *right* thing to do, or any combination of these basic levels of motivation. Furthermore, as suggested earlier, understanding the motivations of others becomes much more complicated when individuals deliberately or unwittingly manifest or articulate one value while being actually committed to another. To know the actual level of commitment, one must look two layers deeper into the 'onion' of Figure 1 to the motivations of the individual for manifesting a particular value. For example, the actual level of commitment to decisions by administrators that are tacitly justified on consequential (e.g., what produces the best learning outcomes) or consensual (e.g., school district policy) grounds could just as easily be grounded in self-interest or personal preference (e.g., if I work this right I'll get the merit pay and promotion), but also occasionally grounded in a transrational motivational base of will or in response to transcendental values of faith or duty. It is the innermost layers of the onion figure that provide the key to understanding the nature and influence of values on life in general and administration in particular.

Between the values layer and motivational base layer of the figure is a separate layer labelled 'available knowledge' or 'understandings.' The kinds of knowledge referenced here are acquired through life experiences, training and reflection, and provide the linkage between the basic motivational bases of the fifth layer, introduced in the previous paragraphs, and the specific values adopted and manifested by the individual. The contention here is that as a result of experience, training and/or reflection, an individual responds to basic motivations by adopting particular value positions that will support the fulfillment of that basic motivation in a specific way, and be operationalized through actions or speech selected by the individual to achieve the valued objective. People vary, of course, in terms of the skills and sophistication they can bring to bear on achieving their objectives, depending on the quality of the knowledge at their disposal. This is generally applicable to all aspects of human enterprise, and an infinite number of examples can be offered. However, for the moment consider how a skilful school administrator, consensually motivated as a professional to achieve a complex set of educational objectives, might employ a carefully orchestrated collaborative school improvement project to achieve those educational objectives. By contrast, a less experienced administrator, with the same consensual motivation, but responding to different knowledge or the absence thereof, might decide a memo is all that is required to achieve the same objective.

As argued in the preceding two paragraphs, the motivational base layer of Figure 1 provides the key to understanding the nature and function of values. This is the motivating force dimension behind the adoption of a particular value which, working out through the layers of the figure, shapes attitudes and potentially the subsequent actions. For the purposes of this chapter, and consistent with Hodgkinson's original value framework, four basic motivational bases are identified. These are (see Figure 2): personal preference or self-interest, an inclination towards consensus, an inclination towards or concern for consequences, and an inclination to respond to ethics or principles. These four motivational bases are relatively broad and arbitrary distinctions and people can manifest a predisposition towards one or more of these motivational bases at the same time when responding to a given situation. As alluded earlier, our recent research conducted on the valuation processes of school administrators in several countries (e.g., Begley, 1999; Begley & Leonard, 1999) suggests that the normative motivational bases for administrative decision-making are the rational domains of consequences and consensus. Self-interest is infrequently acknowledged as a motivation, possibly because professional activity is usually publicly accountable, and ethics and principles tend to be employed under special circumstances.

Needs   >>>   Motivational >>> Available >>> Specific Value >>> Action/Speech
                    Base   Knowledge

Four Motivational Bases:
    Consequences Based
    - focus on desirable outcomes
    - can be rationally justified
    (e.g. 'The Internet is good for research,' 'standardized testing')

    Consensus Based
    - conformity with group norms, peer pressure, expert opinion
    - can be rationally justified
    (e.g. 'Ministry approved curriculum,' 'the research says')

    Preferences / Self-interest Based
    -experience, memory, comfort
    - personal good, no rational justification required
    (e.g. 'I like teaching Phys Ed,' 'Macs are best')

    Ethics / Principles Based
    - wisdom of the ages (e.g. 'the golden rule', 'honesty is best policy')
    - established cultural norms (e.g. "democracy")
    - entrenched societal values, no rational justification required

Figure 2. Hodgkinson's Original Value Framework.

Hodgkinson (1996) argues that motivational bases are at the core of the being of individuals, and that values held by an individual reflect these motivational bases. This implies the limited utility of conducting research that merely describes or lists the values manifested by individuals whether they are administrators, teachers, students, citizens, neighbours, or members of the family. It may be interesting and much easier to determine what people value, but why they do so is often most crucial. Much of the early empirical research on values in the field of Educational Administration is descriptive of the values held and reveals little that is conventionally verifiable about motivation.

The final layer at the centre of the figure is the *self*, or essence of the individual --the biological self as well as the existential or transcendent self. There is not a great deal known or that can be said about this inner core of the individual. Some would describe it as the soul, the life-force or spark of life. It is included in the figure primarily as a conceptual placeholder for such matters.

To summarize the discussion in this section with a metaphor used elsewhere to illustrate the nature of values (Begley, 1996), the attitudes and actions manifested by individuals may be construed as observable ripples and splashes on the surface of a body of water. It is important to keep in mind that the intentions behind these observable actions may alternately be transparently obvious, superficial, or running deep to the core. They can also remain fully obscured below the surface of the self, the organizational structure, or the society. Existing research evidence (see Begley, 1999; Begley & Leonard, 1999) on the values of school administration suggests that the non-rational motivational bases of personal preference and transrational principles occur much less frequently than do the rational motivational bases of consensus and consequences. The relevance of principles or ethics to a given administrative situation seems to be prompted by particular circumstances where an ethical posture is socially appropriate (e.g., the role of the arts), where consensus is perceived as difficult to achieve (e.g., an issue involving ethnic bias), or when urgency requires quick action (e.g., student safety). Furthermore, it may be that the weak influence of personal preferences on administrative practice can be viewed as a good thing. After all, principals are, in the end, "agents of society" and accountable to society for their actions. While values of personal preference are definitely evident as influences on some administrative processes, Begley (1999), and Begley and Leonard (1999), suggest they are less frequently articulated by administrators, probably because of a prevailing social bias towards the rational value types. This rational bias is perhaps an outcome of organizational socialization and cultural expectations.

The arenas of valuation: Sources of values and value conflicts. Although much of the leadership literature is fundamentally organizational in context and emphasis, the full environment of administration is actually much more complex. Any school administrator who attempts to lead and manage without reference to the broader environmental context will quickly encounter difficulty. The values of profession, organization, community and society are not necessarily consistent or compatible with each other. Figure 3 illustrates what can be usefully termed the arenas of valuation. These are the interactive environments within which valuation processes and, by extension, administration occur. There are also important dynamics that occur among these arenas. Seven arenas can be identified to conceptualize the environment of administration.

The term arena itself is helpful in that it highlights the multiple domains and functions of administration. Conceptualizing administration as something that involves multiple arenas, each with potentially competing or incompatible values, is useful for managers or leaders who wish to reflect on the appropriateness of their own actions, the actions of others, and to begin to predict social reactions to their actions. Within Figure 3, the individual is represented within the centre ring as self. In a practical sense, this arena highlights the role of the individual as an entity with a potentially unique influence within a social or organizational enterprise. It also conveys the potentially intensified influence of one individual when he or she is a leader. This highlights 'the power of one', the capability of one person to have impact as a leader. Also acknowledged, however, is the potential for influence on processes by individuals when conditions of distributed leadership exist, or when leadership influence is exerted by individuals without vested authority in the less formal ways which Lindle (1994), for example, has termed micro-politics.

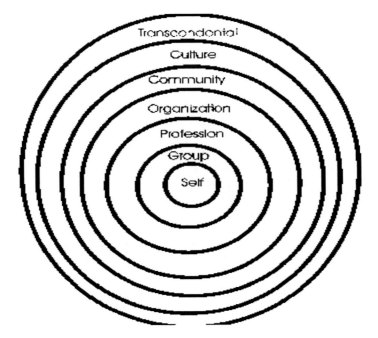

Figure 3. Arenas of Administration.

The second ring from the centre represents the arena of groups, collective entities of various types. This arena acts as a place-holder for collectives such as family, peers, friends and acquaintances. The third ring, profession, represents a more formal arena of administration that is closely related to the second ring, but is given special emphasis here because of its relevance to school administration. The fourth ring represents the arena traditionally of most concern to academics and practitioners in the field of educational administration, the organization. Indeed, much of the traditional literature of educational administration and most of the corporate literature are grounded within the organizational perspective. As such a degree of 'over-weighting vividness' (Leithwood & Steinbach, 1995, p. 202) is often attributed to this arena. Moving further outwards in the figure, one encounters the arenas representing the greater community, society, and culture. Within the last decade, school administrators have learned that it is necessary to pay a lot more attention than before to the community as a relevant administrative arena and source of influence on school leadership (Leithwood, Begley, & Cousins, 1992). The increasing diversity of our societies and a general trend towards globalization has similarly highlighted society and culture as relevant arenas of administrative activity. A final, seventh ring is included to accommodate notions of the transcendental -- God, faith, spirituality. This is an arena of considerable importance to many people, even though it does not get a lot of attention in the literature of administration. Administrators who do not subscribe to a spiritual dimension as a relevant source of personal influence would do well to keep this arena in mind, if only because at least some individuals associated with their followership certainly do. The spiritual dimension can be a significant influence on valuation processes for many people and a leader who wants to understand the motivations of the followership will be sensitive to this potentially significant category of influence.

Figure 3 serves two important functions. It suggests the various sources of values, conveying how values can be derived from multiple external and internal environmental sources. Although some values may potentially be acquired through biology as well as existential processes, values are perhaps predominantly acquired from more collective sources: family, friends, peers, acquaintances, a profession, organizations and formal associations, the community, social culture, and through the transcendental. Figure 3 conveys these multiple sources of values, but also it suggests the sources of value conflicts. For example, although value conflicts can certainly occur within a single arena of administration, consider how the personal values of the individual might conflict with those of the community, or professional values might conflict with organizational values.

Tools for authentic leadership. The discussion and concepts presented here, especially the two onion figures, are offered as tools that will contribute to the conceptualization of authentic leadership practices by school administrators. This is perhaps an ambitious and idealistic view of administration, but not a new one. The innovative dimension being proposed is the adoption and application of a values perspective to make authentic leadership an objective that is more understandable, compelling and achievable. In a fundamental way, authentic leadership is living the examined life as Socrates advised so long ago. More recently, Hodgkinson added this corollary: "if the unexamined life is not worth living, the unexamined value is not worth holding" (1996, p. 8). The skills of authentic and expert leaders will extend beyond management. All leaders consciously or unconsciously employ values as guides to interpreting situations and suggesting appropriate administrative action. This is the artistry of leadership.

NOTES

[1] This chapter is a revised and updated version of a paper originally presented at the Conference of the UCEA Centre for the Study of Values and Leadership, Bridgetown, Barbados (Begley, 2000). It has also been previously published as an article in a special issue (Vol. 4, No. 4, pp. 353-365) of the *International Journal of Leadership in Education* (2001).

REFERENCES

Beck, C. (1990). *Better schools: A values perspective.* New York: Falmer Press.
Beck, C. (1993). *Learning to live the good life.* Toronto: OISE Press.
Beck, C. (1999). Values, leadership and school renewal. In P.T. Begley & P.E. Leonard (Eds.) (1999) *The values of educational administration*(pp. 223-321). London: Falmer Press.
Begley, P.T. (1996). Cognitive perspectives on values in administration: A quest for coherence and relevance. *Educational Administration Quarterly, 32*(3), 403-426.
Begley, P.T. (Ed.) (1999). *Values and educational leadership.* Albany, NY: SUNY Press.
Begley, P.T. (2000). Values and leadership: Theory development, new research, and an agenda for the future. *The Alberta Journal Of Educational Research, 46*(3), 233-249.
Begley, P.T., & Johansson, O. (1998). The values of school administration: Preferences, ethics and conflicts. *The Journal of School Leadership, 8*(4), 399-422.
Begley, P.T., & Leonard, P. (1999). *The values of educational administration.* London: Falmer.

Campbell-Evans, G.H. (1991). Nature and influence of values in principal decision-making. *The Alberta Journal of Educational Research*, *37*(2),167-178.

Cohen, B. (1982). *Means and ends in education.* London: George Allen & Unwin.

Evers, C.W., & Lakomski, G. (1996). *Exploring educational administration.* Toronto: Pergamon Press.

Frankena, W.K. (1973). *Ethics.* Englewood Cliffs, NJ: Prentice-Hall.

Grogan, M., & Smith, F. (1999). A feminist perspective of women superintendents' approaches to moral dilemmas. In P.T. Begley (Ed.), *Values and educational leadership*(pp. 273-288). Albany, NY: SUNY Press.

Hodgkinson, C. (1991). *Educational leadership: The moral art.* Albany, NY: SUNY Press.

Hodgkinson, C. (1996). *Administrative philosophy.* Oxford, UK: Elsevier-Pergamon.

Leithwood, K.A., Begley, P.T., & Cousins, J.B. (1992). *Developing expert leadership for future schools.* London: Falmer Press.

Leithwood, K.A., & Montgomery, D. (1986). *Improving principal effectiveness: The principal profile.* Toronto: OISE Press.

Leithwood, K.A., & Steinbach, R. (1995). *Expert problem solving.* Albany, NY: SUNY Press.

Leonard, P. (1999). Examining educational purposes and underlying value orientations in schools. In P.T. Begley (Ed.), *Values and educational leadership*(pp. 217-236). Albany, NY: SUNY Press.

Lindle, J. (1994). *Surviving school micropolitics; Strategies for administrators.* Lancaster, PA: Technomic.

Parsons, T., & Shils, E.A. (Eds.) (1962). *Towards a general theory of action.* New York: Harper.

Pirsig, R. (1991). *Lila: An inquiry into morals.* New York: Bantam Books.

Sergiovanni, T.J. (1992). *Moral leadership: Getting to the heart of school improvement.* San Francisco, CA: Jossey-Bass.

Shapiro, J., & Stefkovich, J. (2000). *Ethical leadership and decision making in education.* Mahwah, NJ: Lawrence Erlbaum Associates.

Strike, K.A. (1990). The ethics of educational evaluation. In J. Millman, & L. Darling-Hammond (Eds.), *Teacher evaluation: Assessing elementary and secondary school teachers*(pp. 356-373). Newbury Park, CA: Sage Publications.

Strike, K. (1999). Can schools be communities? The tension between shared values and inclusion. *Educational Administration Quarterly*, *35*(1),46-70.

Willower, D. (1992). Educational administration: Intellectual trends. In *Encyclopedia of educational research, 6th edition*(pp. 364-375). Toronto: Macmillan Publishing.

Willower, D. (1994). *Educational administration: Inquiry, Values, Practice.* Lancaster, PA: Technomic.

Willower, D. (1999). Values and valuation: A naturalistic approach. In P.T. Begley (Ed.), *Values and educational leadership*(pp. 121-138). Albany, NY: SUNY Press.

Wilson, E.O. (1998). *Consilience.* New York: Alfred P. Knopf.

ROBERT J. STARRATT

DEMOCRATIC LEADERSHIP THEORY IN LATE MODERNITY:
AN OXYMORON OR IRONIC POSSIBILITY?[1]

Abstract. This chapter is intended to enrich and expand scholarly reflection on democratic leadership theory. Leithwood and Duke (1999) make the claim, in their review of the literature on school leadership, that contemporary philosophy of educational administration has made no significant contribution to leadership theory. However, one can argue that contemporary philosophy has indeed implicated educational administration and the assumptions of enlightenment/modern philosophy that support its practice. The chapter begins with the question of the possibility of democratic leadership theory after the postmodern critique of democracy, epistemology and all meta-narratives (Maxcy, 1991). The question is posed whether democratic leadership theory is thereby defeated, or significantly chastened. It goes on to ask whether democratic theory may overcome its own contradictions through a self-consciously ironic pragmatism.

The next section of the paper explores the limits and constraints on leadership theory after Postmodernism. Leadership theory and its proponents have to agree to a continuous evaluation by a hermeneutic of suspicion, a continuous deconstruction of its treatment of power and authority. It has to respond to the unavoidable issues of racism, sexism, classism, and other oppressing ideologies.

INTRODUCTION

I must begin with several qualifications. In referring to 'democracy', I am restricting myself to considerations of democracy in the United States, the primary cultural landscape of my work. I recognize that there are many democracies represented by various nation states, and that there is no single interpretation of democracy that applies to all of them. Thus, I do not mean to disparage democracy as it is understood and practiced in other countries. Neither do I mean to disparage other scholarly discussions of education for democracy (e.g., the work organized by Ichilov, 1990) or the leadership of such efforts in other countries. I speak only within the American context; scholars from other democracies may find some useful applications of my analysis, but I offer no initial expectations that that will be the case.

The political form of democracy in the United States is representative democracy where the people exercise their sovereignty in electing citizens to represent them at various levels of government (Tarcov, 1996); however, there is another traditional usage of the word that refers to more social forms of democratic living together as equals under the law, citizens with moral bonds to one another, yet each free to pursue one's own interests. When I speak about democratic leadership, I wish to include both the political and more socio-cultural senses of the term.

In what follows, there will be a lot of criticism about schooling in the United States. This criticism differs from the criticism that teachers and administrators face in the press on a regular basis: teachers are lazy, administrators are indecisive and incompetent, students can do whatever they want in school, there are no

13

P.T. Begley and O. Johansson (eds.), The Ethical Dimensions of School Leadership, 13–31.
© 2003 *Kluwer Academic Publishers. Printed in the Netherlands.*

standards, courses lack rigor, and so forth. The criticism offered in this paper is of a different nature. It is a criticism of the way schooling in general is carried out in this country; it is a criticism of some of the purposes schools are asked to serve. It is a criticism of how schools trivialize learning and waste so much of the time of youngsters. I am well aware that schools are served by dedicated and well-meaning educators, people who consciously or unconsciously work against all the obstacles that schools present to learning, against all the ways that schools humiliate children, and who succeed in making learning interesting and fulfilling for children. I am not criticizing the educators. My target is the institutional form, the political form, and the cultural form that schools take; that is what makes me ask the question about the moral possibility of leading these institutions democratically. I raise the question of the morality of an educator claiming to lead a school, when what schools do to altogether too many teachers and children is indefensible. And, of course, the question comes back to me as well, as a professor of educational administration. Is my participation in the preparation of educators to 'lead' schools implicated in an immoral charade?

My argument suggests that a qualified form of democratic leadership of schools is not only possible, but necessary. The argument for a qualified form of democratic leadership can be supported —within the philosophical tradition of American Pragmatism, especially as found in John Dewey. The argument goes on to link Dewey's Pragmatism to the concept of constructivism as that has been recently developed in the sociology of knowledge and culture. I argue, however, that constructivist theory must include the process of deconstruction as a necessary component of the constructivist sociology and psychology of learning, in order to develop a qualified theory of democratic leadership for those practicing school administration. The argument includes the category of irony as employed by a contemporary spokesman of pragmatism, Richard Rorty (1989), for the ironic sense employs deconstruction even while it attempts a pragmatic construction of a response to the social and political context.

DEMOCRATIC THEORY

The history of democratic political theory in the United States has seen a continuous argument over the meaning of democracy and over the appropriate institutional forms it might take. The Founders sought, on the one hand, to avoid the tyranny of the rule of a small elite over the masses, and on the other, to avoid the anarchy of rule by the masses. Representative government was their compromise between those two extremes. As Barber (1998) noted, "The compromise of representation   permitted the many to choose the few, but vested governing power in the few, thereby filtering out the passions and prejudices of the sovereign many" (p. 162).

The Founders, however, had inherited both a religious and an Enlightenment view of human nature. For them, human nature was a fixed philosophical concept; human nature followed "natural" laws. The Founders' religious background, together with their study of the history of republics, led them to believe that passion in humans tended to rule the rational side of humans' nature, thus leading to a repetitive cycle of tyranny, revolution, the growth of new tyrannies and further revolutions in the political history of nations and republics. Their Enlightenment background tended to wed them to the primacy of the individual over the social in human affairs. The authors of the Federalist Papers resolved the problem of designing a self-governing democratic republic, populated by self-interested individuals and governed by passions, by promoting a republic driven by economic and political self-interest. They gambled that, in a republic, where various factions of individuals promoted competing economic interests, these factions would impose checks and balances on each other's power and influence over the representatives. The Founders also carefully divided the governing power among three branches of government, so that each would act as a check on the others. Further, a two-party political system would come to represent a variety of viewpoints, thus allowing competing voices to be heard and to influence public policy.

Shklar (1991) also points out that the Founders represented a class of men who saw liberty as the opposite of servitude. Liberty, from their perspective, was grounded in people's ability to work for themselves, to earn good livings through hard work. By building up personal wealth, individuals earned the liberties that wealth can provide. With wealth, people had the liberty to pursue the finer things in life and had periods of leisure to enjoy social and cultural involvements. They would earn the right to be called "free men" through their work. Their work was an expression of their citizenship in a democratic economy where men were free to pursue personal wealth. Shklar would not have us think that the Founders were interested so much in political democracy, where people would spend much of their time debating contested public policies. That was an occupation for politicians, the ones they elected to do this work. Ordinary citizens had their work to do, namely to secure those liberties they could by engaging in wealth-producing work.

Shklar (1991) went on to point out that the unity of this republic was not a unity of blood, of tribal affinity, of traditions, or of interests. The unity of the republic was based upon the guarantee of equal rights. Everyone in this democratic republic was protected by the state, by virtue of their citizenship, from having these guaranteed rights infringed upon. It was a democracy of citizens with equal rights, rights that enabled them to pursue their personal interests as long as they did not illegally interfere with the rights of their fellow citizens. In the minds of some contemporary scholars, this view of democracy falls far short of a more communal, fraternal, collaborative expression of democracy.

Barber (1998) is perhaps correct in his perspective on the fate of democracy. The founding of the United States defined both a point of origin and a destiny. Democracy, as defined in the Declaration of Independence and the Constitution, was not a clearly defined and commonly accepted doctrine, but much more an "… artificial ideal. Not something to be built upon but something to be brought into being and accomplished over time." (Barber, 1998, p. 167). Shklar (1991) maintained that a fuller expression of democracy was achieved primarily through the courts, rather than through legislation, as various groups sought to have their rights, guaranteed under the constitution, but denied in social and political practice, affirmed and validated.

The meaning of democracy has been debated extensively in a recent flurry of publications in the 1980s and 1990s (Allen & Regan, 1998; Barber, 1984, 1988; Bellah, Madsen, Sullivan, Swidler, & Tipton, 1985; Burns & Burns, 1991; Elkin & Soltan, 1993; Elshtain, 1995; Hunter, 1994; Kymlicka, 1995; Marty, 1997; Sandel, 1996, 1998) The liveliness of the debate and the diversity of voices leads Charles Taylor (1998, p. 214) to comment, "I think we suffer in modern philosophy from an absence of alternative models: models of how people can associate and be bonded together in difference, without abstracting from these differences." Marty (1997) similarly believes that the debate about democracy is not resolvable by reasoned arguments in conditions of postmodernity. It is, he claimed, no longer possible to find a common ground in rational argument, eighteenth century style. He cites the earlier work of John Courtney Murray (1960, p. 130): "The fact today is not simply that we hold different views but that we have become different types of men (sic), with different styles of interior life."

So where does that leave the professor of Educational Administration who is promoting the notion of leadership of democratic schools? One can stand on the sidelines pointing out all the ways schools are not democratic. One can also engage in the use of democratic rhetoric in courses and in essays without bothering to ground that rhetoric in a well thought-through analysis of democracy that might be taught and practiced in schools. If I have no theory as a professor, however tentative, to ground my teaching and writing, then I am left with a purely functionalist basis for teaching my students. Herein lies the problem; there is no intellectual or moral justification available in functionalism, other than it is in some senses effective. At the same time, I cannot ignore the critique of schools and the critique of the leadership of all social institutions in the United States, as I try to build such a theory. Therefore, I have to try to uncover deeper values and different perspectives than those provided in an "eighteenth century style" rational argument. In the next section, I will try to lay out some premises for such a theory.

FIVE PREMISES FOR A QUALIFIED THEORY OF DEMOCRATIC EDUCATIONAL LEADERSHIP

The first premise is there is a philosophical tradition, older than the Enlightenment, that asserts the intrinsically social nature of human beings. This argument may have some appeal to a broad range of people. The position is well articulated by Charles Taylor (1998, p. 214):

> It is the idea of humanity as something to be realized, not in each individual human being, but rather in communion between all humans. The essence of humanity is not something which even in principle a single human being could realize in his or her life. And this is not because of the finitude and limitation of this life, since we couldn't make up for the limitation of one by laying other lives, as it were, along side it, until human variety is exhausted. The fullness of humanity comes not from the adding of differences, but from the exchange and communion between them. They achieve fullness not separately but together.

Taylor goes on to elaborate using the metaphor of an orchestra. Musicians create the full richness of the music in the space between them. This position does not deny relationships of power among humans, but power from this perspective can have a positive as well as a negative quality. This position offers a positive power between people to create something that no one could alone. This position seems compatible with an expansive view of democracy, and indeed with a view of learning.

The second premise is that, as Marty (1997) suggests, I accept the incommensurability of rational attempts at interpretations of democracy. I back away from attempting a conclusive, rational argument for democratic, educational leadership, and focus instead on the work in front of us. That work flows from our mutual need to share a common, public space, since we are all tossed together. That common space is productively occupied by our stories, not by our rationalizations of our convictions about theories of democracy. We will find common ground in stories about our lives and our communities, stories that will generate bonds of affection and sentiment. Instead of seeking to become a community in which we share uniform commitments to common goals, values, and cultural expression, we might seek a more modest goal of accommodation and acquiescence so that we can collectively get on with our public lives. We do not, as Marty (1997) counsels us, need to demand consensus as the all-compelling principle of politics, but rather honor differences of perspectives and interpretation in the interests of arriving at more modest agreements about sharing the public space while living within our own community of preference. The phrase "e pluribus unum" can mean a limited unity for the pragmatic exigencies of public life, while maintaining a rich diversity of plural communities where deep human fulfillment can be found. Sharing in public life with more modest expectations may soften the jagged edge of difference and indeed generate bonds of civility, respect, and even caring. While this pragmatic posture may be embraced in the present, it is open to the future possibility (but not necessity) of stronger bonds of community based more on sentiments of loyalty and appreciation than on rational arguments over principle.

The third premise is that any form of democratic living requires "civic virtue"; namely the ability to forego, at least on some occasions, self-interest on behalf of a particular other, or on behalf of a more general common good. Democratic living does not automatically happen because one has read a treatise on democracy and is intellectually convinced of its logic. Democratic living requires a suppression of the impulses of greed, impatience, lust, and psychological projection, in favour of a mature acting out of a generous portion of altruism. Such civic virtue is learned. Families and other social institutions must socialize the young into habits of civic virtue. As Barber (1998, p. 163) commented, "the actualization of liberty required much more that being born". We may have certain rights that are ours by birth, but birthrights do not equate to the ability to exercise them. That requires a person educated in the arts of citizenship (Galston, 1995). Democracy is a moral as well as a political and social enterprise. It has to take account of the cruelties and humiliations and hypocrisy of its past as a warning of the self-delusional possibilities of its future.

The fourth premise is that at present, at least, democracy as participation in communal self-governance can be enacted in its most generous sense at the local level, in small communities, in small organizations like schools, neighbourhood churches, synagogues, mosques, voluntary associations, and professional groups.

Beyond the local level, issues of power politics, mass administration, well-financed special interest groups and lobbies, national political parties, media oversimplification and distortion, and finally the rhetoric of ideological dogmatism tend to diminish, if not entirely suppress, the ability of most individuals and small groups to participate in any meaningful sense. On the other hand, members have an opportunity in smaller organizations to get to know one another as fuller human beings, have opportunities to prolong conversations and debates over longer periods of time, and can share a common focus on a limited number of public issues which are close, familiar and amenable to intentional, planned change. The dimension of smallness does not mean uniformity. It does mean that ideological or genuinely different perceptions and interpretations may be accommodated even while pragmatic agreements about needed local improvements on sewage treatment or the location of public clinics are concluded.

The fifth premise concerns a framework for thinking about the *leadership* of democratic organizations. Rather than emphasizing a framework of technical rationality, in which goals and objectives are set and then appropriate means are operationalized for their efficient and effective achievement, I want to emphasize leadership as "cultivation." By this, I mean that democratic leadership is primarily concerned to cultivate an environment that supports participation, sharing of ideas, and the virtues of honesty, openness, flexibility, and compassion. Democratic educational leadership should be focused on cultivating school environments where Taylor's richer and fuller humanity is experienced and activated by people acting in communion. People with many different talents, backgrounds interests and abilities can bring these together in a common public work; namely a rich quality of learning by all members. Moreover, the concept of cultivation may be considered central to the learning process itself. Thus teachers could speak more about cultivating the cognitive virtues rather than teaching thinking skills, cultivating civic virtues rather than engaging in classroom management, cultivating attitudes of stewardship, cultivating relationships, cultivating respect for plurality and diversity, cultivating time and space for human endeavour, cultivating authenticity, cultivating the human spirit, etc. The metaphor of cultivation carries a much richer configuration of meanings when applied to teaching and learning than "delivering instruction," "achievement," "academic excellence," or "developing individual potential".

With these as foundational premises to a qualified theory of democratic educational leadership, I want to argue that we may ground this theory in some aspects of traditional American pragmatist philosophy as well as in more recent developments of constructivist theory (giving it a twist of postmodern deconstructionist activity for good measure). This points the way towards a pragmatic, ironic democratic educational leadership theory. There are two shaping elements.

American Pragmatism

For purposes of brevity, I have to assume that the reader is familiar with the general contours of American Pragmatism, especially as that philosophical school is represented by John Dewey. For our purposes, we may focus on the relationship

Dewey made between pragmatism as a way of constructing knowledge and pragmatism as a way of democratic living. For Dewey, knowing served a mediating function for pursuing human interests (Dewey, 1948, 1958; Westbrook, 1991). Knowledge was something individuals, groups and communities constructed on their way to solving mutual problems. In this regard, Dewey's theory of knowledge opposed both the realist and the idealist epistemologies of his day, and he was severely attacked by critics from both schools. Thus, pragmatism abandoned the traditional concern to uncover and clarify "ultimate reality", and focused much more on the everyday world of human beings.

Dewey proposed that a generalized methodology of science offered a model for constructing knowledge in the social sphere. Thus, reflective thought proceeded through five steps: 1) a felt or perceived difficulty or problem; 2) the clarification of what the difficulty appeared to be; 3) a search for possible solutions to the difficulty; 4) a reasoned projection of the possible consequences of each solution; and 5) the choice of a solution and an assessment of its actual consequences, leading to the acceptance of the solution or its rejection. This methodology was not simply the reflective production of knowledge by the individual. On the contrary, for Dewey, the production of knowledge was necessarily a social process, involving multiple perspectives and opinions in the clarification and solution of the problem. To be sure, individuals would use this methodology of intelligence in solving individual problems, but their solutions would necessarily have to take into consideration the social context of the problem, as well as the social consequences of any given solution. This normative methodology was to remove capriciousness, selfishness or impulsiveness from the generation of responses to human problems, to ensure a greater probability of the solution actually serving human interests.

Dewey closely linked this view of knowledge to his view of democracy. For him democracy "required a belief that ordinary men and women might possess the intelligence to effectively direct the affairs of their society" (cited in Westbrook, 1991, p. 149). The pragmatic use of intelligence to deal with the everyday problems and conflicts that arise among people who claim to have equal rights as citizens would guide them in the public discussions and debates about the appropriate course of action to follow. Furthermore, given Dewey's acceptance of the theory of natural evolution, he saw this democratic, social intelligence developing over time. He accepted the necessary incompleteness of pragmatic knowledge constructed in the course of human affairs. Nonetheless, the ongoing pursuit of a clearer interpretation of what everyday conditions demanded of citizens enabled them, through the use of the general method of deliberation (which he identified loosely as scientific), to transform their present experience into something more serviceable for their human interests. His notion of the continuous transformation of social experience became the process whereby people living in a democracy could progressively improve and direct the affairs of their society.

While Dewey promoted a methodology of socializing intelligence, he was not a naive rationalist. Dewey coupled his method of intelligence with an analysis of civic virtue. That analysis was founded on an analysis of the morality of the individual, which Dewey characteristically situated in what was, for him, the naturally *social* nature of human beings. The morality of the individual was intrinsically connected with the good or harmful effects of the individual's choices on others. Social interests become moral interests, Dewey argued, when they are permeated by an instinctive sympathetic affection towards others (Dewey, 1958; Westbrook, 1991). Thus "every natural capacity, every talent or ability, whether of inquiring mind, of gentle affection, or of executive skill, becomes a virtue when it is turned to account in supporting or extending the fabric of social values" (Dewey, cited in Westbrook, 1991, p. 161).

Dewey projected his individual morality onto the collective morality of a democratic society. This would be a morality not of doing good *for* others, but *with* others. Dewey proposes a lofty moral ideal in the "moral democracy." In such a society, the moral person not only adjusts his or her choices to accommodate the choices of others, but acts in such a way as to call out and make effectively possible the activities of others so that they will fully exercise their talents and interests, and achieve their moral fulfillment. Thus, a moral democratic society would be the ideal society for individuals to find their greatest human fulfillment. This moral ideal appears to go beyond even the Golden Rule, and Dewey acknowledged the difficulty of a society ever reaching that ideal in any consistent and extensive practice.

Other commentators have also insisted that public life in a democracy requires the cultivation of civic virtue (Galston, 1995; Sandel, 1996; Sullivan, 1995). Habits of tolerance, respect, mutual trust, honesty, obedience to law, attentive listening to the opinions of others, even when disagreeing with those opinions - to mention but some of these virtues - make the social intercourse of members of a democracy possible. The difficulty that all proponents of civic virtue face however is the question of the foundational principles and logic that stand behind and support and legitimate the moral claims of citizens. Dewey eschewed such foundationalism. He argued that the virtue is in the doing and in the living out of the consequences of choices.

We don't know ahead of time what is right in any absolute sense. We may know the consequences of certain choices from our past experience, or we may argue as to the negative and positive possible consequences and therefore make more enlightened choices. Dewey would argue that we need to take account of the needs of the community and of the people immediately involved in the choosing and try to anticipate the consequences of one decision over another. This "taking account" would involve not simply some cold calculation of effects, but would be suffused by sympathy for the feelings and possibilities of those involved. It is important to note that Dewey usually argued for the moral ideal, rather than that which described the way people actually functioned in society. His point, however, was that a moral democratic way of living, which was for him the most authentically moral way of living, was always out in front of us. It was the potential of the democratic ideal to inspire new insights into each day's possibilities that attracted him, rather than a torn and tattered expression of democracy at a point in history. Dewey advocated moral imagination as well as moral habits, encouraging us to probe beyond what present circumstances appear to require, to look beyond what is to what might be.

Dewey was never able to translate his pragmatic philosophy into an actual political institution. Without going into a detailed analysis of why his ideas never took immediate hold, Dewey himself believed it was due to the widespread "identification of liberty with the maximum of unrestrained individualistic action in the economic sphere, under the institutions of capitalistic finance" (Westbrook, 1991, p. 436). Democracy had become a captive of the development of American capitalism, in Dewey's judgment. Those who controlled the means of production, the banking system, transportation systems, and the means of communication effectively ruled the life of the country. The small elite who controlled such vast resources held a substantially disproportionate influence over regional and national governments and political parties, and they used that influence to further their own interests. One need only to follow the funding of current political campaigns in the United States to recognize the influence of these elites on state and national politics, and one might also add, on the state and national policies regarding education.

It is fair to say that schools exist in a democracy that is partially compromised by an undemocratic economy, by undemocratic communications and media industries, by undemocratic cultural institutions, as well as by a form of representative government many see as serving special interests and itself more than the broad needs of the people. The theory of democracy does not look particularly appealing in practice, or in what passes for its practice (Barber, 1998). On the other hand, we may take encouragement from three sources.

One source of encouragement is the growing attention being paid to the topic of democracy, at least among scholars. After Dewey's death, we saw the ascension of the political realists who simply presented the practice of politics in the United States as democracy. Gradually, the description of politics in the United States came to be seen as the way democracy was supposed to work, so once the Cold War ended there was talk about exporting or bringing democracy to the countries dominated by Soviet Communism. What was exported was the ideology of free market economics, not democracy. The same may be said of efforts to bring democracy to developing countries. In the past two decades or so, however, there has been a resurgence of interest in democratic theory. The proliferation of historical and analytical studies promises to create a larger conversation about continuing the struggle to achieve a greater realization of democracy in American public life. The topic has also been related to schools (Soder, 1996). A second source of encouragement is the historical development, however slow, of democratic ideals enacted into law in the form of increased civil rights granted to groups previously denied those rights. There remains, however, a long way to go.

The third source of encouragement is the globalization of politics and economics, along with the globalization of attention to the environment. The phenomenon of globalization is not an automatic guarantee of the spread of democracy; indeed, in the United States, globalization all too often is equated with the pursuit of commercial advantage driven by a globalized ideology of Social Darwinism. Nevertheless, the multiple realities of globalization force the pursuit of democracy into new spheres of international discourse and influence, which have the potential to breathe new life into its understanding and practice at home.

Constructivism

The Twentieth Century brought an ever-increasing clarification to the conflict between idealism and realism in art, literature, science and philosophy. Without going into the various aspects of that conflict, we may oversimplify the issue for purposes of expediency and say that the conflict was resolved, more or less, by striking a middle ground between two contrary positions. This middle ground holds that what we claim to know about the world, the knowledge which is expressed in ordinary or specialized language, are linguistic and conceptual tools by which we interpret the world around us, with which we begin to make sense out of the world of immediate experience. Holding this position does not deny the existence of an exterior reality "out there." Rather, it asserts that what we know about the external world is always and necessarily contingent; knowledge both reveals and distorts; it is partial and fallible. Furthermore, our knowledge is inescapably social; it relies on the distributed intelligence among human, institutional, and cultural resources in our immediate environment. We never know anything fully and completely. We "know reality", but from various perspectives. The usefulness of our knowledge is very much conditioned by historical circumstances. Before the inventions of the telescope and the microscope, our knowledge of the material world was limited to direct observations of the human eye; before the invention of the computer, certain medical diagnoses were not possible; before advances in genetics and microbiology, other medical applications were not possible. Fifty years from now, the knowledge made possible by these inventions will be reinterpreted in the light of new knowledge.

The cultural embeddedness of language means that translations of meanings and metaphors across languages and dialects are limited and imperfect. More precise studies of language revealed the historicity of language development, revealed how humans of various centuries changed words, played with new meanings by making metaphors out of old words. Studies in the history of science revealed how often it was the reflective rationalization after the fact that revealed the potential significance of the results of an experiment, rather than a prior, logical prediction of a result that led to the experiment. Studies in urbanization, in the founding of institutions, in the transformation of institutions - all revealed how they came about through the construction of human beings, usually through the disconnected constructions of a multiplicity of human beings over a period of time. Culture itself came to be seen as a multidimensional fabric created over the slow evolution of human societies, a fabric always in a dynamic and unpredictable process of change. The source of change was not always reason and logic; in fact, change came about as much through force, violent conflict, chance natural disasters, the introduction of new viruses or foreign technologies, or unexpected consequences of inventions intended for other purposes.

More recently, research in cognitive psychology focusing on the learning of young children reveals a diversity of ways young people construct knowledge. Often the knowledge they construct is not the approved knowledge of the curriculum. When the children are asked to explain what they were doing, however, they can offer plausible explanations that make partial sense, once the researchers imaginatively enter the world of the child. For example, one wise, experienced teacher was puzzled by a child's comment that he "had committed adultery." The teacher assumed that the child did not know the accepted meaning of the term, but knew that the child was making some kind of connection in his mind. When the teacher asked the child to explain what the word adultery meant, the child answered, "You know, it's when a kid criticizes an adult."

Although constructivist research is still in its infancy, it has caught the attention of professors in teacher preparation programs, causing them to revise many of their assumptions about the work of teachers as conveying knowledge or "delivering curriculum", toward the assumption that teachers design learning activities in which *students* have a good chance to construct knowledge through a variety of scaffolded learning activities. While the knowledge constructed will still reflect its embeddedness in the cultural context and developmental capabilities of the child, it will nevertheless be the authentic knowledge of that child. By providing cooperative learning opportunities, the knowledge being constructed by each child will by influenced by the knowledge and perspectives of other children, and thus be corrected, refined, reinforced nuanced, stretched. Subsequent learning opportunities will continue to expand, qualify, enrich that knowledge during the schooling years and beyond.

Research in other areas of human development such as identity formation within ethnic and racial communities involves a dialectic of the self being shaped and of the self shaping the self through conscious choices. A similar dialectic is found in research in gender identity. Thus, constructivist theory proposes a two-dimensional dynamic: the historical and cultural context plays a crucial role in constructing individuals; the individual, in turn, through the various experiences and encounters with his or her world, responds, makes choices, seeks goals, pursues interests, uses developing talents. Thus in tacit as well as intentional ways the individual constructs him or herself, using the cultural meanings, language, and symbolic interpretive and expressive systems. To posit an exclusive explanation relying on either dimension - the external shaping influences, or the internal choices and activities of the individual - would be to reduce the life course of human beings to either fatalistic determinism, or anarchic and solipsistic individualism.

Research in constructivism seems to reveal a kind of three-step process. First, the individual absorbs cultural, linguistic, religious, class, and gender shaping influences through the socialization process which begins even in infancy. These influences are received without much questioning, although there are clearly affective responses of acceptance or resistance even in infants. Second, as the child develops, however, there is more and more deliberation about the outside shaping of his or her identity, rejecting some of this influence as obsolete, embracing other aspects of this influence, resisting with increasing vigor the confining effects of other cultural influences, while nonetheless using the cultural tools to effect that resistance. In this deliberation, the child is both reconstructing him or herself in the light of past influences, and constructing him or herself using new influences. What seems to be going on, at least tacitly, is critique of external influences, partial acceptance, partial rejection, and an increasingly intentional construction of the self. Third, in healthy humans we find a continuous cycle of the construction of knowledge, the self, the other, the world; the deconstruction of knowledge, the self, the other, the world; the reconstruction of knowledge, the self, the other, the world.

Larger Significance of Constructivist Theory

The perspectives offered by constructivist theory and research seem to suggest that the world as humans know it is continually being constructed, either to replicate and interpret the world as it was known the day before (Giddens, 1984), or to modify that world in however small adjustments, in order to make that world more intelligible, more user friendly, more functional, more just, more caring (Starratt, 1993). Knowledge is both the medium and product of this constructing. Culture is both the medium and the product of this constructing. The self is both the medium and the product of this constructing. The social sphere, "society", is both the medium and the product of this constructing. Institutions are both the medium and the product of this constructing.

The school, as are all other social institutions, are constructs put together by human beings. There is no Platonic, ideal school; there are only schools that particular communities create and sustain. This means, at least, that not all schools have to be the kinds of schools that postmodern critics disavow. It means that one can accept The Left's critique of the modernist naïve assumptions about knowledge, progress, capitalism, democracy, rationality, individualism, the social contract, economic liberalism, as well as The Right's critique about the need for standards and norms in schools, and a concern for preparing youngsters for productive adult lives in society. Both groups point to deficiencies in schooling practices and theoretical assumptions underlying those practices.

If we take constructivism seriously, then we have to admit that everyday, we "play school" according to scripts that we did not write, but which we have come to accept as defining what is possible. Schools are both the medium and the product of our activity. The critiques of schooling point to ways that we should *not* be running schools; they suggest, if only by implication, the kinds of scripts we should be writing for the conduct of schooling. Constructivist theory suggests that, since the script is a human construction, it is possible for a group of human beings to rewrite the script. The rewriting, however, will involve the dialectic suggested above. We have to recognize the strong cultural influences on the interpretation and meaning of the current script. We have to critique the assumptions behind those cultural influences to explore what is counterproductive, humiliating, stereotypical, unsupportable, contrary to crucial political beliefs, obsolete, unjust, and simply an ineffective waste of everybody's time. To do this, however, we have to probe the deeper values, ideals, and convictions of the very culture we are critiquing to find the positive values and ideals for the rewriting. We might adapt the familiar quotation from the Peanuts comic strip: we have met the culture and the culture is inside us. We have to recognize that the language we use to rewrite the script is the language of the old script. That will require a reexamination of the meanings behind or within the language we use, because our prior use of that language tended to express certain assumptions which now, we realize, need a second look.

That second look may lead us to embrace much that the culture holds sacred; for example, the sacredness of individual rights, the dignity of the individual, the ideals of civil liberties and equal rights before the law. It may lead us to reject aspects of the culture that are dysfunctional and conditioned by historical circumstances that no longer exist (for example, racial, class, and sexual subordination). It may also lead us to reinterpret other aspects of the culture which might usefully be restated and therefore retained (for example, the duties of citizenship, or freedom of religion). In other words, the work of rescripting the work of schooling will necessarily be a more evolutionary than a revolutionary process, not only because a revolution is politically impossible, but also because those doing the rescripting are working within the very cultural perspectives they want to challenge. Even Dewey appeared to have reflected cultural bias in his research on segregated African-American schools and on the supposed resistance of Polish-American communities to being Americanized.

The work of the cultural transformation of a school requires the continuing clarification of those meanings about learning, knowledge, productivity, excellence, democracy, equity, community, assessment, efficiency and effectiveness that are needed to set new directions for schooling. This work will involve struggle, time, and patient and respectful conversation among many people, for the work involves a two-fold effort. The reconstruction of schooling involves both a deconstruction of meanings, values, and assumptions - the analysis of their negatives and their positives, of what is to be rejected and what is to be kept - *and* a reconstruction, an invention of new meanings, new metaphors, new organizational dynamics, new institutional processes which will carry the playing of school into a more humanly satisfying and morally fulfilling story. The process of deconstructing the familiar script will teach two lessons. One lesson is that our knowledge is always historically conditioned, and therefore limited, and eventually antiquated. Another lesson is that our culture inescapably reflects relationships of power: not only the power of wealth and control over the instruments of violence, but the power of defining what things mean in the culture, what is considered natural, normal, acceptable and what is considered deviant, unnatural, and unacceptable. Frequently those powers coalesce into powers of domination, and when such power comes to be accepted by those in power as the natural order of things, their responsibility for the oppression of others becomes invisible to them.

The process of deconstruction needs to teach educators the humbling lesson that knowledge and power are mutually reinforcing. That is good news and bad news. The knowledge gained through science enables a people to understand how the natural world works, and enables them to make choices about how they will use that knowledge to improve the human condition while honoring environmental balance. The knowledge gained through science, however, is itself limited, and can lead a group of people to make short-sighted decisions about the exploitation of natural resources without understanding the long-term consequences on the environment and the human community. All knowledge can lead to pride, the pride that one now knows all one needs to know about life, success, nature, human relationships, even God. The acquisition of knowledge may also lead to its misuse for selfish or cruel motives, for torture, for terror, for revenge, for asserting superiority or domination over others.   In other words, the work of the constructivist, which includes the work of deconstructing the presently accepted script, must be carried on with the awareness of the possibility, and more important, the likelihood that one will believe that he or she has the right answer for everyone, has the final solution to the cultural problem of equity or gender relations or the distribution of public resources. This is the warning issued so consistently by Richard Rorty (1989): knowledge is contingent, fallible and dangerously misleading, and therefore one has to remind oneself continually of the irony involved in the human quest for knowledge.

Knowledge can seduce one into the illusion of certainty, can lead to the illusion of control over what one knows, can lead to the exclusion and silencing of all other points of view. We have to accept the irony of knowledge - that it distorts in the very process of revealing reality - and understand that its pursuit requires that we perform a simultaneous act of deconstructing of our knowledge even while we are constructing it. In other words, we have to recognize that what we do not know is always much larger than what we know, and that what we know sometimes prevents us from seeing other important aspects of reality to which our new knowledge blinds us. Thus, the constructivist attempt to rescript the process of schooling must retain the ironist attitude that the rescripting will contain distortions, omissions, latent power relationships. The rescripting, ironically, will more than likely lead to unforeseen future problems even while it addresses current problems. Further, rescripting schooling for others without their participation in the conversation will almost certainly make matters worse.

This larger perspective on the construction of knowledge that includes a never-ending process of constructing, deconstructing, and reconstructing, offers a depth to Dewey's pragmatic method of intelligence. It carries that method into a second level of deliberation, namely that the issue in front of us may be problematic, not because of conflicts between two desirable course of action, but because our naming of the problem itself may be too limiting, too one-sided, too biased by unquestioned assumptions. It offers an ironic quality to Dewey's optimistic pragmatic democracy, namely the awareness that today's agreed-upon solution will bring about next week's new problem, but that next week we will deal with that one as well.

The Argument for A Postmodern Theory of Democratic Educational Leadership

Let me try to pull this commentary together. I will lay out what appear to me to be "givens". Then I will argue that we can make something out of these givens that provide a *reasonable* foundation for an ongoing effort to build a theory that might begin to legitimate the practice of democratic leadership in schools.

Givens
1)   Schools in the United States cannot presently be called democratic institutions, and the governance and leadership of these institutions cannot be called truly democratic. Those who call themselves democratic leaders or administrators are using misleading terminology.
2)   The postmodern critique of modernity has illuminated the logic of power and the mythic assumptions behind the practice and the theory of democracy.

3) The conditions of postmodernity, which reflect the shattering or rejection of all metanarratives, make the development of a widely accepted, revised theory of democratic leadership of any social institution, including schools, very unlikely.

4) The postmodern critique nevertheless requires a reconstruction of democratic theory and practice that is enlightened by that critique, chastened by that critique, and to a degree encouraged by that critique. We still need to chart a course through the wasteland, even though no one knows a clear path or a final destination. The path will go where we go, day by day, and the destination will be what we agree and want it to be. Making a path, rescripting the play is our burden and our responsibility and our blessing.

5) There resides in American pragmatism a useful set of perspectives on democratic life, the social construction of knowledge and morality, the cultivation of civic virtues, and the conduct of education.

6) Constructivist theory provides a sufficiently developed body of literature to support and enlarge the pragmatist understanding of the construction of knowledge and virtue within social institutions of democracy.

7) The postmodern critique would suggest intentionally using a "hermeneutic of suspicion" to analyze all decisions before they are implemented in order to check for evidence of self-serving interests involved in the decision.

8) The postmodern critique would suggest an ironic attitude toward all leadership initiatives; namely that leaders recognize ahead of time the unavoidable fallibility and fragility of institutional arrangements including the very exercise of leadership, and the likelihood that they will need continuous further adjustment in the foreseeable future.

9) The present arrangements of politics nationally, regionally, locally will remain as it is for some time; so too, the influence of economic and cultural elites on government policies and operations; so too, the existence of widespread social injustices and unjust institutional structures.

10) Within the literature on organizational studies, there is sufficient agreement on the leader's dependence on "distributed intelligence" to argue that organizational leadership (in our case, educational leadership) requires a much more consultative, participatory, inclusionary stance in arriving at internal school policies and major operational decisions, a stance that on the surface, at least, appears consistent with democratic leadership.

A PRAGMATIC, IRONIC, THEORY OF DEMOCRATIC EDUCATIONAL LEADERSHIP

A reconstruction of democratic educational leadership theory posits that such leadership would:

a) reflect the local context, history, and chemistry of the people at the school. The local context will determine the limits and possibilities on any given day of democratic leadership in the school, even while school leaders are making strides in transforming the local school environment into something more democratic than it was before. What is possible in Bridgetown, Barbados, differs from what is possible in Boston or Buffalo.

b) establish a variety of consultative procedures and processes that will involve major stakeholders in the construction of school policies. In the establishment of these procedures, major attention will be given to the democratic spirit embedded in these procedures, as well as a method for assessing and revising these procedures. The stakeholders shall specifically be concerned with providing free inquiry, toleration of diverse opinions and free communication, and will solicit the opinions of those under-represented groups in the school community.

c) expect that conflicting opinions and proposals will surface in the course of deliberations and hold to the conviction that the deliberations will be richer and more promising thereby. If the school is to be a self-governing community (as far as the management of its internal affairs is concerned) then it will develop ways to negotiate, arbitrate, and at least temporarily resolve such conflicts, for this is one of the realities of democratic living in an increasingly pluralistic society.

d) be willing to critique both the manner and the content of its decisions and to have others critique them in order to keep the focus of decisions on the good of the community, especially on the enrichment of quality learning for all students, rather than on expediency, favouritism, or some other inappropriate reason.

e) expect that decisions will be regularly evaluated against their intended effects and modified and reversed in the light of that evaluation.

f) continually integrate decisions within a larger sense of purpose and value to support and improve the learning being pursued at the school, especially the learning of increasingly mature attitudes and skills of citizenship (the civic virtues), and those skills and understandings that facilitate their full participation in social and economic life.

g) attempt to have the school exhibit the qualities of a democracy in miniature, so that the school functions as a learning laboratory for democratic living, which insures that students and teachers will have multiple opportunities to practice democratic leadership with their fellows in contributing to the life and well being of the school.

h) ensure that both individual and group academic learning projects may frequently be targeted to make some contribution either to the school or the civic community.

i) establish specific proactive processes and procedures in the daily and weekly functioning of the school that address problems and issues around the ideal of democratic living.

j) expect misunderstandings and violations of rights to occur; provide a variety of ritual processes for reconciliation when they do, and use these opportunities to explore how to prevent such future occurrences.

k) ensure that a variety of public spaces are available for all voices to be heard, for the sharing of life stories, for celebrating the differences that contribute to the make up of the school community. At the same time provide for other spaces to be available for sub-communities to nurture their own identities.

l)   provide for students and teachers to govern their own affairs as much as possible, while at the same time preserving a concern for the overall common good of the entire school community.

m)   ensure that the school teaches appropriate lessons about the way democracy currently functions in our society, and explores how the conditions of public life may be improved within democratically constituted procedures and traditions. Teach how current arrangements of power operate, and help all members of the community to use power constructively for the common good.

n)   ensure recognition and reward for a variety of talents, contributions and achievements of individual members and groups in the school community.

o)   try to instill the long view about the development of democracy, for democracy will never be a final achievement; it will always be an ideal that calls us to transform our present condition into something more collectively satisfying and morally fulfilling.

p)   recognize that most of the time you do not know what you are doing, and that you are probably, however unwittingly, often doing some harm or hurt to somebody. Be assured that there is always someone in the community who does not appreciate or benefit from your leadership. Always remember the fable of the Emperor's clothes.

IMPLICATIONS FOR THE PREPARATION AND CONTINUING EDUCATION OF SCHOOL ADMINISTRATORS

Briefly stated, I see four implications for university programs that prepare and further educate school administrators.

1)   Begin the program by admitting that neither the professors nor the students know how to reform schools. If the previous analysis and argument has any validity, then no one person or group of person knows the answer—certainly not the answer for all or most schools. To the question of how to reform schools, everyone should respond, I don't know   but I have some ideas I'd like to put on the table for discussion." This instantly removes the phony aura of wisdom that graduate courses appear to have, and enables the group to work on what appear to be useful ways to lead the schools out of the doldrums.

2)   The members of each class construct, deconstruct and reconstruct what they think they know through a vigorous and extended discussion of their ideas about school transformation.

3)   In the process, the class reflects on what it is they are learning about the process of democratic deliberation, and about the pragmatic construction of frameworks for action.

4)   Student papers, and their dissertations, be evaluation reports of their attempts to engage in the process of democratic leadership of their own school's renewal.

CONCLUSION

As I conclude this chapter, I know that I will continue to deconstruct and reconstruct this effort at a theory of democratic leadership of schools. For the time being, the key points I wanted to stress are here: (a) a pragmatic approach to addressing the transformation of schooling; (b) a self-imposed moral wariness that always takes a second look for self-serving or domineering motives; (c) an acceptance of limited rationality in decisions and the concomitant expectation of continuous adjustments; (d) a focus on teaching youngsters the rudiments of democratic living through realistic experiences of the obstacles and joys in the struggle to achieve it; and (e) permeating all of it, a belief that the moral fulfillment of working towards a democratic community is worth the struggle for its imperfect realization.

NOTES

[1] This chapter is a revised and updated version of a paper originally presented at the Conference of the UCEA Centre for the Study of Values and Leadership, Bridgetown, Barbados. It has also been previously published as an article in a special issue (Vol. 4, No. 4, 333-352) of the *International Journal of Leadership in Education* (2001).

REFERENCES

Allen, A.L., & Regan, Jr., M.C. (1998). *Debating democracy's discontent: Essays on American politics, law, and public philosophy.* New York: Oxford University Press.

Barber, B. (1984). *Strong democracy.* Princeton, NJ: Princeton University Press.

Barber, B. (1988). *The conquest of politics.* Princeton, NJ: Princeton University Press.

Barber, B. (1998). *A passion for democracy: American essays.* Princeton, NJ: Princeton University Press.

Bass, B. (1981). *Stogdill's handbook of leadership.* New York: The Free Press.

Bellah, R.N., Madsen, R., Sullivan, W.M., Swidler, A., & Tipton, S.M. (1985). *Habits of the heart: Individualism and commitment in American life.* New York: Harper Collins.

Burns, J.M. (1978). *Leadership.* New York: Harper & Row.

Burns, J.M., & Burns, S. (1991). *A people's charter: The pursuit of rights in America.* New York: Alfred A. Knopf.

Dahl, R. (1989). *Democracy and its critics.* New Haven, CT: Yale University Press.

Dewey, J. (1958). *Democracy and education.* New York: Macmillan.

Dewey, J. (1948). *Reconstruction in philosophy.* Boston, MA: Beacon Press.

Elkin, S.L., & Soltan, K.E. (1993). *A new constitutionalism: Designing political institutions for a good society.* Chicago, IL: University of Chicago Press.

Elshtain, J.B. (1995). *Democracy on trial.* New York: Basic Books.

Galston, W.A. (1995). Liberal virtues and the formation of civic character. In M.A. Glendon & D. Blankenhorn (Eds.), *Seedbeds of virtue: Sources of competence, character, and citizenship in American society* (pp. 35-60). Lanham, MD: Madison Books.

Giddens, A. (1984). *The constitution of society.* Berkeley, CA: University of California Press.

Hunter, J.D. (1994). *Before the shooting begins: Searching for democracy in America's culture wars.* New York: The Free Press.

Kymlicka, W. (1995). *Multicultural citizenship: A liberal theory of minority rights.* Oxford: Oxford University Press.

Marty, M.E. (1997). *The one and the many: America's struggle for the common good.* Cambridge, MA: Harvard University Press.

Maxcy, S. (1991). *Educational leadership: A critical pragmatic perspective.* New York: Bergin & Garvey.

Murray, J.C. (1960). *We hold these truths.* New York: Sheed and Ward.

Rorty, R. (1989). *Contingency, irony, and solidarity.* Cambridge: Cambridge University Press.

Sandel, M.J. (1996). *Democracy's discontent: America in search of a public philosophy.* Cambridge, MA: Belknap/Harvard University Press.

Sandel, M.J. (1998). *Liberalism and the limits of justice, second edition.* Cambridge: Cambridge University Press.

Shklar, J. (1991). *American citizenship: The quest for inclusion.* Cambridge, MA: Harvard University Press.

Soder, R. (Ed.) (1996). *Democracy, education, and the schools.* San Francisco, CA: Jossey-Bass.

Starratt, R.J. (1993). *The drama of leadership.* London: Falmer Press.

Sullivan, W.M. (1982). *Reconstructing public philosophy.* Berkeley, CA: University of California Press.

Sullivan, W.M. (1995). Reinstitutionalizing virtue in civil society. In M.A. Glendon & D. Blankenhorn (Eds.), *Seedbeds of virtue: Sources of competence, character, and citizenship in American society* (pp. 185-200). Lanham, MD: Madison Books.

Tarcov, N. (1996). The meaning of democracy. In R. Soder (Ed.), *Democracy, education and the schools* (pp. 1-36). San Francisco, CA: Jossey-Bass.

Taylor, C. (1988). Living with difference. In A.L. Allen and M.C. Regan, Jr. (Eds.), *Debating democracy's discontent: Essay on American politics, law, and public philosophy* (pp. 212-226). New York: Oxford University Press.

Westbrook, R.B. (1991). *John Dewey and American democracy.* Ithaca, NY: Cornell University Press.

Westbrook, R.B. (1996). Public schooling and American democracy. In R. Soder (Ed.), *Democracy, education and the schools* (pp. 125-150). San Francisco, CA: Jossey-Bass.

MALCOLM J. RICHMON

PERSISTENT DIFFICULTIES WITH VALUES IN EDUCATIONAL ADMINISTRATION: MAPPING THE TERRAIN

Abstract. This chapter examines scholarly work in the area of values and Educational Administration, and maintains that academic inquiry into values has proceeded over the past several decades in the absence of any broadly shared conceptual agreement as to what values actually are or might be. It is argued that this conceptual incoherence hampers practitioners' efforts to understand the role values might play in their professional lives, and ultimately hinders the development of meaningful reflective practices. To this end, it is suggested that greater clarity is needed with regards to the dimensions of difference which characterize values inquiry. Four key dimensions are proposed and discussed: knowing values, framing values, investigating values, and informing values.

Recent scholarly attempts to better understand the work of principals and superintendents has accorded the study of values increased prominence (Begley, 1999a). This does not suggest, however, that the interest in values is particularly new. Indeed, questions surrounding truth, goodness, and moral rightness can be traced back to the ancient Greeks, and related axiological concerns have been raised in philosophical inquiry for several centuries. Yet over the past several decades, scholars of educational administration have began to recognize the importance of values for those individuals we charge with running schools, evidenced by the formation of two affiliated academic centres, OISE/UT's Centre for the Study of Values and Leadership, and the University of Virginia's Centre for the Study of Leadership and Ethics. Moreover, recent texts edited by Begley and Leonard (1999) and Begley (1999b), further illuminate the vast and at times divergent interests in values.

As a basic assumption, it can be acknowledged that values are important to academic inquiry into educational leadership. As Willower (1992) points out, "a significant portion of the practice in educational administration requires rejecting some courses of action in favour of a preferred one" (p. 369). Nonetheless, while scholarly work in educational administration has increasingly embraced the term 'values', this shared focus is largely illusory, belying the actual level of coherence in academic approaches to studying values. Perhaps the two most rudimentary questions of the field remain highly contested: *what are values and how can we best understand them?*[1]

Greenfield explains:

> the fundamental problem in knowing and understanding social reality is of the place values shall play in inquiry. For nearly two decades this question has troubled the theory and knowledge promulgated in the field of educational administration (in Greenfield & Ribbins, 1993, p. 169).

Central to Greenfield's point is that there is a lack of any widely-shared understanding of what values actually are or might be. In examining the extant

P.T. Begley and O. Johansson (eds.), The Ethical Dimensions of School Leadership, 33–47.

literature on the subject, Nicholas Rescher (1969) compiled a non-exhaustive list of nearly a dozen distinct, and at times, contradictory descriptions of values. Similarly, Frankena (1967) stresses this lack of coherence, explaining that:

> the terms 'value' and 'valuation' and their cognates and compounds are used in a confused and confusing but widespread way in our contemporary culture, not only in economics and philosophy but also and especially in other social sciences and humanities (p. 229).

More recently, in a discussion of the conceptual dimensions of values, Green (1999) describes the host of alternative ways in which 'values' have been understood, entitled rather discouragingly, "The Grand Delusion" (pp. 123-147). While Green, driven by an interest in moral education, makes quite a concerted effort to be clear as to what he means by 'values', it would seem that many scholars of educational administration have been somewhat less conceptually fastidious. Indeed, a great deal of literature in educational administration refers to 'values' rather obliquely, providing little or no account of what is meant by the term.

Superficially, then, it may seem unlikely that values inquiry can meaningfully serve to examine administrative phenomena in the absence of any basic conceptual agreement as to the nature of what "values" actually are. As the literature on values has been informed by an exceptionally wide range of assumptions about "values", it should only be expected that the accumulation of scholarly work in the field is remarkably diverse. Thus, inquiry into values is not simply heterogeneous, but might even be said to be examining entirely different phenomena under the singular and dubious banner of 'values'.

CONCEPTUALIZING THE DIFFICULTIES WITH VALUES IN EDUCATIONAL ADMINISTRATION

It might be safely stated that, at this point in the development of the field, it is not likely, or perhaps even desirable, that universal agreement regarding the conceptual dimensions of values be pursued. If this is indeed the case then, at a minimum, there is a need for more clarity about the differences among competing perspectives which inform values research. To this end, I attempt to examine systematically the differences across perspectives in values research, "mapping the terrain" as the title of this chapter suggests. Of course, it would be nothing short of a Herculean effort to propose a comprehensive overview of perspectives which have their roots in centuries-old philosophical debates. Rather, the intention is to seek greater clarity than currently exists, by identifying and examining themes in the literature which embrace a broad range of theoretical understandings embedded within scholarly work on values in educational administration.

The benefit of this approach is essentially twofold. Firstly, I submit that the literature on values in educational administration is to a great extent fragmented, and while conceptually meaningful unification of dissimilar perspectives may not be feasible, clarity with the regard to their differences is essential. Secondly, and perhaps most importantly, accounting for the persistent differences which underpin scholarly inquiry into values may assist practitioners - those charged with the formidable task of running schools and school systems - in assessing how particular values perspectives may or may not apply to their work.

This chapter provides an analytic orientation to values perspectives advanced and pursued in the literature over the last several decades. More specifically, a four-part framework is applied to the analysis of existing approaches to conceptualizing values, in an attempt to identify and compare persistent themes. Though no exhaustive review of all values literature is possible, the sources used in this paper were selected based on several criteria including citation frequency, scholarly contribution, and breadth of perspective.

The analytic framework identifies four fundamental issues which will be examined within the literature on values and leadership. Expressed as questions, these four interrelated issues are: (a) what does it mean to know values? (b) how can values be conceptually framed? (c) how can values be investigated? and (d) how can values be informed?

Knowing Values - All social science research is informed by an epistemological perspective, essentially a position on what it means to "know", or purport to "know" social phenomena. Inasmuch as all knowledge claims about values are embedded in assumptions about the nature of how social knowledge can be acquired, a description of these often unarticulated positions is of paramount importance.

Framing Values - As a point of departure, inquiry into values typically utilizes particular frameworks which inform and guide research. Since these frameworks provide the scaffolding for a great deal of empirical research into values, they are essential in shaping understandings surrounding the phenomenon.

Investigating Values - At the most rudimentary level, it is necessary to consider the role that values play in research efforts to describe social phenomena. Insofar as educational leadership focuses on the work of principals and superintendents in schools, the prominence of values in administrative inquiry illuminates a crucial perspective on understanding values in administrative work.

Informing Values - The relationship between scholarly work on values and administrative practice is of central importance. Indeed, the study of values in educational administration should, at least in some way, be aimed at offering meaningful insights to school leaders. Of particular importance in this area is the ethical content of values inquiry which provides the normative substance that may serve to guide administrative action.

Although this chapter is essentially an examination of existing theoretical literature, it is an interest in supporting practitioners that drives the analysis. The basic premise is that values theory, being highly prolific and diversified, remains overly inaccessible to practitioners. A clearer and more systematic understanding of the breadth and scope of values literature may enable them to better appreciate how values may or may not relate to their day-to-day work. I propose that a better understanding of values can assist school leaders in discriminating between competing tenets embedded in the literature, and hence heighten their sensibilities in drawing upon elements of scholarship which best reflect their own personal "values philosophy". Inasmuch as values inquiry in educational administration is frequently predicated on the notion that school leaders are indeed valuing agents, it is imperative that scholars in the field accord school leaders the opportunity to do just that - determine the relative "value" of contending theoretical perspectives which purport to inform their work.

KNOWING VALUES

Begley (1999b) rightly points out that values literature is characterized by "epistemological wrangling" (p. 117). Yet values seemed to be less troubling in the middle of the twentieth century, when the field of educational administration was undergoing a transformation most often referred to as the Theory Movement. The Theory Movement, at its core, sought to develop a science of educational administration, in which law-like generalizations could be developed to guide practitioners in their work (Evers & Lakomski, 1991; Greenfield & Ribbins, 1993). As Getzels explains, "systematic research requires the mediation of theory - theory that will give meaning and order to observations already made and will specify areas where observations still need to be made" (cited in Culbertson, 1988, p. 15).

This era reflected "a general doctrine of positivism which held that all genuine knowledge is based upon sense experience and can only be advanced by means of observation and experiment" (Cohen & Manion, 1994, p. 11). In this conception of knowledge, there are believed to be universal laws guiding human conduct, and hence organizations operate within seemingly functionalist frames. By identifying the relationships between empirically grounded variables, it was suggested that the fundamental truths of administration could be discovered. Yet this emerging administrative science viewed people as highly determinable, and notions of values were eschewed in favour of more material and observable organizational variables. Herbert Simon's work (1945) was among the driving forces behind this movement, which proposed administration as, essentially, a value-neutral activity. Inquiry then, "was to be properly studied on the basis of objective observations informed by operationally defined concepts and directed and ordered by explanatory theories" (Allison, 1989, p. 12).

The ideals of the Theory Movement, however, have become increasingly criticized over the last three decades. In his famous address to colleagues in Bristol in 1974, Greenfield launched an attack on the positivistic tenets of an administrative science in what would be later recognized as "the epistemological shot that was heard around the world of educational administration" (Hodgkinson, 2000, p. 12). Greenfield (1975) argued that social reality is not a 'naturally' occurring phenomenon; rather, it is construed by individuals in different ways. Knowledge, he argued, should be recognized more tentatively, within subjective frames. In this view, humans are not moral ciphers but valuing agents, and prone to be influenced by these values. The goal of theory, then, would be to describe the ways in which individuals give meaning to their world, and make sense of their actions. Initially, constructivist-subjectivist[2] approaches came under heavy criticism, particularly from those vested in the development of a more traditional administrative science (e.g., Willower, 1980).

Greenfield's assault on the Theory Movement was bolstered by Christopher Hodgkinson, who challenged strictly technical-rational conceptualizations of educational administration by suggesting the work of school leaders to be morally artful, rather than simply functional.   Much of Hodgkinson's substantial contribution to the field can be found within four books (1978; 1983; 1991; 1996) to which Peter Ribbins (1999) refers to as the "Victorian Quartet" of values literature.   Perhaps the most contentious and yet essential component of Hodgkinson's work is his conception of the naturalistic fallacy, which posits that values can not be reduced from objective facts, or as more commonly expressed, you can't get an "ought" from an "is". Viewed in this way, if administration is indeed a value-laden enterprise, and values could not be discerned from facts, then there could be no science of administration (Evers & Lakomski, 1993).

It would be largely incorrect to suggest that subjective-constructive epistemologies simply subverted the dominant positivist thinking of the Theory Movement. What emerged in actuality was a new post-positive perspective, "a contingent positivism that attempts to accommodate the most problematic criticisms of the former" (Begley, in preparation under contract). The extent to which post-positive inquiry differed substantially from the scholarly work of the preceding era is questionable. Allison (1989) explains that:

> while Greenfield certainly laid the original optimistic hopes for a theoretical science of educational administration to final rest, his first shots at the positivistic beasts that had come to graze in [the] field of academic educational administration during the age of the New Movement scarcely wounded, let alone dispatched, them. Indeed, even a cursory glance through the pages of any recent issue of Educational Administration Quarterly . . . will show that the key notion of studying organizational functioning and administrator behaviour as objective, quantifiable, predictable, phenomena is still very much alive, and even kicking. (p. 13)

Post-positive perspectives frequently recognize the valuing nature of individuals, but view this as non-problematic insofar as values, like organization variables, can also be determined and accounted for, and hence provide but another variable for inquiry into administrative phenomena. This is starkly opposed by Greenfield's view that "values lie beyond rationality . . . they lie beyond quantification, beyond measurement. They are not 'variables'" (as cited in Greenfield & Ribbins, 1993, pp. 183-184). Moreover, recent analyzes of paradigms of inquiry suggest that positive and post-positive perspectives frequently exclude the notion that values play a central role in educational research, while constructivist perspectives acknowledge and interrogate this role (Guba & Lincoln, 1994). It is perhaps for this reason that some scholars of educational administration might suggest, quite astonishingly, that contemporary philosophical work has contributed little to the development of the concept of leadership (e.g., Leithwood & Duke, 1999). One might suspect that the scholarly treatment of values as mere variables in our understanding of organizational processes is related to the view that conducting research itself is a relatively value-neutral enterprise, a position untenable to those who adopt more constructivist or subjectivist frames of inquiry.

Recently, Evers and Lakomski have proposed a theory of naturalistic coherentism over the course of three books (1991; 1996; 2000). In their approach, they "adjudicate a naturalistic definition of 'good' in terms of the role it plays in promoting the virtues of coherence in the theory, or system of statements, in which it figures" (Evers & Lakomski, 1993, p. 147). The promulgated coherentist virtues, which are instrumental in the naturalization of 'values', include: simplicity, explanatory power, testability, question resolving power, and congruence with existing beliefs. Theories are viewed as webs of belief, and as such, factual and value claims can both be embedded within them. Values (and related ethical claims), exist within the very same neuronal networks described by cognitive neuroscience as facts do.

While impressive in scope, Evers and Lakomski's work is essentially geared at proposing coherentist criteria for justifying theory selection. Although the sophisticated attempt to marry facts and values within a shared web of understanding represents a rather innovative way of conceptualizing values, it is similar in many ways to more recognizable and accessible post-positive perspectives, as it offers a sterile notion of values which can be determined and 'weighed'. More troubling is that Evers and Lakomski's theoretical approach offers little justification of its coherentist virtues, claiming they are "super-empirical" (1993, p. 145). Expectedly, naturalistic coherentism has been the subject of a great deal of critique (e.g., Allison, 2001; Allison & Ellett, 1999; Donmoyer, 2001; Maxcy, 2001; Stapleton & Long, 1995).

Though the epistemic debates that have ensued (and will invariably continue to ensue in perpetuity) in the study of values and educational administration are contentious, they are a necessary consideration for appreciating how values are understood differently from different perspectives.

FRAMING VALUES

Among the more contemporary scholars in axiological philosophy is Gaus (1990). Gaus argues that, at a minimum, theoretical perspectives should provide a clear and coherent conceptual framework for understanding values phenomenon. Gaus proposes this conceptual clarification can take three basic forms: description, stipulation, and reconstruction with justification. In the first form, theorists aim to describe values by identifying a wide range of salient features related to the phenomenon. The second perspective, the stipulative account, views values as being characteristics, and the aim of this perspective involves stipulating the qualities of what is valued. Both of these perspectives, Gaus suggests, are inadequate. He reasons that not only are these approaches unlikely to provide a highly nuanced account of values, they are primarily descriptive, offering little insight into *why* values are held. Gaus advocates for a reconstructive-justification approach to values, which aims not only to provide a conceptually coherent system of values, but legitimate, normative grounds on which to discriminate between competing values.

At the very least, Gaus provides an ambitious direction for those inquiring into values. The most widely recognizable conceptual framework relating to values in educational leadership is essentially a descriptive account (with some attempt at justification) proposed by Hodgkinson.

Hodgkinson suggests that values can be held at three basic motivational levels (Table 1). Type III values, or *subrational* values, are grounded in preference. "Type III values are self-justifying, since they are grounded in individual affect and constitute the individual's preference structure" (1991, p. 98). Type II values, or *rational* values, are grounded in either consequences (type IIa) or consensus (type IIb).   Values of consequence involve "a reasonable analysis of the consequences entailed by the pending value judgment [directed at] some future resultant state of affairs" (1991, p. 98), while values of consensus concur "with the will of the majority in a given collectivity" (1991, p. 98).   Type I values, or transrational values, are grounded in more metaphysical principles, taking "the form of ethical codes, injunctions, or commandments" (1991, p. 99).

Table 1. Analytic Model of the Value Concept
(Adapted from Hodgkinson, 1991, p. 97).

(Deontological-Nomothetic-Discipline Dimension)			
Grounding	*Psychological Correspondences*	*Philosophical Correspondences*	*Types of Value*
Right Principle (I)	Conative	Religionism Existentialism Ideologism	Transrational
Consequences (IIa)		Humanism	Rational
Consensus (IIb)	Cognitive	Pragmatism Utilitarianism	
Good Preference (III)	Affective	Logical Positivism Behaviourism Hedonism	Subrational
Axiological-Idiographic-Indulgence Dimension			

Although Hodgkinson's framework was - and continues to be - highly influential, it has been strongly criticized (Evers & Lakomski, 1993; Lobb, 1993).

Ashbaugh and Kasten (1984) provide an alternative framework for considering values, which they acknowledge was highly influenced by Hodgkinson's work. The framework describes three main categories of values: personalistic, organizational, and transcendent. *Personalistic* values, as the name suggests, are highly idiographic and typically emerge from an individual's experiences.   This type of value subsumes an individual's sense of personal style, patterns of human relations with others, and understandings about the nature of schools. *Organizational* values, alternatively, are related to "organizational norms, systems concerns and professional ethos" (p. 199).   These values may reflect perceptions about organizational goals, professional concerns, and organizational efficacy. Lastly, *transcendent* values are rooted in more ethereal conceptions of (supposedly) broadly based codes of conduct.   The values are believed to be highly generalizable, and grounded in philosophy or religion.   While Ashbaugh and Kasten's framework was inspired by Hodgkinson's model, it has received less attention in the literature, although it has been used in some qualitative studies on values (e.g., Leonard, 1996).

Beck (1993) envisions a system of values in which there are no absolute values, but rather values are in a state of constant negotiation, and hence are difficult to relate directly to action. Beck describes six categories of values, though he does not explain at any length how these categories were developed. *Basic* values relate to rudimentary areas of human needs, and include "survival, health, happiness, friendship . . . [and] freedom" (p. 24). *Spiritual* values embody more ethereal affective qualities, such as "awareness, breadth of outlook, integration, wonder, gratitude, hope, detachment, humility, love [and] gentleness" (p. 24). *Moral* values relate to ethical sensibilities such as honesty, reliability, and fairness. *Social and political* values refer to sensibilities dealing with general social functioning, such as justice, participation, and citizenship. *Intermediate-range* values reflect personalized sensibilities in a broad sense, including valued views on "fitness, sporting ability, music appreciation, [and] good family relationships" (p. 24). Alternatively, *specific* values relate personal sensibilities surrounding almost any particular thing, such as the value of a certain song, a football player, or a bicycle.

Leithwood, Begley, and Cousins (1994) modify Beck's framework, proposing three similar categories of values, *basic human* values, *general moral* values, and *social and political* values. To this, they add *professional* values, which embeds the roles and responsibilities of educators into the framework.

Although the values frameworks described here represent a range of conceptual classification systems for studying values, they share a highly descriptive function, in that values are categorized based on characteristics of the value itself[3]. Insofar as scholars of educational leadership are interested in how values influence administrative action, it may seem surprising that existing conceptual approaches to values do not focus more specifically on the interface between values and action. Though Gaus (1990) contends that reconstruction-justification frameworks serve to best relate values to the action of individuals, it is likely necessary to first develop a conceptually robust account of what values are or might be.

INVESTIGATING VALUES

Since educational researchers approach values from different epistemological perspectives, and adopt different conceptual frameworks for their research, it is not surprising that the role of values in administrative inquiry is highly divergent (Begley, 1996). What is most obvious in the treatment of values in administrative inquiry is the centrality of values in the research effort - that is to say how "important" values are to the study.

Post-positive inquiry into administrative phenomena has slowly begun to recognize the valuing nature of individuals in organizations. Yet the spirit of much of this work relegates values to a position of relatively minor importance, a single variable within a greater theoretical frame. By acknowledging the complexity of values, though, functionalist organizational and behavioural research can account for unexpected variation in results; values might provide an attractive, though superficially treated, subterfuge for phenomena not adequately treated within the original theoretical tenets of the research effort. Alternatively, values have also been recovered in deterministic inquiry by simply treating them as non-problematic. Leithwood, Jantzi, and Steinbach (1999), for example, consider the function of values in the problem-solving processes of administrators. Yet the treatment of values is a rather pedestrian one, where values are suggested to be "enduring . . . a standard to guide one's actions and thoughts" (p. 105). Moreover, Leithwood, Jantzi, and Steinbach consider values as an accessible and quite knowable cognitive phenomenon, and consider the effect of values on action benignly, as almost entirely indirect.

If values are a "fly in the ointment" for those working within deterministic frames, to those working in more constructive-subjective frames, values are the ointment itself. In this view, values are central to the research, "the very stuff of leadership and administrative life" (Hodgkinson, 1991, p. 11). Indeed, a great deal of inquiry has been directed at uncovering administrators' values and examining how these values are articulated and acted upon. Among the more significant and well agreed-upon findings that have resulted from these efforts is the notion that administrators tend to articulate the motivational bases which underpin their values in rational terms concerned with consensus and consequences (Begley & Johansson, 1998; Campbell-Evans, 1991; Leonard, 1997).

Of course, values research is not easily balkanized into strict camps. Administrative scholars have become increasingly interested in the valuing dimensions of leadership, to varying degrees (e.g., Maxcy, 1993; Sergiovanni, 2000). In many cases, values are treated as an organizational phenomenon rather than an individualistic one. Essentially, when values are assumed to be functionally equivalent across people within an organization –hence, 'organizational values'– they can be used to describe general belief systems that characterize organizational members without considering the more troublesome, yet more interesting, idiographic nature of values and individuals. In one study, Holmes (1991) offers a comparative analysis of attitudes and beliefs between matched samples of chief education officers and private sector CEOs, and provides illustrative general characteristics of both groups, though he offers little attention or insight into the relative impact of values for individual participants.

It is important to recognize, of course, that values still remain largely absent from a great deal of the scholarship in educational administration and leadership. Across a wide range of currently popular topics on school improvement, school effectiveness, best practices, and program evaluation, notions of values are frequently ignored. Ironically, there is little doubt that values assumptions are embedded throughout these works. Yet much of the aforementioned research concerns itself primarily with concrete measures of organizational effects as they relate to student achievement data. Perhaps this is to be expected, though. After all, if an administrative science could be realized, it would provide exceptional instruments of control over people in organizations. As Ryan (1988) points out, a shift away from an administrative science involves letting go of the potential power it offers:

> It comes as no great surprise that most in the field would be reluctant to part with a conceptual scheme that promises to fulfill this mandate. To abandon this mechanical metaphor would be to relinquish the power which accompanies an (alleged) ability to forecast the future and control human beings and establish bona fide truth. (p. 19)

Values research carries an intrinsically greater burden. Greenfield explains (with reference to Hodgkinson's work) that to consider values:

> ... is to consider questions for which there are no easy answers . . . it is to think hard
> thoughts and to look at things painful to bear. The strong and the compassionate,
> however, will see the relevance of this work, the truth of the realities described, and
> their force in everyday administrative affairs. (cited in Greenfield & Ribbins, 1993, p.
> 162)

As Greenfield correctly suggests, values are difficult to investigate not only on account of their ethereal nature, but as a matter of virtual distress for those scholars who rise to the challenge. Thus the diversified treatment of values in literature comes as neither a surprise nor a peculiarity.

INFORMING VALUES

In considering the conceptual incoherence surrounding values, Kluckhohn (1954) writes "the only general agreement is that values somehow have to do with normative as opposed to existential propositions" (p. 390). Despite the general consensus that values are related to normation, ethical claims are invariably the most contentious areas of values inquiry. We can take comfort, though, that problems surrounding ethics have permeated philosophical discourse for centuries, and it is unlikely that they can ever be resolved with unanimous satisfaction (Gensler, 1996). Inasmuch as research on values might seek to inform the practice of educational leaders, it is necessary to recognize the problems in doing so.

At the heart of the disagreement with regard to the professional applicability of values theory is a longstanding debate dealing with objectivist-subjectivist tenets. Moral subjectivism or moral relativism, in a strict sense, provides for ethical claims to be made by individuals as in the following generic example:

'X is good or right' means that 'I (the speaker) approve of X.'

'X is bad or wrong' means that 'I (the speaker) disapprove of X.'

Yet if these two statements are true, and rightness and wrongness could be established by individuals merely by believing them to be so, then no one could ever be wrong in moral judgments[4]. While this may seem counterintuitive, it is essentially the normative content provided by Hodgkinson (1978; 1983; 1991; 1996).

Hodgkinson offers a single normative postulate regarding his model; that is, the model represents a hierarchy of values. Type I values are "superior, more authentic, better justified, of more defensible grounding than type II" (1991, p. 103). Similarly, type II values are superior to type III values. Type III values are at the axiological end of the values axis representing what is *good*, while type I values are at the deontological end of the axis representing what is *right*. In Hodgkinson's model, then, transrationally held values are more defensible than rational ones. Accordingly, violent radicals and extreme fundamentalists –true believers– are afforded loftier "ethical" providence than the deliberate, rational politician or even the self-interested individual. In professional domains, if not in political ones, this position is rather difficult to imagine.

In critiquing moral subjectivism, Schick (1988) explains "despite its popularity, there are probably fewer subjectivists among professional ethicists than there are creationists among biologists. Why? Because as ethical theories go, subjectivism is as bad as they come" (p. 32). Not surprisingly, many contemporary scholars in educational administration promote standards for ethical conduct, although admittedly, for school leaders, such standards remain elusive (Campbell, 1999). Yet there are those who believe that objective ethical reasoning is possible. Strike, Haller, and Soltis (1998) relate moral reasoning to ethical reflection and justification, and propose guiding ethical principles such as liberty, equality, and due process. They are optimistic - perhaps painfully so - that "it is possible to give reasons for our choices, to decide objectively on the basis of these reasons, and to *persuade others* who are willing to judge our evidence fairly *that our views are correct*" (emphasis added, p. 3). Needless to say, questions surrounding the arbitrary nature of prescribed ethical criteria challenge an objective ethical perspective. Such criteria are always sentient in nature, social constructions of "rightness" that fail to consider culturally and anthropologically relevant factors, which influence their construction. In the absence of any naturally occurring ethical criteria, morality must either be individually or socially constructed. On the one hand, it is expected that people behave in certain ways, and hence normative prescriptions in the form of laws and regulations serve to define legitimate parameters of human conduct. In contrast, we expect values to reflect the subjectivity of individuals. Quite clearly, we do not consider people's preferences for certain foods, types of music, or recreational pursuits, to provide only few examples, to be a matter of right or wrong but to reflect individual tastes. Moreover, there is little evidence that the codification of professional ethical responsibilities has any substantive influence on practice. Intuitively, it would seem that professional codes of ethics subvert the very human deliberation that characterizes moral behaviour by mandating it.

The debate surrounding ethics, and particularly professional ethics, continues. Yet more recently, notions of professional reflection have offered an alternative approach to addressing this debate (Schon, 1990). Works by Starratt (1994) and Begley (in preparation under contract) provide a potentially more auspicious direction for the application of values, suggesting that discourse, dialogue, introspection, contemplation and reflection, *in and of themselves* may have redemptive properties for practitioners, ameliorating administrative sensibilities and elevating ethical capacities without giving dogmatic primacy to the *rightness* of some values over others[5]. A process oriented focus on values *contemplation* seems to be gaining momentum, and in some ways, provides a far more promising direction for the future, than calls for the objectification of values through rational, arbitrary criteria.

PERSISTENT DIFFICULTIES

What emerges from the analysis is a broad framework for understanding the differences that exist in research on values in educational administration (Table 2).

In an attempt to consolidate these findings, I draw on a framework adapted from Cohen and Manion (1994). It should be noted that this framework does not intend to show absolute linear relationships across the areas of analysis, but rather to illustrate the breadth and scope of the domain relating to values.

Table 2. Breadth and Scope of Domain Relating to Values
(Adapted from Cohen & Manion, 1994).

Epistemic Foundation	Constructivism Subjectivism Relativism	Naturalistic Coherentism	Post-Positivism	Positivism
Knowing Values	- social reality is interpreted differently across people - knowledge is constructed in different ways hence tentative and incomplete	- natural and social science exist in a web of belief - knowledge exists within neuronal networks in the brain	- limited sense of determinable social action - identify relationships between values and variables or conditions	- humans are determinable - identify laws governing social action
Framing Values	- descriptive accounts of values with some attempt at justification	- values exist in the same web or system of belief as 'facts' do	- values as variables within larger theoretical frameworks	- values are largely ignored
Investigating Values	- values play a central role in understanding human behaviour	- values are considered along with theory as they relate to coherentist principles	- values are a single variable within a study - values account for variation - values determinable - values broadly shared	- values are largely ignored
Informing Values	- moral subjectivism or relativism - values reflection and contemplation	- adjudication of ethical claims embedded within the global theory	- moral objectivism, logically and rationally driven - specific criteria for ethical action	- ethics outside the science of administration

There is little doubt that more detailed and comprehensive reviews and analyzes of values phenomena related to educational administration can be found elsewhere. The central intent of this chapter, however, has been to suggest that more effort needs to be directed at developing a conceptual framework which accounts for the areas of persistent difficulty in the field. The underlying advantage of such a framework is to allow educational leaders to recognize and appreciate the often unarticulated assumptions about knowledge, theory, and research which inform values literature. At the very least, this can assist educational leaders in discriminating between contending approaches to values, and allows them to critically reflect and to determine which approaches may best inform their practice. While there may indeed be benefits to reflecting on one's practice within a particular framework, it is possible that the very recognition that multiple values perspectives exist enhances this reflection and promotes more authentic and sophisticated contemplation of personal factors which influence professional practice.

While values have entered the collective conscience of scholars of educational administration and leadership, what values are and how they should be studied remains a disputed issue. We might still be optimistic, though, that inquiry into values and related leadership phenomena will serve to galvanize scholarly efforts towards a new and more authentic approach to leadership. Yet this prospect has been consistently met with resistance by those who still seek out steadfast truths about our social world. Perhaps it is an intimidating prospect that values, troublesome as they are, might very well be the true substance of administrative life. After all, if this is the case, then those charged with the preparation of future school leaders are responsible for not only instructing aspiring leaders, but *edifying* them as well. In the absence of any widely shared agreement as to the best way to lead today's schools, perhaps it can be agreed that better people will beget better educational leaders.

NOTES

[1] I have argued elsewhere that scholarly work on leadership –which 'values' inquiry ostensibly informs—is also conceptually incoherent, compounding the problem even further (Richmon, 2000).

[2] There is, of course, good reason to be sensitive to the differences between epistemic terms such as subjectivism, constructivism, and relativism. While the 'spirit' of these positions collectively challenged the dominant frames of deterministic inquiry, they are not without nuanced meanings. It seems, however, that epistemic labeling is more descriptively helpful than functionally useful. In many cases, such labeling is used to meet rhetorical ends. Howe (1986) for example, associates subjectivism with narcissism. Elsewhere, Willower (1999) characterizes Hodgkinson's writing as idealist-subjectivist.

[3] It should be noted that in this examination of conceptual classification systems for values, I have excluded frameworks which can be found in the literature on professional ethics, insofar as their scope treats 'values' in a more parochial sense.

[4] This argument presupposes that the qualities of 'rightness' exist outside of the experiences and judgments of people.

[5] Burgeoning work into values contemplation moves beyond mere 'reflective practice' and sterile notions of applied ethical theory and values clarification. Starratt (1994) describes the qualities of autonomy, connectedness and transcendence which foster the 'ethical person'. Begley (in preparation under contract) describes the contemplative capacities of the 'authentic leader'.

REFERENCES

Allison, D. J. (1989, April). *Toward the fifth age: The continuing evolution of academic educational administration*. Paper presented at the annual conference of the American Educational Research Association, San Francisco.

Allison, D. J. (2001). Riding the E and L roller coaster, or: How I came to fear natural coherentism. *Journal of Educational Administration, 39*(6), 539-553.

Allison, D. J., & Ellett, F. S. (1999). Evers and Lakomski on values in educational administration: Less than coherent. In P.T. Begley (Ed.), *Values and education leadership* (pp. 183-208). Albany, NY: SUNY Press.

Ashbaugh, C.R., & Kasten, K.L. (1984). A typology of operant values in school administration. *Planning and Change, 15*(4), 195-208.

Beck, C. (1993). *Learning to live the good life: Values in adulthood.* Toronto: OISE Press.

Begley, P.T. (1996). Cognitive perspectives on values in administration: A quest for coherence and relativism. *Educational Administration Quarterly, 32*(3), 403-426.

Begley, P.T. (1999a). Guiding values for future school leaders. *Orbit, 30*(1), 19-23.

Begley, P.T. (Ed.). (1999b). *Values and educational leadership.* Albany, NY: SUNY Press.

Begley, P.T. (in preparation under contract). *Authentic leadership: The moral intentions of educational administration.* London: Paul Chapman - Sage Publishing.

Begley, P.T., & Johansson, O. (1998). The values of school administration: Preferences, ethics and conflicts. *The Journal of School Leadership, 8*(4), 399-422.

Begley, P.T., & Leonard, P.E. (Eds.). (1999). *The values of educational administration.* London: Falmer Press.

Campbell, E. (1999). Ethical school leadership: Problems of an elusive role. In P.T. Begley (Ed.), *Values and education leadership* (pp. 151-163). Albany, NY: SUNY Press.

Campbell-Evans, G.H. (1991). Nature and influence of values in principal decision making. *Alberta Journal of Educational Research, 37*(2), 167-178.

Cohen, L., & Manion, L. (1994). *Research methods in education, fourth edition.* New York: Routledge.

Culbertson, J. A. (1988). A century's quest for a knowledge base. In N. J. Boyan (Ed.), *Handbook of research on educational administration*(pp. 3-26). New York: Longman.

Donmoyer, R. (2001). Evers and Lakomski's search for leadership's holy grail (and the intriguing ideas they encountered along the way). *Journal of Educational Administration, 39*(6), 554-572.

Evers, C., & Lakomski, G. (1991). *Knowing educational administration.* Toronto: Pergamon Press.

Evers, C., & Lakomski, G. (1993). Justifying educational administration. *Educational Management and Administration, 21*(3), 140-152.

Evers, C., & Lakomski, G. (1996). *Exploring educational administration.* Oxford: Pergamon Press.

Evers, C., & Lakomski, G. (2000). *Doing educational administration: A theory of administrative practice.* Oxford: Pergamon Press.

Frankena, W.K. (1967). Value and valuation. In P. Edwards (Ed.), *The encyclopedia of philosophy* (pp. 229-232). New York: Macmillan.

Gaus, G. (1990). *Values and justification: The foundations of liberal theory.* Cambridge: Cambridge University Press.

Gensler, H.J. (1996). *Formal ethics.* New York: Routledge.

Green, T.F. (1999). *Voices: The educational formation of conscience.* Indiana: University of Notre Dame Press.

Greenfield, T. (1975). Theory about organizations: A new perspective and its implications for schools. In M. Hughes (Ed.), *Administering education: International challenge*(pp. 71-99). London: Athlone Press.

Greenfield, T., & Ribbins, P. (1993). *Greenfield on educational administration: Towards a humane science.* London: Routledge Press.

Guba, E.G., & Lincoln, Y.S. (1994). Competing paradigms in qualitative research. In N. K. Denzin & Y. S. Lincoln (Eds.), *Handbook of Qualitative Research*(pp. 105-117). Thousand Oaks, CA: Sage Publications.

Hodgkinson, C. (1978). *Towards a philosophy of administration.* Oxford: Basil Blackwell.

Hodgkinson, C. (1983). *The philosophy of leadership.* Oxford: Basil Blackwell.

Hodgkinson, C. (1991). *Educational leadership: The moral art.* Albany, NY: SUNY Press.

Hodgkinson, C. (1996). *Administrative philosophy: Values and motivation in administrative life.* Oxford: Pergamon.

Hodgkinson, C. (2000). Then-now-next: A postmodern peek at everything. *Journal of Educational Administration and Foundations, 15*(1), 10-22.

Holmes, M. (1991). The values and beliefs of Ontario's chief education officers. In K. Leithwood & D. Musella (Eds.), *Understanding school administration: Studies of the contemporary chief education officer* (pp. 154-174). New York: Falmer Press.

Howe, K.R. (1986). A conceptual basis for ethics in teacher education. *Journal of Teacher Education, 37*(3), 5-12.

Kluckhohn, C. (1954). Values and value-orientations. In T. Parsons & E. Shils (Eds.), *Toward a general theory of action* (pp. 388-433). Cambridge: Harvard University Press.

Leithwood, K., & Duke, D. (1999). A century's quest to understand school leadership. In J. Murphy & K.S. Louis (Eds.), *Handbook of research on educational administration, second edition* (pp. 45-72). San Francisco, CA: Jossey-Bass.

Leithwood, K., Begley, P., & Cousins, B. (1994). *Developing expert leadership for future schools.* Bristol: Falmer Press.

Leithwood, K., Jantzi, D., & Steinbach, R. (1999). The problem-solving processes of transformational leaders. In *Changing leadership for changing times* (pp. 99-114). Buckingham, UK: Open University Press.

Leonard, P. (1996). Variations in value orientations in the implementation of multi-grades: Implications for moral leadership. *Canadian Journal of Educational Administration and Policy, 5*(1).

Leonard, P. (1997). *Understanding the dimensions of school culture.* University of Toronto: Unpublished doctoral dissertation.

Lobb, W. M. (1993). *Hodgkinson's values model: A question of ethical applicability.* University of Western Ontario: Unpublished master's thesis.

Maxcy, S.J. (1993). *Educational leadership: A critical pragmatic perspective.* Toronto: OISE Press.

Maxcy, S.J. (2001). Educational leadership and management of knowing: The aesthetics of coherentism. *Journal of Educational Administration, 39*(6), 573-588.

Rescher, N. (1969). *Introduction to value theory.* New York: Prentice-Hall.

Ribbins, P. (1999). Foreword. In P.T. Begley & P.E. Leonard (Eds.), *The values of educational administration* (pp. ix-xvii). London: Falmer Press.

Richmon, M.J. (2000). *Toward a conceptual framework for leadership inquiry.* University of Western Ontario: Unpublished master's thesis.

Ryan, J. (1988). Conservative science in educational administration. *Journal of Educational Administration and Foundations, 3*(2), 5-22.

Schon, D. (1990). *Educating the reflective practitioner.* San Francisco, CA: Jossey-Bass.

Sergiovanni, T.J. (2000). Leadership as stewardship: Who's serving who? In (unedited) *Educational Leadership* (pp. 269-286). San Francisco, CA: Jossey-Bass.

Schick, T. (1988). Is morality a matter of taste? Why professional ethicists think that morality is not purely subjective. *Free Inquiry Magazine, 18*(4), 32-34.

Simon, H. (1945). *Administrative behaviour.* New York: Macmillan.

Stapleton, J. & Long, J. (1995, June). *Administrative decision-making in education: A critique of the Evers-Lakomski naturalistic coherentist propositions.* Paper presented at the annual meeting of the Canadian Association for the Study of Educational Administration, Montreal.

Starratt, R.J. (1994). *Building an ethical school.* London: Falmer Press.

Strike, K.A., Haller, E.J., & Soltis, F.J. (1998). *The ethics of school administration, second edition.* Teachers College Press: Columbia University.

Willower, D. (1980). Contemporary issues in theory in educational administration. *Educational Administration Quarterly, 16*(3), 1-25.

Willower, D. (1992). Educational administration: Intellectual trends. *Encyclopedia of Educational Research, sixth edition* (pp. 364-375). Toronto: Macmillan.

Willower, D. (1999). Values and valuation. In P. T. Begley (Ed.), *Values and education leadership* (pp. 121-138). Albany, NY: SUNY Press.

CYRIL P. COOMBS

REFLECTIVE PRACTICE: PICTURING OURSELVES

Abstract. Professional literature portrays reflective practice as deliberately inquiring into one's thoughts and actions to better examine a perceived problem so that a response might be reasoned and tested. Using a camera metaphor, this chapter examines reflective practice by comparing elements of reflective practice consistently identified in professional literature to the perceptions of six school principals. Issues examined include situations and concerns that prompt reflection, reflective timing, and the influence of values, training and experience in reflection.

Findings are based on field research data collected in the spring of 1999 with six principals in eastern Canada. Participants were interviewed about their perceptions of reflection and were requested to reflect on two vignettes pertinent to their work. Additionally, they were asked to reflect with the researcher on two situations of their own choice. The researcher also observed each participant for approximately five hours and then collected individual think aloud responses to these observations. This paper specifically addresses the practical application of values in reflective practice.

The fast paced environment of modern schooling makes the role of principal a complex one. Trends towards decentralized decision making and centralized accountability have increased role ambiguity and conflict. Principals often seem to be in an impossible predicament as they attempt to navigate new directions, or even simply try to hold fast to an existing course. Their existing procedural maps may be outmoded or no longer applicable to the shifting currents of education, while the absence of direction from external reference points may seem even more problematic and dangerous. More than ever, principals must know and consider their intentions before taking action in an environment where they will inevitably be judged by these actions. How then, do principals come to know and interpret their intentions and the subsequent actions in response to these intentions? Over the past few decades there has been a range of educational research conducted on this topic. Though the concepts vary, for example, action theory (Argyris & Schon, 1974), praxis (Wilson, 1994), problem solving (Leithwood & Steinbach, 1995) and cognitive apprenticing (Prestine & Legrand, 1991), many fall within the realm of reflective practice.

Although reflective practice has attained increased status as a topic for inquiry, McNiff (1995) highlights the need for research that will reveal the process of reflection. She states that much research literature emphasizes the need for reflection but is "impoverished in actual examples" (p. 86). This itself is a source of irony to McNiff, since one aim of reflective practice is to close the gap between theory and practice. The intent of this paper is to illuminate reflective practice by comparing and contrasting some practitioners' perspectives about reflective practice with portrayals presented in professional literature. More specifically, the following questions are examined:

Question 1: What is reflective practice?
Question 2: What is the nature of reflective practice among select school administrators?

P.T. Begley and O. Johansson (eds.), The Ethical Dimensions of School Leadership, 49–65.
© 2003 *Kluwer Academic Publishers. Printed in the Netherlands.*

Question 3: On what basis do select school administrators choose to reflect?
Question 4: To what extent is reflective practice among select school administrators a function of their values, training and experience?

The findings presented herein are part of a much larger study conducted in 1999.

RELEVANT LITERATURE ON REFLECTIVE PRACTICE

To understand the nature of reflective practice, I first conducted a review of professional literature. Peters (1991) recognizes that reflective practice involves critical thinking and learning, both of which are processes that can lead to significant self development (p. 89). Barnett (1990) posits that reflection is the ability to bring past events to a conscious level, to make sense of them, and to determine appropriate ways to act in the future (p. 67). Adding to the variety, Osterman (1991) regards reflective practice as a professional development process that goes beyond imparting knowledge to creating action change.

Van Gyn (1996) asserts that most notions of reflective practice are based in "Dewey's theoretical perspective on critical inquiry and how that relates to practice" (p.105). Dewey proclaims "reflective thought is the 'active' persistent, and careful consideration of any belief or supposed form of knowledge in light of the grounds that support it and the further conclusions to which it tends" (Dewey in Van Gyn, p. 105).

Definitions appearing in literature of recent decades continue to be derivatives of Dewey's. For example, Loughran (1996) views reflection as:

> the purposeful, deliberate act of inquiry into one's thoughts and actions through which a perceived problem is examined for order that a thoughtful, reasoned response might be tested out (p. 21).

Loughran, citing Dewey (1933), further asserts that such a process involves five phases, *suggestion, problem, hypothesis, reasoning and testing*. Suggestions are action ideas or possibilities that come to minds of individuals as a puzzling situation arises, creating the need to suspend judgement. As individuals come to see the puzzle as a whole, rather than as small parts, they begin to better understand the situation's perplexity and the problem itself. The suggestions are then reconsidered in terms of what can be done with a more adequate and refined sense of the problem. This is referred to as the hypothesis stage. Then through reasoning, ideas and experiences are linked to expand suggestions further. The hypothesized end result is tested to corroborate or negate the idea (p. 5). Loughran contends that the five phases overlap considerably and that some may be omitted or expanded, depending on the nature of the problem and the timing of the reflection.

During the past several decades the field of education has not only seen increased interest in reflective practice but the development of a plethora of reflective methods. Paradigmatically they contrast sharply, particularly in purpose and method. Van Manen (1977) and as cited in Reagan, Case, Case, and Freiberg (1993) offers a hierarchical model for understanding reflective practice by teachers with three distinct levels of reflectivity:

1) effective application of skills and technical knowledge;
2) reflection about the assumptions underlying specific classroom practices and their consequences;
3) critical reflection, the questioning of morals, ethical and other types of normative criteria (pp. 265-66).

Over time, as teachers move through the three stages, their perspective of teaching tends to broaden while the examination of their experience deepens.

Grimmett (1989) identifies three variations of reflective practice in professional literature. Each perspective is sorted according to its purpose and method, clearly distinguishing divergent epistemological differences. The first, *instrumentally mediated action*, characterizes approaches that tend to be positivist, where technical problems can be tinkered and adjusted. Knowledge is used to technically direct practice. *Deliberating among competing ends*, too, has elements of deciding among various lines of action. Grimmett emphasizes, however, this type of reflection is more contextual, experientially based and collaborative. The third category, *reconstructing experience*, also tends to be personally and experientially rooted, but is aimed at transforming practice through self enlightenment. This may come about through restructuring any combination of personal experience, the situational context, image of self as teacher or personal assumptions held about professional practice.

Loughran (1996) considers the temporal nature of reflection relative to experience. Subscribing to Dewey's (1933) phases of reflection (suggestion, problem, hypothesis, reasoning, and testing) he advocates that the weight of each stage depends on when the reflection occurs in relation to the pedagogical experience. Loughran contends that reflection can occur before, during and after an event, and believes that the 'when' of reflection influences the learning that might be drawn from experience. Consequently, he uses three distinct time elements, *anticipatory, contemporaneous* and *retrospective* that respectively correspond with reflection for, in and on action.

Sergiovanni (1991) also pursues the development of a reflective practice model to illustrate how knowledge is used in practice. His model has three critical and interrelated components, *practice episodes, theories of practice* and *antecedents* (p. 10). For the larger context, practice episodes are influenced by theories of practice that he poetically calls "bundles of beliefs and assumptions . . . " about one's perceptions of how things work, consequently functioning as "mindscapes and platforms" (p. 10). Antecedent conditions extend the context of reflective practice even further by considering one's values and know how.

CONCEPTUALIZING REFLECTION

A conceptual framework was developed based on the issues and themes derived from the preceding literature review. Using the metaphor of a camera, the scholarly thinking discussed in the preceding section can be consolidated in Figure 1 to present the many interconnected dimensions of reflective practice. Behind a camera lens, various shutters work together to create and control an aperture. Reflected light enters an otherwise light proof box when this aperture is existent, making an image onto film. The size of the aperture is determined by the synergy of the shutters, since each does its part to systematically open or close the camera box, enabling rays of light to focus onto an action frame. The image of this action frame is influenced greatly by the amount of light. Too much light causes overexposure and a blurring of boundaries while too little light creates shadows and dullness. Expert photographers use this light effectively, to capture not only action but the very essence of humanity.

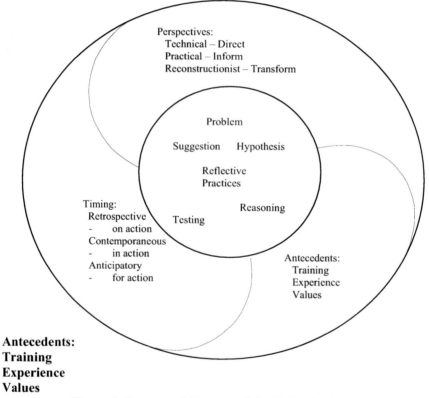

Figure 1. Conceptual Framework for Reflective Practice.

Reflective practice, happening within the camera's aperture, occurs with the synergetic opening of its shutters. These shutters, *perspectives, antecedents* and *timing* determine the nature and extend of reflective practice through the activation, size and control of this aperture. Three perspectives and related purposes are identified: *technical - directing practice, practical - informing practice* and *reconstructionist - transforming practice*. For example, the purpose of reflection from a technical perspective is to direct practice; however, a practical perspective views reflection as informing practice by emphasizing the contextual basis. Meanwhile, the reconstructionist perspective of reflection attempts to transform practice.

The *antecedents* and *timing* shutters are variations of ideas presented earlier. Antecedents form and shape theories of practice and include such variables as one's values, training and experience. Timing, on the other hand, indicates when the reflection occurs in relation to the situation or event being reflected upon. Reflection can be retrospective, contemporaneous or anticipatory respectively corresponding to reflection-on-action, reflection-in-action, and reflection-for-action.

METHODOLOGICAL CONSIDERATIONS

Six principals participated in the study. They were at least at the midpoint of their careers, varied in gender, training and administrative experience, and worked in schools with different grade configurations. I wanted to consider the place of background factors such as training, experience, gender and job description in reflective practice, so I selected participants who varied in this regard. Interviews were conducted with each of the six participants to collect their views and perspectives. During each interview, I asked participants to describe reflection, what caused them to reflect, when they reflected in relation to an event, the process they used, the kinds of information they included in their reflection and the place of their values, training and experience in reflection. Questions also focused on their perceptions about the usefulness and prevalence of reflective practice among school principals. All interviews were audio taped, transcribed and entered into *Ethnograph v5.04,* a computer software program designed for the analysis of text based data. This software is an analytical tool that helps compile, organize and manipulate data by importing and numbering transcripts, coding specific segments and then sorting and analyzing the various codes (Seidel, 1998). As Marshall and Rossman (1995) emphasize, each stage of data analysis represents data reduction and interpretation. A grounded approach was used to identify and determine codes that represented various categories, themes and patterns. Although the review of the literature helped establish initial patterns, categories were not limited to a specific reflective stance. Some findings supported elements of existing theory while other findings contributed to the development of new ideas.

REFLECTION PRACTICES OF SIX PRINCIPALS

I begin a discussion of the research findings with brief biographies of each participant as an introduction to the six voices presented throughout the findings, and to serve as a guide when sorting various perspectives that are presented. Pseudonyms are used for all participants and in some cases, minor details are altered to better preserve the anonymity of their identities.

The Principals

Cam, approaching fifty, is a seasoned principal with almost twenty-five years educational experience. About ten of these years have been in an administrative capacity with the last four being in his current position of principal. Cam holds Bachelor of Arts, Bachelor of Education and Master of Education (Curriculum and Instruction) degrees. He has also served in the military reserve over the past twenty-five years. Paul, unlike Cam, has acquired most of his experience outside the city and with a board different from his current one. Paul is also approaching fifty and has twenty-six years. Of all participants, he has the most administrative experience, having worked nineteen years in educational administration, three in his current position of principal. Paul holds Bachelor of Arts, Bachelor of Arts (Education) degrees, and a Master of Education (Educational Administration) degree. He has been at his current school for the past sixteen, years and served as assistant principal for five years before becoming principal.

Roy has passed his fiftieth birthday and has reached the twenty-seventh year of his career. He has worked at his current school for the last twelve years, seven as assistant principal and five as principal. He holds Bachelor of Arts, Bachelor of Education and Master of Education (Educational Administration) degrees. As well, he has done extensive graduate work toward a Master's degree in theology. Beth is in her mid-forties and has been teaching for about twenty-five years; however, this is Beth's first year in her current school and her first year as a principal. She has worked as an assistant principal in three other schools and had her Master of Education (Administration) degree completed before beginning work as an assistant principal. She also holds Bachelor of Arts and Bachelor of Education degrees, with most of her teaching experience at the junior high level.

Jon is currently principal of a high school that accommodates students from grades nine to twelve. He is in his early forties and has been an educator for the past twenty years. Jon is also unique to this study in that most of his experience has been acquired with another school board in a region far removed from the city. This is his first year at this school and with this school board. He has spent the last eight years in educational administration, five of these as a senior high school principal. Jon currently holds Bachelor of Science and Education degrees and a Master of Education (Educational Administration) degree.

Kay, nearing forty, has worked for sixteen years in the education profession. The last six have been in administrative positions at three different schools. She is presently a principal in a kindergarten to six school that has a student population of 180 and a teaching staff of nine. Kay teaches half time and does not have an assistant principal and is the only site-based administrator at her school. This is Kay's first year as principal and her first year at this school. She has a Bachelor of Education degree and two graduate degrees: Master of Education (Teaching and Learning), and Master of Arts (Christian Spirituality). She also pursued training at a technical institute before entering university.

How Practitioners Define Reflection

I initiated discussions about reflective practice by asking participants first to share their understanding of the idea. There is remarkable definition similarity among participants and between their comments and findings of the literature review. Kay describes reflection with a series of verbs such as "rethink, mull over, probe, ponder and pick apart," to ask "what if?, why?, how come?, and what about?" in an effort to "come to grips with a situation." Beth, Jon and Roy approach their definitions by asking a sequence of questions, similar to "Where are we?, What are the possibilities?, How are we going to get there?" Beth, Cam and Roy respectively emphasize pausing, taking time to stop, collecting their thoughts, putting things on hold, and giving more thought before or after situations. All three emphasize reflection as being able to cut through everyday tasks to ask this sequence of questions.

Reflective Timing

Most definitions offered by participants emphasize reflection before or after action, not during action. Paul, for example, describes reflection as "past thinking through" and Beth says it is asking "what can we do to make things better down the road?" Cam stresses the element of planning in his reflection, and contends that reflection is mostly about what needs to be put into action. Roy and Jon do, however, refer to the contemporaneous nature of reflection. Roy asserts that one function of reflection is to put things on hold to give more time for thought and Jon adds that reflection is always happening, suggesting instances of reflection-in-action.

Although most participants say they do not reflect-in-action, there was evidence to suggest otherwise. Cam, for example, states, "I am not quite sure if I reflect on present events, I am probably reflecting on some instances just intuitively, as you are doing something." Later in the interview he reveals, "I could be in a conversation and say, now this isn't going well and I shouldn't have started this." Although Cam may not realize it, this is an example of thinking in action.

Reflective Prompts

The group of six gave consistent responses to circumstances and events that prompt reflection. Usual suggestions included unanticipated events, critical events, conflict, interpersonal tensions, crisis events, extremely positive or negative happenings, and events that directly affect the participants' welfare. Although most participants said that they reflected about everything, there were individual differences. Beth was more inclined to state that she reflects when negative outcomes occur, especially unexpected ones. She also names other prompters such as 'interpersonal conflict' and 'personal life changes' such as illness. Cam, with a strong planning orientation, is prompted to reflect when anything that impacts the school's effectiveness and achievement arises. This ranges from the management of a crisis to accommodating individual student learning needs. Similar to Beth, the unexpected, especially in the form of a crisis, is an immediate prompter.

Kay contends that an extreme experience sets her into a reflective mode; ". . . extremely positive experiences or really negative experiences cause me to reflect most frequently, and the general run of the mill experiences that I have, I don't find that I reflect as frequently on these." Roy is prompted into a reflective mode when he receives an adverse reaction to his decisions or actions. Jon also identifies personal criticism as a prompter, acknowledging that this kind of reflection "sticks with you or hurts something . . . it probably hangs on a little bit longer that the positive things that go on." Roy also identifies concerns related to change as an initiator of reflection.

Another aspect of reflection that yielded interesting findings was when and where participants reflect. Most participants adamantly state that most of their reflection occurs outside their school day. Beth claims that there is no time for reflection from the time she enters school in the morning until the last event is finished after 5:00 p.m. Outside that, she contends she could reflect anywhere. Jokingly, she states that it is not always quietly, with "candle light, a journal and those sorts of things." She describes how sometimes at night she cannot sleep, or could wake up thinking about a particular thing.

Cam has a cabin outside the city and claims that most of his reflection occurs here. Jon, who believes that we reflect all the time, asserts that there is no best time to reflect. He holds the belief that it depends on the issue and the degree to which deep or uninterrupted thought is needed. Reflection could occur for Jon anywhere or at anytime, from the staff room to the evening drive home.

Kay places the most emphasis on the need for solitude when reflecting. She usually sets time aside at the end of her day, or sometimes at the start. Reflection could also occur during leisure activities such as gardening or exercising. Paul, on the other hand, enjoys the opportunity to reflect at conferences and professional development seminars. He observes that he has opportunity to think and talk with colleagues in an environment where he is not directing the activity. Attending professional development sessions also helps him see his work in a different light once he returns to school.

Roy vividly describes why reflection is difficult at school by detailing the start of a normal day. "The first minutes in the morning there could be ten decisions, all of varying levels of concern and every person who comes to you, that's their major problem right now." He finds the evening time best for his reflection, when he is "just sitting down and everything is quiet." Roy adds, though, "I don't sit down and say, 'well, I'm going to think about how things are going now'." For Roy, reflection comes to him when circumstances are right, it is not something he schedules.

Roy, like Paul, comments on the reflective importance of collegial gatherings. He says that when he is with other principals, he is constantly "running things by them, you are snatching a minute here and there. What do you think of this or what did you do about that?" Roy contends these kinds of questions automatically prompt a level of reflectiveness.

Reflective Processes

Questions to participants about their reflective process produce many detailed and intricate comments. Beth begins reflection-on-action by first creating a mental picture of the event. She includes as much detail as possible, such as where people were located, what they said, and even their body gestures. Next, she gives thought to what happened, and why it happened in this way. Beth acknowledges that she plays these questions repeatedly to herself, "just like a tape recorder." She questions not only how things could have been done differently, but also how she could be a better support to others. Beth deems the setting, conversations, feelings and emotions all to be important elements of reflection. Once Beth feels that she has analyzed the event she considers next what has to be done and more specifically, what her role is to be. Beth remarks "then I will practice in my head how I am going to go at this, when I am going to have to do this . . . and what is going to be done."

Kay, similar to Beth, emphasizes recalling vividly, situational detail including the conversations and the feelings of those involved. Kay begins reflection by recounting detail such as the conversational atmosphere, the colour of clothing that individuals wear and their facial expressions. Recounting physical characteristics then brings to light the conversation, which in turn causes Kay to think about how she felt during different parts of the conversation. "I will probably say I felt intimidated there, or I felt a great sense of peace there, I felt guilty there, I felt intimidated and insecure when such a person said that part of the conversation." Kay not only thinks about the conversation and related feelings. She also tries to delve into why she experiences these feelings, particularly the negative ones. She claims that usually she is attentive to her feelings and for the most part "can attribute them to a cause."

Roy posits that when reflecting on specific situations, his first step is to try to understand better what is happening. "Do I have the facts straight . . . or am I exaggerating something?" Next, he tries to discuss the situation with other persons to be certain that he has considered it from all angles and that his interpretation is accurate. Then he develops a course of action that considers to whom he has to talk and in what order. Roy also explains that reviewing how he has handled similar experiences is helpful in this process. Next, the reflection moves to taking a course of action. During this part of the process, how to fairly take a stand without judging others is a key issue for Roy.

Cam focuses much of his reflection process on future events. He poses the following questions in rapid fire order: "What has to be accomplished? Who is doing what? Is the plan effective? Is necessary communication in place? Is some other information needed? Does everybody understand? Does anything else need to be put in place?" Cam claims that sometimes he reflects mentally, but usually reflects better "on paper." Consequently, he commits many of these questions to paper and finds that he needs to have concrete evidence of planning. He declares that he needs to look at his schemata to decide if everything is included, otherwise "I tend to miss things in my head."

Improving Decisions Through Reflection

Given that participants express clear views on what constitutes reflection and the processes they employ, I extended the discussion by soliciting their opinions about whether reflection leads to better decisions. For a variety of reasons, they gave a resounding "yes." Beth claims that she gets herself into more trouble when she acts without "taking it all in and thinking about it." She contends that many people misread her when she has to decide in a rush because she is not able to make decisions "on her feet." Consequently, she tends to rethink and backtrack on rushed decisions. She adds that, unfortunately, reflection can also be seen as "indecisiveness" or "wishy washy." Rarely, Beth claims, does she "speak off the top of her head," unless it is to a trusted person.

Paul says that it is important to be able to show how he arrives at decisions. He comments that reflective practice must be used to decide action and reiterates that if reflection is not used to improve action, it is wasted time. Roy's response summarizes the views of others when he adds "the decision that I ultimately make may not be the best decision, . . . but at least I can go back and say I thought it through, and it was the best thing that I could come up with at the time."

When prompting others to reflect, most participants say they avoid using the term "reflection" because for many, it is a foreign word. Kay illustrates this point by adding, "If I say think about, mull over, ask yourself, what have you learned, what would you do differently the next time, I think some of these synonyms will help further clarify what I mean by reflect."

The Evolving Quality of Reflection

Kay holds the belief that the quality of her reflection has found more depth and breadth over time. She notes that in the early stages of her career, reflection would take the format where she would be simply recalling events, their circumstances and probably verbatim what happened. Now she contends that she delves more, to go beyond the "what" to the "why," theorizing that the why gives her more insight and understanding about others and herself. She says, "I don't think I had that depth in the beginning."

Paul claims that with experience, the purpose of his reflection has broadened considerably. In his formative years Paul reveals, ". . . it was probably reflecting but really in a negative sense, in the sense of trying to look good and not being relaxed in what I was doing." Today, for Paul, reflection is more about listening and being attentive to others, to help motivate people and to develop ideas. Paul claims that today, he also reflects about his reflections pondering "Am I using it enough? Is it impacting? Is it making a difference?"

In a similar way, Cam describes reflection in his beginning years as "worry and torment," mainly because he felt that when things did not go as planned, it was a reflection on himself. He suggests that now, he has gotten over taking things personally and regards reflection today as a generally positive exercise. Cam states, too, that reflection comes to him more naturally; it is not a chore or a task that has to be done.

Beth contends that more exposure to different situations and "getting gray" has made her reflections more open and more focused on human elements, and less on accountability; however, she acknowledges that she sometimes waivers between the two, when she tries to focus more on human issues. Beth also voices the belief that she now reflects more than she has in the past and that some of this reflection is actually about how and why she reflects. She asks of herself, "Why are you reflecting? (laughing) How are you reflecting? Sometimes I just walk away and not do that." Beth remarks that, with time, she has learned more about herself, and this, she adds, has helped her reflect even better.

Jon believes as he gets more experience and more knowledge of various situation, the better he can handle conflict. Jon contends that knowledge from experience is obtained by deliberately relating present situations to past events. He postulates that the more he does this, the more likely he is to keep on doing it, and the more likely he is to handle future conflicts better.

I asked Roy if he has considered the effectiveness of his ability to reflect, and as his response unfolded, he seemed astounded that he had not previously considered this question. Within moments, this astonishment turned to excitement as he considered the possibilities; ". . . it would be interesting to try to think out (pause) and if I had a list of skills, . . . and say well (pause) do you use this, this and this (pause), and really I would be able to trace it back to that, but I've never consciously thought about it." Roy continued to wonder about how well he was reflecting and if indeed he should have other skills.

The Relevance of Training and Experience

Early in the interview process, I asked participants to identify their relevant experience and training. Later, I extended this discussion, and asked how this experience and training was useful in their reflection. Initially, most participants downplayed the usefulness of professional training. A closer examination of commentary about training reveals that its importance is often overshadowed by the importance of experiences. For example, Jon's diplomas are prominently displayed in his office but when I asked him about the importance of them, he said that they were not really that important, "a lot of it is learning on the job and mentoring"; however, after the interview was over and the tape was stopped, he indicated that he wanted to go back to the training question. He added that he has acquired much technical know how through his training. An example he cited was his knowledge of school law. Jon claims that his training in this area shapes his responses when liability concerns arise. He further illustrates the importance of his training in student evaluation, program development and human resource management. Jon contends that his training has been especially helpful in developing the technical knowhow needed in his work.

Cam states that his training has positively shaped his reflection. Interestingly, Cam counters that some of his best training has been professional development since completing his Master of Curriculum degree. He acknowledges that his Master's degree has well-prepared him for classroom issues; however, since becoming an administrator, he has had to seek more specific training in areas such as technology. Cam specifically credits his military reservist training as especially useful to his work.

Beth claims that she has learned much from the first year she worked as an assistant principal. Often, she thinks back to the experiences of that year when facing new and similar situations. She comments that in other schools, her administrative partners were not as inclined to reflect but were willing to take time to hear her out. Despite her experience as an assistant principal, Beth feels that she was not adequately prepared for the principal position she finds herself in this year. She wishes that she had more experiences to include in her reflections.

Cam asserts that "unless you have no pulse," personal experiences "have got to prepare you better to reflect." He believes that he has learned a great deal from his experiences, and deliberately "brings them to bear on the present and on the future." Cam stresses the need to tap into the "collective wisdom" of principals. He calls collective wisdom "not something learned in a course necessarily," but things learned through "living your principalship, through living with diverse personalities and abilities." Cam is adamant that all administrators have something to share, and since the opportunities to do it are scarce, sharing usually happens incidentally.

Jon and Roy state similar views. Jon says when a situation arises, he consciously considers how he has handled past situations, either positively or negatively. In times of decision making, he claims, knowledge and experience come together. Roy emphasizes not only reviewing his own experience, but trying to tap into the experiences of other principals. He asserts that as experience is accumulate, "you kind of trust your experience of the past more, and your analysis of it."

Espoused Values

Participants' espoused values were coded using Leithwood and Steinbach's (1991, as cited in Leithwood, Begley, & Cousins, 1994) classification scheme as presented in Table 1. This scheme was derived from their revisions of earlier research and identifies sixteen values across four categories. These value classifications were not actually presented to participants, but were used to organize, sort and analyze participants' responses.

Espoused values of participants tended to be more similar than dissimilar. An overview reveals that the six participants emphasize, in descending order from most to least important, *basic human, social and political, professional* and *general moral values.* Within *basic human values,* respect received overwhelming support and was the single most identified espoused value. Happiness, for self or for others, also received attention in this set, particularly by Kay, Paul and Roy. The value of participation received most priority in the *social* and *political values* set. Participants who espoused social and political values also tended to identify with *basic human values.* Within the *professional values* set, they gave most attention to general and specific role responsibilities. Although participants articulated some consequence values, they usually made these statements as an explanation of their role responsibilities. Of Leithwood and Steinbach's (1991, as cited in Leithwood, Begley, & Cousins, 1994) sixteen values, fairness and courage received little acknowledgment by participants.

IMPLICATIONS FOR PRACTICE

The literature portrays reflective practice as a process involving critical thinking and learning that in turn, leads to significant self development. Finding meaning through the questioning of ideas and existing patterns, is emphasized, too. Images presented by the participants were very much like this portrayal. This was especially so when participants presented reflection as a series of questions that revolved around developing a better understanding of situations or events. Self questioning, usually aimed at examining existing thought and developing alternate perspectives, often helped participants to better understand their reality and to consider how to make necessary changes.

Table 1. A Classification of Values and Illustrative Statements
(Leithwood, Begley & Cousins, 1994, p. 103).

Categories of Values		Illustrative Statement
Set 1.	**Basic Human Values**	
	* Freedom	Staff is not forced to supervise dances by the Education Act ... I would not force people to do this
	* Happiness	Most people felt pretty good about those goals
	* Knowledge	I would collect as much information about the probable suspects as possible
	* Respect for others	In a blanket approach you could offend many fine teachers
	* Survival	I don't think you can let an issue like this dominate a lot of time
Set 2.	**General Moral Values**	
	* Carefulness	(Check) to indeed see if whether or not we have a problem
	* Fairness (or justice)	Make sure that some people who are a little unsure of themselves also have an opportunity to speak
	* Courage	Their responsibility is to speak out when vandalism occurs
Set 3.	**Professional Values**	
	* General Responsibility as Educator	Your value system is interfering with the mandate that we have in education
	* Specific Role Responsibility	Staff have to feel they are supported by the office

	* Consequences . . .	Kids deserve a certain number of social events
	* Consequences (other)	There's an impression that . . . students aren't under control
Set 4.	**Social and Political Values**	
	* Participation	Involve groups such as Heads' Council, Special Education, Student Services
	* Sharing	Allow people to get things off their chests-talk about the problems they perceive
	* Loyalty, Solidarity and Commitment	We (admin. team) have to be seen as being philosophically in tune
	* Helping others	Let's help each other (school and parent) deal with that child

Participants consistently stated that they did not reflect during their work day; rather, they reflected outside the day when immediacy for action was not present. They also suggested that they did not plan a time to reflect, that it just happens when conditions are right, and participants like Jon know their right conditions. These conditions usually include being away from job responsibilities, being in comfortable surroundings and perhaps in the quiet company of a trusted friend; however, participants asserted that often they need to work things through in solitude before including others in their reflective process.

No literature references were found about where participants reflect, though all participants have strong views on the matter. Most participants, for example, comment that reflection occurs at professional development sessions. Although these sessions may appear crowded, busy and noisy, participants say it gives them opportunity to step back from their work, and alternately introspect and socialize with colleagues. They are able to confidentially discuss concerns and thoughts during unstructured times.

Wilson (1994) and Leithwood and Steinbach (1995) identify the importance of social interactions in learning and in the development of expertise. Wilson argues, for example, that praxis is to be done as a community of inquirers, while Leithwood and Steinbach emphasize Vygotsky's (1978) zone of proximal development. The credit that participants give to their gatherings acknowledges the ideas of these theorists. Whether through a formal agenda or via incidental discussions at break time, participants thrive as a community of learners at conferences and meetings. As Cam says, "it solves a whole bunch of unnecessary individual reflective time, to which you would not get the same results."

Similar to the literature review, all participants identified the need to have a trusted friend. This friend usually had no immediate involvement in the problem situation and generally had a long-standing rapport with the participant. Many reflective strategies, such as Costa and Kallick's (1993) critical friend or Barnett's (1990) peer assisted leadership (PAL), are based on similar principles. Such strategies help participants develop critical and alternative perspectives in a trusting and supportive atmosphere.

The findings about reflective prompters can be linked to values research to explain the prevalence of values and ethics in reflective practice. Begley and Johansson (1997) found that values were important in deciding action, particularly in providing structure for problem solving. This was especially so when principals lacked information, considered the problem unique or when principals were pressed to act quickly. Leithwood and Steinbach (1995) also found that expert principals, in comparison to non-experts, were much clearer about their values and could use them as substitutes for knowledge, when domain-specific knowledge was lacking. Additionally, they found that values served as a perceptual screen, influencing what principals chose to notice and how they defined problems.

Literature findings about when principals increase reliance on their values are similar to circumstances that prompt participants of this study to reflect. Additionally, the functions of reflective practice and valuation overlap considerably. They are both used to detect and resolve difficult situations. Since a fundamental goal of reflective practice is to frame a problem situation properly and to resolve it affably, the use of values in this process is a natural fit. On the other hand, reflective processes facilitate the inclusion of value considerations.

The findings of this study have relevance for practitioners in a number of ways. The first has to do with the nature of principals' work. Clearly, if principals do not build reflective opportunities into their work, it will probably occur by chance. One participant said that he did not just sit and say, "I am going to reflect now." Participants knew the conditions that facilitated their reflections. It might be through deferring a decision, taking a ten-minute reprieve for silent thought, or conferring with a trusted friend. In fact, any number of reflective strategies are pertinent to the realities of principals' work. So, practitioners need to consciously create conditions and use processes that enhance their ability to reflect.

Not only do practitioners need to organize their work for "reflective rests", they need consciously to think about their experiences if they are to learn from them. Filby (1995) contends that learning does not automatically come from experiences. It occurs when the learning is consciously thought about. Some participants even suggest they extend their reflection by recording their thoughts in some manner. This, for instance, could mean attaching a notation to a file for future use. When the situation or event again occurs, the practitioner can then reference it as retrospective reflection.

The three shutters of the conceptual framework also have implications for practitioners. It is important that participants think about their training, experience and values, and how these shape their reasoning process. Working in environments where values conflicts are commonplace, administrators must know the sources of these conflicts. Aside from this, they must also recognize how their own values, training and experience shape their actions. It is equally important that administrators assess the consistency of their intentions and actions, and better know their motives and biases. Similarly, administrators must be able to interpret the action and intentions of others, especially in these post modernist times (Hoy, 1996).

The literature review indicates that an individual may reflect on an event or situation from any temporal perspective. Although there are differences in each type, all three forms are effective; however, contemporaneous reflection seems to be the key link, where participants either bring past events to a situation, or notice features of the present situation for future decision-making. Consequently, it is never too late or too early to reflect. Practitioners need to consider the temporal dimensions of reflection and preferably use all three; however, they could also develop a preferred temporal style, and routinely apply it to their work.

The literature findings about the purpose of reflection also have direct relevance for practitioners. Grimmett (1989) suggests that practitioners can operate at any reflective level, depending on purpose and method. Not all reflection involves reconstructivist thinking. Some very experienced participants in this study used reflective practice to technically direct their practice. Although many participants reported that, with time, the purpose of their reflection has broadened and deepened, they were not adverse to using it for fundamental purposes. This in itself suggests that no area is off-limits for reflection, as asserted by Willower (1994).

CONCLUSION

These findings illustrate the need for principals to examine the daily organization of their work to find opportunity for reflection and to make it an integral part of the day. Given growing role ambiguity and conflict, principals will continue to be pressed for time to reflect, let alone to critique the quality of these reflections. They also support the greater use of reflective strategies in professional development. Such a move not only encourages principals to develop their use of reflection, but it would enable them to be more open to the critique of others and to change practices in view of better rationales.

Despite the possibilities of reflective practice, it must be acknowledged that not all reflection is effective. Dewey (1933) postulates that reflection can be so extensive that it leads to inaction. Bright (1996) expresses concern that practitioners may limit areas open to reflection, thereby restricting its depth and quality. A similar observation is noted by Campbell (1996), who states that because one has reflected before making a decision does not infer that the decision will be good or ethical.

The main purpose of reflective practice is to increase our relative awareness of factors that influence planning and action. In many ways this is an ethical undertaking, however tentative the planning and action. Dewey (as cited in Willower, 1994) concludes that if reflection is to play a part in making everyday moral choices, that it has to be an internal habit of mind. In essence, to develop reflective practice is to develop habits of mind so that we might picture ourselves more clearly.

REFERENCES

Argyris, C., & Schon, D.A. (1974). *Theory in practice: Increasing professional effectiveness.* San Francisco: Jossey-Bass.

Barnett, B. (1990). Peer-assisted leadership: Expanding principals' knowledge through reflective practice. *Journal of Educational Administration, 28*(3), 67-76.

Begley, P., & Johansson, O. (1997, April). Values and school administration: Preferences, ethics and conflicts. Paper delivered at the annual meeting of the American Educational Research Association, Chicago.

Bright, B. (1996). Reflecting on "reflective practice." *Studies in the Education of Adults, 28*(2), 162-184.

Campbell, C. E. (1996). *Ethical leadership: Problems of an elusive role.* Paper delivered at the Toronto Conference on Values and Educational Leadership, Ontario Institute for Studies in Education/University of Toronto.

Costa, A., & Kallick, B. (1993). Through the lens of a critical friend. *Educational Leadership, 51*(2), 49-51.

Dewey, J. (1933). *How we think.* New York: Heath and Co.

Filby, N. (1995). *Analysis of reflective professional development models.* Columbia: ERIC.

Grimmett, P. (1989). A commentary on Schon's view of reflection. *Journal of Curriculum and Supervision, 5*(1), 19-28.

Hoy, W.K. (1996). Science and theory in the practice of educational administration: A pragmatic perspective. *Educational Administration Quarterly, 32*(3), 366-378.

Leithwood, K., Begley, P., & Cousins, B. (1994). *Developing expert leadership for future schools.* London: The Falmer Press.

Leithwood, K., & Steinbach, R. (1995). *Expert problem solving: Evidence from school and district leaders.* Albany, NY: SUNY Press.

Loughran, J. (1996). *Developing reflective practice: Learning about teaching and learning through modeling.* London: The Falmer Press.

Marshall, C., & Rossman, G. (1995). *Designing qualitative research.* California: Sage Publications.

McNiff, J. (1995). How can I develop a theory of critical self reflection? *Studies in Continuing Education, 17*(1&2), 86-96.

Merriam, S. (1988). *Case study research in education: A qualitative approach.* Oxford: Jossey-Bass.

Osterman, K. F. (1991). Reflective practice: Linking professional development and school reform. *Planning and Changing, 22*(3&4), 208-217.

Peters, J. M. (1991). Strategies for reflective practice. *New Directions for Adult and Continuing Education, 51*(Fall), 89-96.

Prestine, N., & LeGrand, B. (1991). Cognitive learning theory and the preparation of educational administrators: Implications for practice and policy. *Educational Administration Quarterly, 27*(1), 61-69.

Reagan, T., Case, K., Case, C., & Freiberg, J. (1993). Reflecting on "reflective practice": Implications for teacher evaluation. *Journal of Personnel Evaluation in Education, 6*(3), 263-267.

Seidel, J. (1998). *Ethnograph v5.0: A user's guide.* Thousand Oaks, CA: Qualis Research.

Sergiovanni, T. (1991). *The principalship: A reflective practice perspective, second edition.* Boston, MA: Allyn & Bacon.

Van Gyn, G.H. (1996). Reflective practice: The needs of professions and the promise of cooperative education. *Journal of Cooperative Education, 31*(2&3), 103-131.

Van Manen, J. (1977). Linking ways of knowing with ways of being practical. *Curriculum Inquiry, 6*(3), 205-208.

Vygotsky, L.S. (1978). *Mind in society.* Cambridge, MA: Harvard University Press.

Willower, D.J. (1994). Dewey's theory of inquiry and reflective administration. *Journal of Educational Administration, 32*(1), 5-22.

Wilson, A.L. (1994). To a middle ground: Praxis and ideology in adult education. *International Journal of Lifelong Education, 13*(3), 187-202.

PART 2:

CONCEPTS OF SCHOOL COMMUNITY AND COLLABORATION

KENNETH A. STRIKE

COMMUNITY, COHERENCE, AND INCLUSIVENESS[1]

Abstract. This paper develops a theory of schools as communities. It argues that the key to a school that is a community is that such schools are rooted in something I call a Shared Educational Project. An SEP is a constitutive vision of the nature of a good education that involves public ends requiring cooperation to achieve. An SEP also generates a conception of the roles to be played by various actors in the school, grounds instructional practice, and informs governance. An SEP also is important in securing what I call the goods of community such as trust, cooperation, belonging and mutual identification. The liability of such communities is that full membership in the community is predicated on agreeing with the SEP. Since the SEP will be rooted in a "thick" conception of human flourishing, agreement cannot be imposed. Hence such communities cannot be fully inclusive and should be formed through free association. I provide examples of several models of such school communities. I also discuss two models of what I call quasi communities. Quasi communities do not have an SEP; however, they may have shared views of good educating (rather than good education), may have a strong commitment to justice, caring and inclusiveness, and may have informal, non-bureaucratic organization forms. I argue that quasi communities may also produce some of the goods of community, and they may be more fully inclusive. Regardless, there are reasons to suppose that they will not be stable and that they will be less successful in generating the goods of community than will schools grounded in an SEP.

In this chapter, I take up a set of issues about the notion that schools can be communities. In the first part, I sketch some hypotheses about how making schools more communal might advance goals that I believe most everyone will value. In the second part, I explore four different metaphors for the notion of a school that is a community. I use these to explore what I call the "thick, thin" dilemma. The thickness of a set of values concerns how robust and life encompassing they are. The essence of this dilemma occurs when the values that constitute community are too thin, they do little useful work; however, as values get thicker, there is also an increased risk that their realization will be accompanied by what I shall call the "bads" of community. Communities may produce a sense of belonging and generate such relational goods as caring or respect; however, they may also produce parochialism, sectarianism, intolerance, and an erosion of autonomy. A suitable conception of community is required if we are to maximize the educational goods to which community can lead while minimizing the bads of community.

Seven Educational Reasons to Care about Community

I want to begin by describing a school that is not a community. Imagine a secondary school that serves a large and diverse student population. There are members of different races, cultures and religions present. Students in this school and their families agree on little about the fundamental aims that a good education should serve. Their conceptions of human flourishing and the ways in which education can serve their visions of human flourishing are characterized by what might be called durable pluralism (Rawls, 1993). How might such a school achieve an educational program? On what might people agree? I imagine them

P.T. Begley and O. Johansson (eds.), The Ethical Dimensions of School Leadership, 69–87.
© 2003 *Kluwer Academic Publishers. Printed in the Netherlands.*

reasoning like this: We cannot and should not root our educational program in some vision of human flourishing. People in our school have widely differing views of what human flourishing consists, rooted in our different religions, cultures, and philosophies. We have to respect this diversity. Hence, we need to be neutral concerning those conceptions of the human good that divide us. What we can do is to search for educational programs that produce knowledge and skills that we all value even if we do not agree about the nature of human flourishing. There are some things we all value because they are instrumental to different and varied conceptions of human flourishing. Whatever people want out of life, it seems that they need to learn to read and to do basic mathematics. Whatever people want, they are likely to need access to further education. Whatever people want, they are likely to need economically valuable skills. Everyone, regardless of their religion or culture, will value such things. Moreover, some subjects do not raise difficult issues about the nature of human flourishing. There is no such thing as Presbyterian math or Native American computer science. Hence, even if not every person or culture values all of what we teach equally, at least, nothing will offend. When we stick to those subjects that are broadly instrumental and broadly acceptable, we can agree on what to teach even if we do not share a conception of the deeper ends that this curriculum serves.

Suppose we do seek for an educational program that all can salute despite significant disagreement about the nature of human flourishing, what will we have done? One thing we may have done is to have privatized the deeper ends of education. We will have come to view schools as though they were like banks. People value banks because they value money, but money is a kind of universal instrumentality. People value it because it enables them to achieve purposes that are their own private purposes. Some will save for a car or for the education of their children. Some will borrow for a home. Still others will want a vacation or an early retirement or the security of a large nest egg. They need not value the bank because they share common goals or a common conception of human flourishing.

A second thing we will have done is to instrumentalize and commodify knowledge. We began with the assumption that we cannot agree on any fundamental characterization of what knowledge is for. We cannot say that we value learning because of how it forms our character or because it is intrinsically worthwhile. We cannot agree to learn for the love or glory of God. Nor can we use the school to affirm or restore our distinctive culture. There are others here with other cultures. As individuals, we may value education when it serves these ideals to which we subscribe, but we cannot collectively agree on such ends. We can only agree to value knowledge when it serves a range of private goals and conceptions of life.

A third thing we will have done is to view education as a competitive enterprise. Knowledge is curious stuff. When we gain some, we do not reduce its availability to others. While the resources on which gaining knowledge depends may be scarce, knowledge is not. On the other hand, to view knowledge as an instrumental good is often to make its value to us depend on our having more of it than others. Gaining admission to a select college or a desired job is often not a matter of possessing a certain quanta of knowledge. It is a matter of having more than one's competitors. So long as knowledge is valuable in this way education will be a scene of competition. We may mitigate this competition in various ways, but we cannot make it go away without reconceptualizing what we are about.

Finally, we will have come to view equality as equal opportunity and this, in turn, as fair competition. We will say that the knowledge and skills we provide are the means to living well in our society, but we will also notice that achievement depends on possessing resources that are scarce. While everyone can, in theory, know that $E=MC^2$, we must also acknowledge that not everyone can have access to a physics class. The attainment of knowledge is a race for goods that not everyone can have or have equally. If so, at least the race must be fair. When we say this, we also construct our interactions as arm's length transactions. Equality is fairness among those seeking their own good. We come to expect justice from others. Benevolence is supererogatory.

Let me summarize the properties of this school:

1. It has no overarching conception of a good education rooted in a view of human flourishing.
2. Agreement on a conception of education is achieved by seeking for knowledge and skills that are broadly instrumental.
3. The deeper purposes that education may serve are private matters beyond the legitimate concern of the school just as the objects for which people save are beyond the legitimate interest of a bank.
4. Relationships in the school are competitive and arm's length and are regulated by a theory of fair competition.

I hope that this intuitive picture will seem familiar. I believe that many schools in our societies are formed by such views even if they do not clearly recognize this. We should be ambivalent about this picture. We need to recognize that it militates against community because it privatizes central values and reinforces competitive relationships. At the same time, it arises from a desire to have schools that all can attend that are not instruments of domination and oppression. Pluralistic societies have good reasons to seek neutrality in public institution.

I do not claim that schools that are formed by such conceptions must be bad schools. Nor do I claim that they cannot in any sense be communities. Nor do I claim that the fact that relationships are conceptualized as competitive and arm's length means that friendships cannot be formed or caring relationships established. Even in banks, tellers sometimes fall in love. But I do argue that such schools are not communities in one important sense. They lack a shared conception of the deeper point of the education they seek to provide, and they lack shared practices through which this conception is realized.

The antithesis of a school of this sort is one that is united not just by some vague sense of shared values. It is a school that is united by a shared non-instrumental vision of a good education rooted in a shared view of human flourishing. Examples of schools that are communities in this way might include schools that emphasize developing democratic character, or religious schools, or schools that emphasize the fine arts.

Should we want such schools? There are certain goods of community that are inherently important to human flourishing. I will call these the *primary goods* of community. They include a sense of belonging, place or membership, they help one to achieve a sense of identity, and they produce attachments with other people such as trust, friendship, loyalty, solidarity, and caring. Schools that are communities may help us to realize such goods.

These primary goods of community are not educational goods. Nevertheless, they may help to establish learning communities in which educational goods are more readily achieved. Consider now seven goals that might be realized by creating schools that are communities.

1. Having schools that are communities is essential to the provision of safe and emotionally secure learning environments. I am not thinking here primarily of physical safety. I am rather thinking of having a sense of belonging and the emotional security that results from belonging. These feelings enable exploration and investigation. In communities, human relationships are more than arm's length. They depend on such things as trust, friendship, mutual affirmation, love, caring, cooperation, and especially a sense of membership. These features of the relationships that characterize communities are also preconditions of growth.

2. Belonging is essential for normation and normation is a precondition of learning. (Green, 1999) Mastery of a subject is not merely a matter of memorizing its facts or even of mastering its cognitive skills. It is a matter of internalizing the intellectual norms (some of which are ethical) of a guild. One becomes a mathematician through initiation into the community of mathematicians. If one has learned some mathematical facts and skills, but has not begun to internalize the standards and norms that regulate the practice of mathematics, one is still a long way from being a mathematician. Intellectual guilds are the custodians of the life of the mind. To master an intellectual practice is to be initiated into such a guild. Mastery depends on normation which, in turn, depends on membership.

3. A sense of community is required for a conception of equality that goes beyond fair competition. A communal sense of equality is one in which each feels a stake in the welfare of all. In community, the other's good is part of one's own. Equality is more than fair competition. Transactions are more than arm's length.

4. A community organized around a shared conception of a good education is often the alternative to the development of a school fragmented by subcultures (Vivian, 2000). When students find themselves in a large and impersonal organization and lack any clear conception of the goods it serves, they are likely to organize themselves into various subcultures, often on racial or socioeconomic lines. The names of some of the groups are familiar. They include jocks, nerds, and druggies. Schools that lack an overarching conception of the values that unite their community may for that reason lack an important resource for uniting such subcultures into cooperative efforts towards common goals. However, schools that lack such an overarching conception do not lack a hierarchy of values. Schools will differentially value groups that are cooperative with the school's program and those that are oppositional. Hence, some of these subcultures will become sources of

resistance to the school's program. Community helps schools resist youth cultures.

5. Community develops socially desirable traits. It is in relationships where one is loved, valued, and cared for where one learns to trust cooperate and care for others (Putman, 1993; Rawls, 1971). Communities of shared purpose are more likely to develop such traits than associations characterized by arm's length agreements.

6. Community is a precondition for reducing bureaucracy. It has become commonplace among educators that one of the things that reduces the effectiveness of educational institutions is an environment that emphasizes bureaucratic compliance over conscientious educating (see, for example, Chubb & Moe, 1990). Among the things that generate bureaucracy are competition and lack of trust. If we exist in institutions where we primarily seek our own good and where we insist on being treated fairly, we are also likely to insist on detailed rules to ensure equitable treatment. If we exist in a community where we share a common perspective and common goals with others, we can trust more and rely on procedures and rules less.

7. Communities foster non-alienated learning. Learning is alienated when it is viewed as an imposed task. In a community, the aims of education are shared. The ends of the school are the ends of the students. If so, the learning is not alienated. When learning is not alienated, there may be more of it and it may be more robust. There may be more of it because students are more likely to learn when they share the ends of learning. It may be more robust because community permits the kind of normation that enables students to go beyond the learning of mere details and fact to an internalization of the point and the ethos of subject matter.

Let me see if I can summarize this view of why community is important in education. Educational communities have an overarching conception of their mission that connects their educational program to a conception of human flourishing. They know what education is for. This overarching conception allows the school to select or socialize students, their families, and their teachers so as to achieve some degree of coherence about what the school's mission is and it permits the school to provide an account of its educational practices to members of the school community in terms of this agreed-upon mission. In such schools, all members of the school are engaged in a shared educational project. This shared educational project can be a means to engender cooperation, trust, and a shared understanding of the basis of action and decision making in the school. Perhaps the best summary of the relationship between community's primary goods and these educational goods is that community produces not only cohesiveness, but also coherence. Both cohesiveness and coherence contribute to good education.

These hypotheses assume a certain conception of what it means for a school to be a community. They assume that schools have a particular kind of shared values. Not every shared value can create a community. In some cases, this is obvious. Everyone in all schools is likely to value good plumbing, but this is unlikely to create an educational community. What are needed are values that are constitutive of the purposes of the school and which can be pursued through shared and cooperative practices. Schools that are communities are like orchestras. While people in orchestras may compete for things such as chairs or solos, fundamentally orchestras succeed or fail as a whole. The success of each is required for the success of the overall project. Schools that are communities have a sense of their educational project that is like that of an orchestra.

In short, schools that are communities work because they have what I shall call a *shared educational project*. Because this notion of a shared educational project is central to my view of community, I want to specify the notion carefully. Here is what I mean: *When a school has a shared educational project, it has a vision of the education it wishes to provide which is known to, and agreed upon by the members of the community. This vision is rooted in a common vision of human flourishing, and it involves aims that require cooperation in order to secure. This shared educational project is the basis of the community's self understanding, and is the basis for articulating roles within the community. It grounds the community's educational practices, rituals, and traditions, grounds the community's governance practices, and is the basis of the community's ability to achieve the goods of community such as belonging, loyalty, mutual identification, and trust.*

Three caveats about this: First, while a shared educational project is essential to educational communities, it may not be sufficient. It may be that there are certain structural variables that are important to whether a school can be a community. Size, or what Coleman (1987, 1988) calls intergeneration closure, are examples. Such schools may also require reasonable autonomy and non-bureaucratic governance. Second, creating a community does not repeal human nature or eliminate all discord. People will still disagree, squabble, compete, behave selfishly, and break the rules. Good communities are not inevitably harmonious, and are maintained by successful practices of deliberation and conflict resolution. What having a community changes is the context in which these human frailties are addressed and in which deliberation and conflict resolution are practiced. Third, there may be "bads" associated with community as well as goods. Communities may enforce homogeneity, stifle debate, and promote sectarianism and intolerance. Not every community is a good community. On this last point hangs a tale.

Four Metaphors of Community

Suppose we take a different approach to the idea that schools should be communities. Communities are held together by what I shall call "social glue." They are more than just associations of people who are united because their individual good is served by cooperation. Members of communities are attached to one another. They are deeply bonded in some way. But what is the nature of this glue that promotes bonding and how is it engendered? I want you to consider the comments of four philosophers that provide four somewhat different visions of this social glue. I will link these views with four metaphors. I will distinguish between communities as tribes, communities as congregations, communities as orchestras, and communities as families.

Michael Sandel (1982) writes:

> And in so far as our constitutive self-understandings comprehend a wider subjectivity than the individual alone…to this extent they define a community in the constitutive sense. And what marks such a community is not merely a spirit of benevolence, or the prevalence of communitarian values, or even certain shared final ends alone, but a common vocabulary of discourse and a background of implicit practices and understandings within which the opacity of the participants is reduced if never finally dissolved (pp. 172-73).

A community, on this understanding, is a group of people linked by a shared consciousness and a shared identity and not just by bonds of mutual regard or attachment. People are transparent to one another because they understand and see the world in the same way. These shared understandings result not just or primarily from shared beliefs, but from common practices. Common identities are rooted in these shared understandings. These common understandings and shared identities are themselves rooted in a shared way of life. Sandel's community is a *Gemeinshaft* community (Tonnies, 1988), a Folk, a people. People in such communities share a way of life. I will call this kind of community a tribe.

John Rawls (1993), on the other hand, characterizes a community as "a society governed by a shared comprehensive religious, philosophical or moral doctrine" (p. 42). In his view, what creates community is a shared creed or common core values that provide a vision of the ends of life or of human flourishing. Rawls's communities are united by shared commitments, but people who share a common set of commitments such as a religion need not be united in a shared form of life. Indeed, many religions value the diversity of races, languages, ethnic groups, nationalities and professions that they can gather into a common faith. A shared doctrine does not require a common way of life. I will call the communities Rawls describes congregations.

Alasdair MacIntyre (1981) says this about community:

> …a community whose shared aim is the realization of the human good presupposes a wide range of agreement in that community on goods and virtues, and it is this agreement which makes possible the kind of bond between citizens which, on Aristotle's view, constitutes a polis. That bond is the bond of friendship…. (p. 146)

MacIntyre seems to agree with Rawls that community requires agreement about some conception of human flourishing, but he adds to Rawls's account the expectation of agreement about the characteristics, the virtues, that people should have in order for the community to realize their shared conception of the aims of the community. Moreover, MacIntyre suggests that sharing goods and virtues is a precondition of developing bonds of friendship. While MacIntyre's example of a community is a polis, MacIntyre also applies these conceptions to groups that are formed by a shared practice. He describes a practice as

> any coherent and complex form of socially established cooperative human activity through which goods internal to that form of activity are realized in the course of trying to achieve those standards of excellence which are appropriate to, and partially definitive of, that form of activity, with the result that human powers to achieve excellence, and human conceptions of the ends and goods involved, are systematically extended (p.175).

Examples of practices are physics, music, and many professions. It is MacIntyre's account of communities of practices that interests me here. A religion is a community united by what Rawls calls a comprehensive doctrine and MacIntyre a tradition. An orchestra, however, is joined by a commitment to a shared practice. I will characterize communities united by a shared practice as orchestras. In this case, it is not clear that MacIntryre's view requires the kind of deep mutual understanding that Sandel's characterization requires. People who play in orchestras need not share a way of life.

In her book, *The Challenge to Care in Schools*, Nel Noddings (1992) compares the school with a large heterogeneous family (p. 45). Here, the bonds that form community are those of caring. Neither a shared culture, nor a shared creed, nor a shared conception of goods to be sought and the virtues to be cultivated seems required.

Here then we have four different metaphors for community: *tribes* who share a common form of life, *congregations* which share a set of core convictions, *orchestras* which share a commitment to the values that inhere in a shared practice, and *families* which are united by caring. All of these can be pictures of what is meant by schools as communities.

I want you to notice three things about these various pictures. First, they vary on a dimension that might be called the "thickness" of the values that unite them. The thickness of values concerns how robust and life encompassing they are. Members of orchestras are united by shared values. So are religious groups. So are those who inhabit a distinct culture or way of life; however, ways of life are far more life-encompassing than orchestras. The kind of community that Sandel calls a constitutive community depends on people sharing a culture or a way of life. They share a wide range of common understandings that bind them together. Because they share a common form of life with its associated ways of understanding, they are psychologically transparent to one another over a wide range of activities and practices. That is, they intuitively understand one another in the way that the English appear to understand cricket and Americans do not. The values that unite constitutive communities are thick, in that they broadly define ways of life and forms of identity.

Rawls's view of community requires that people share a set of core convictions. These core convictions may provide criteria or standards for many of life's decisions, but ordinarily they are not as life-encompassing as is a way of life. Similarly, a practice is less life encompassing than a way of life and, typically, than a religion.

Noddings' view of community is thin in that caring is not life encompassing. I do not mean by this that caring is somehow weak or deficient. Rather, I mean that when we care for another, on Noddings's account, we need not share a wide range of other commitments. Her image of a large, heterogeneous family suggests a picture of communities where members may be culturally and religiously different. And it may be that this is a good thing, since it enables us to have strong communities that do not constrain people with respect to the life commitments that must be possessed or taken on in order to be a member of a community. I will, however, argue below that this is unlikely.

The second thing to consider is these different visions of the values that form community are associated with different visions of the nature of the "social glue" that binds the members of community together. What binds people together in Sandel's constitutive communities is a deep mutual understanding and a shared identity. Members of constitutive communities are the same in a deep way. They are psychologically transparent to one another. When they meet each other, they meet people who are a part of some larger We in which each participates. Other people are not psychologically transparent in the same way. They are not Us. They are strangers.

For MacIntyre, what creates bonds of friendship is shared practices that are rooted in sharing of a vision of human flourishing.

The social glue that binds those who share a common religious, moral or philosophical outlook – what Rawls calls a comprehensive doctrine – is likely to be the trust and mutual regard that flows from the cooperation required to pursue shared ends as well as the enjoyment of participating in shared practices. Members of a common faith pray and worship together. They cooperate in sustaining institutions and efforts that serve ends in which they believe.

For Noddings, the glue that sustains community is what might be called unmediated caring. That is, caring itself is the principal value, and caring need not flow from other shared commitments or practices.

The third thing to consider is that these different views of the values that help form community have implications for the inclusiveness of community. Inclusiveness has to do with how open the community is to diverse members. Sandel's constitutive communities are likely to be life-encompassing, and will tend to sharply distinguish between insiders and outsiders, between Us and Them (Barber, 1998). If we think of schools in this way, we are likely to be drawn to one of two options. Either we will try to pretend that there is a national constitutive community to which we all belong, or we will aspire to create a plurality of school communities in which each community serves its own members and where all such school communities are treated equally. Either view has serious problems. I do not believe that there is any national constitutive community in most multicultural and pluralistic societies. If we pretend that there is one, we are likely to impose some vision of what a national community should be like on members of other cultures. On the other hand, if we opt for a plurality of constitutive communities we run the dangers of parochialism and sectarianism, of tribalism.

If we seek school communities that are built around shared core values, our schools will still fail to be inclusive. We will still need to choose between asserting that there are some core values that everyone does or should share and which are thus able to create fully inclusive communities, or we must opt for a plurality of school communities each formed by its own core values. In this second case, we should note that such schools may be inclusive in many ways. They may be diverse with respect to race, culture, social class, and perhaps, depending on what their core values are, religion. Nevertheless, if a school does have a set of core values, sharing these values will be a litmus test for full membership. If so, there will still be insiders and outsiders, members and non-members, Us and Them. Is there a danger of parochialism and sectarianism in such schools? Surely, but perhaps to a lesser degree.

Arguably, the kinds of school communities Noddings seeks can be fully inclusive. Her large, heterogeneous family need exclude no one. Caring need not create insiders and outsiders, members and non-members, Us and Them. Here two points should be considered. First, it is not self evident that caring is fully inclusive. I have suggested that almost every vision of community values caring or its functional equivalent. No reasonable person, it seems to me, can be against caring. Noddings, however, argues for more than caring. She argues for an ethic of caring – a perspective in which caring, if not the only thing, is the main thing. It is not just a value, it is a *summa bona*. It is not quite as obvious that all reasonable people should favour an ethic of caring (see Strike, 1999a, b). If not, then caring itself is a comprehensive doctrine, a set of core values, and a school built on an ethic of caring is not likely to be fully inclusive. Here, however, my more pressing concern is that the social glue that "unmediated caring" provides may not be strong enough to bind people together in community given significant cultural and religious diversity between community members. We may grant that caring in families is often strong. But Noddings' heterogeneous school is not, in fact, a family. It is an aggregation of people who may be quite different in many ways and who need share little beyond caring. Little in human experience suggests to me that people are likely to come to care deeply about those with whom they share little by way of kinship, common culture, or common purpose.

These comments suggest four connected hypotheses we might want to entertain about communities and school communities. These are:

1. The thicker the social glue is that constitutes a community, the more durable and robust will be the bonds of community.
2. The thicker the social glue is that constitutes a community, the less inclusive the community will be.
3. The thicker the social glue is that constitutes a community, the more risk there is that the community will produce what I shall call the bads of community.
4. The thicker the social glue is that constitutes a community, the stronger the demand for free association will be in forming community.

The import of these hypotheses can be developed from considering two figures. These are, of course, egregious oversimplifications. I hope, nevertheless, that they will prove revealing.

Table 1 concerns the basis for attachments. What should be noticed is the chart arranges attachments from the thickest to the thinnest. Tribes share a common life. This is the basis of their identification with one another.

Table 2 suggests how my four hypotheses above work out for the four metaphors of community. It suggest that when the social glue that binds people together is quite thick, then their communities tend to be cohesive; however, thick communities also tend to exclude non-members from participation. Because the community is rooted in a shared way of life that must be nurtured and protected, thick communities may also tend to run a high risk of such "bads" of community as sectarianism, reduction of individual autonomy, and intolerance. Because schools that seek to be communities in this sense are suitable only for members, a high level of freedom of association is required for the formation of school communities. Members need to be able to form their own school and to exclude others.

Table 1. Basis of Attachment.

Community Metaphor	Basis of Attachment	Character of Attachment
Tribe	common life shared understandings, common identity	identification
Congregation	common convictions shared ends	trust, mutuality
Orchestra	common aims shared practice	friendship
Family	extended natural sentiments	care

Table 2. Hypotheses about Community.

Community Metaphor	Cohesion	Inclusiveness	Risk of "bads"	Demand for Free Association
Tribe	high	low	high	high
Congregation	moderate	moderate	moderate	moderate
Orchestra	moderate	moderate	moderate	moderate
Family	low	high	low	low

The Amish can illustrate these points. In *Wisconsin v. Yoder,* the U.S. Supreme Court exempted the Amish from compulsory education laws after the age of fourteen, and permitted Amish children to be educated in the Amish community via informal mechanisms. In my sense of the term, the Amish are a tribe. They are bound together through sharing a way of life. In *Yoder,* the Amish argued that the education provided by the typical high school was predicated on values alien to the Amish way of life and tended to generate defections from the Amish community. Those who opposed the right of the Amish to separate their children for a distinct Amish education claimed that such an education diminished the autonomy of Amish youth and eroded their capacity to become good citizens (see Gutmann, 1987). Certainly, the Amish do not value some things that many would find to be important features of a good education, such as a marketplace of ideas or developing the capacity to choose and to construct one's own conception of a good life.

Hence, it seems reasonable to believe that generally, if not inevitably, thick communities will tend to be more cohesive, have lower levels of inclusiveness, have a higher risk of producing the bads of community, and have a higher demand for freedom of association in producing a school community. This suggests that schools that seek to fit into the picture of community as tribe may have some serious drawbacks. I do not think that this is a compelling argument against them. There may be cases in which having "tribal" schools is a condition of the survival of a way of life. We should also note that on my definition of a tribe, there are few tribes in modern, technologically-advanced, liberal democratic societies. African Americans, for example, are not a tribe. African Americans are members of different faiths, may speak different languages, are from different ethnic groups, and work in different professions. While there may be some distinct features of an African American culture and there are interests that African Americans share as a group, these do not, I suspect, amount to a shared way of life. An Afrocentric school would be closer to a school as congregation than a school as a tribe.

Note that I have suggested that the cohesion of communities that are modeled on families is low. Let us suppose that real families are bound together by what David Hume has called natural sentiments (Hume, 1967). That is, there is a natural tendency for members of families to care for one another. Parents are inclined to love their children, and when they do this, their love is reciprocated. If, however, such sentiments are to be extended to those strangers encountered in schools, we must believe that these natural sentiments can be developed and extended so that people become able to care for those who are not members of their families. Not only this, but they must come to care for these people who are, at the outset, strangers in the absence of any of the commonalities that form attachments in other types of communities and often in the face of considerable difference. It is my hunch that in the absence of factors that generate attachments in other communities, things such as a shared culture or shared convictions, it will be difficult to create a community in which caring is not fragile and easily undermined by cultural differences or conflicts of interest.

Caring, however, is widely thought to be central to community. And it is. My concern is not with caring, but with the view that caring is able to create community in the absence of other uniting factors. I suspect, however, that caring receives emphasis because it is high on inclusiveness, low on the risk potential for the bads of community, and low on the demands for freedom of association. If we look at many public schools with their diverse populations and conflicting perspectives, we may easily conclude that such institutions cannot be tribes, congregations or orchestras. They can only be families. Caring may be the only basis for community available in many cases.

If so, then we have a dilemma. It seems that we can arrange different forms of community on a continuum. On one end are communities that are thick. The cohesion of these communities may be high, but they will be difficult to achieve apart from significant freedom of choice, they will fail to be inclusive, and they will pose the risk of generating the bads of community. On the other end are communities that can be produced without freedom of association, that are inclusive, and that do not risk the bads of community. But these communities will be fragile. They lack important resources that make cohesiveness possible.

How about the middle groupings? Should we want communities to be like congregations or orchestras? In fact, I believe that this is where we should look for community. I will suggest several reasons. Before I do so, I want to provide some examples of schools that would fall into these middle categories. Those schools that would fit into the community as orchestra picture would be those that emphasize some particular practice. This would normally be some subject matter or some grouping of subject matters. Schools that emphasize science, or the arts, or some vocation would be examples. Schools that fit into the schools as congregations picture might include religious schools, democratic schools, or schools that focus on the centrality of the life of the mind. I have sketched models of these schools in Appendix 1 below.

What is the case for these schools? First, these schools may be able to create what I described above as the primary goods of community. Because they provide a context in which people can work together to achieve shared aims requiring cooperation for their achievement, they may be able to produce such goods as trust, friendship, loyalty, and belonging. Second, because they produce these goods and because they are able to achieve coherences about their mission, they may also be able to produce educational goods. Third, while these schools do run the risk of producing the bads of community, this risk is less than thicker communities, and it can be minimized.

Why do communities run the risks of producing the bads of community? There are two central reasons. First, neither schools that are congregations nor schools that are orchestras can be fully inclusive. Schools that are congregations will include those who accept their overarching sense of their educational mission and the vision of human flourishing that grounds it. Others will not be admitted or will be marginalized. Schools that are organized around some practice will, of course, be inclined to attract and value those interested in or skilled in the practice, and not others. The lack of inclusiveness itself can produce the bads of community. Schools that emphasize some practice such as the arts or science, may be parochial merely by virtue of providing inadequate exposure to other activities. They will also attract those whose values systems are attuned to the goods internal to the practice pursued. Such individuals may be parochial in the ways captured by C.P. Snow (1959) in his description of the two cultures (the humanities and the sciences) that he claims divide modern universities.

The failure of inclusiveness in schools as congregations may be more problematic. Such schools will hold at least a partially comprehensive doctrine - a distinct vision of human flourishing that grounds their vision of education. Those who do not share this vision will not be there or will be marginalized. This can be the source of loss of autonomy, parochialism and sectarianism. The marketplace of ideas - the free and open discussion of ideas - is a primary mechanism of autonomy and the enemy of parochialism and sectarianism (see Callan, 1997). The lack of inclusiveness necessarily truncates the marketplace of ideas because those voices who reject the view of human flourishing that is central to the school's shared educational project will not be there.

The second reason why schools that are congregations may produce the bads of community is that a school's constitutive doctrine may itself generate them. Some religions are intolerant as a matter of principle. Nor is intolerance unique to religious convictions; I have sat in on one meeting of an alternative democratic school where teachers at other local schools were routinely referred to as "the fascists."

Nevertheless, we should not overstate these difficulties. Let me note a few reasons. First, it is important to note that while schools in this middle group of communities as congregations and orchestras may not be fully inclusive, they may nevertheless be highly inclusive. Congregations are not tribes. They may include people from different races, ethnic groups, professions, and political persuasions. Many religious groups emphasize the creation of inclusive communities. Religions do not preclude much diversity of outlook. This is all the more the case for schools as orchestras. Moreover, schools that seek to be congregations may be decently welcoming to those who do not share some features of their vision. Catholic schools are a useful illustration (see Bryk, Lee, & Holland, 1993). They have significant numbers of non-Catholic students, and have become effective educators of poor minority youth. Many appear to wish to establish communities that are not narrowly Catholic, and are comfortable places for children from other faiths. Granted, this does not add up to equal time for Protestants and atheists. Nevertheless, Catholic schools now seem to take care not to coerce or otherwise violate the conscience of those who are not Catholic.

Second, schools that are congregations may still value a marketplace of ideas. They may even do so for religious reasons, perhaps from a conviction that an examined faith will be a better faith. I attended a religious school as an undergraduate where I was a philosophy major. When I went on to do graduate work in philosophy, I discovered that the difference between the philosophical education I received compared to that of my peers who had attended secular universities was that I was literate in philosophy of religion. The education I received was broad. I read not only scholars of different faiths and theological persuasion, but Hume, Huxley and Kant, whose arguments were fairly represented and seriously considered, if not accepted. The issues these views debated had not been on the table for most of my peers.

Consider that part of the ethos of many modern Catholic schools is a kind of Aristotelian humanism filtered through Aquinas and other modern Catholic thinkers (Bryk et al., 1993). This strain of Catholic thought affirms the life of the mind. Is it better to have religious issues on the table in a school that has a view, or not on the table at all, as is the case in most public schools? This is a question I shall not answer here. Merely to ask it is to see that it cannot be uncritically assumed that schools that seek to be communities inevitably truncate a marketplace of ideas and that secular schools promote one.

Third, we need to attend to the fact that while there are intolerant comprehensive doctrines that might become the basis of schools, there are also very many others that are tolerant and humane. Religious views fall on both sides of this divide. We should remind ourselves that Christianity is the source of the parable of the Good Samaritan, one of the most vivid manifestations of universalism available in our culture. Most major religions have similar views. What is most important about schools as congregations is not that they have a vision. It is the vision that they have.

The manner in which a comprehensive doctrine is held is also important. I believe that there is a crucial difference between communities that view their overarching doctrine as a tradition, and those that view it as a dogma. To view one's comprehensive doctrine as part of a tradition is to see it as something mutable, something that can change over time as the result of the deliberations and experience of members of the community as well as the result of assessing external criticism. Traditions change and learn, and they value the deliberations that promote reflective change. Dogmas are viewed as immutable and as things to be protected against discussion and isolated from criticism. A school that is rooted in a tradition is far less likely to generate the bads of community than one rooted in a dogma.

The conclusions we should draw are that schools as congregations and schools as orchestras do run some risk of generating the bads of community, but that these are risks, not inevitabilities. Creating community in schools is a project that can be worked on, one whose risks can be minimized.

How are we to do this? There is much to be said. Here I want to discuss the idea of free association. I have said that the thicker a school's constitutive doctrine is, the more freedom of association is required. Why? There are two reasons. First, a school cannot maintain and pursue its vision if it cannot select teachers and students who share it. Second, the visions that are constitutive of school communities are not likely to be universally shared and are not properly coerced. Schools that are communities are oppressive unless they are chosen.

It does not follow that schools that are communities must be private schools operated out of public space. What is needful is to invent institutions that permit appropriate forms of free association in public space (see Strike, 1999a, b). Charter schools are one example. Properly done, they permit schools that have a distinctive vision while providing some public regulation. Schools within schools, comprised of small and distinctive learning communities, are another. We can envision institutions that permit students to freely associate to pursue some purposes and to associate with diverse individuals for others.

Trying to make schools that are communities involves risks. We sometimes hide these risks from ourselves through vague and unspecific talk about shared values, or by pretending that we can have community if we only become less bureaucratic or if we try to care more. Less bureaucracy and more caring are good things. I do not think that more vague talk about the importance of shared values will get us anywhere. We need to face both the benefits and the risks more squarely. We need to recognize that if we change institutions to permit more community that tradeoffs will be involved. In thinking through these tradeoffs we need to avoid the dual evils of romanticizing community, or of pretending that real public schools are models of democratic polity and liberating discourse.

I think that we need to value the goods of community more. Schools are too alienating and lonely for too many children, especially adolescents. This is a reason for making community a project. But it should be a cautious and thoughtful project. There are bads to be avoided as well as goods to be attained.

NOTES

[1] The research reported in this article was made possible, in part, by a grant from the Spencer Foundation. The data presented, the statements made, and the views expressed are solely the responsibility of the author.

REFERENCES

Barber, B. (1998). *Clansmen, consumers and citizens: Three takes on civil society.* Rutgers University: Working Paper #4.

Bryk, A.S., Lee, V.E., & Holland, P.B. (1993). *Catholic schools and the common good.* Cambridge, MA: Harvard University Press.

Callan, E. (1997). *Creating citizens: Political education and liberal democracy.* Oxford: Oxford University Press.

Coleman, J.S., & Hoffer, T. (1987). *Public and private schools: The impact of communities.* New York: Basic Books.

Coleman, J.S. (1988). Social capital in the creation of human capital. *American Journal of Sociology (Supplement), 94,* S95-S120.

Chubb, J.E., & Moe, T.M. (1990). *Politics markets and the American school.* Washington DC: The Brookings Institution.

Green, T. (1999). *Voices: The educational formation of conscience.* South Bend, IN: University of Notre Dame Press.

Gutmann, A. (1987). *Democratic education.* Princeton, NJ: Princeton University Press.

Hume, D. (1967). *A treatise of human nature.* Oxford: Clarendon Press.

MacIntyre, A. (1981). *After virtue.* Notre Dame, IN: University of Notre Dame Press.

Noddings, N. (1992). *The challenge to care in schools: An alternative approach to education.* New York: Teachers College Press.

Putman, R. (1993). *Making democracy work: Civic traditions in modern Italy.* Princeton, NJ: Princeton University Press.

Rawls, J. (1971). *A theory of justice.* Cambridge, MA: Harvard University Press.

Rawls, J. (1993). *Political liberalism.* New York: Columbia University Press.

Sandel, M. (1982). *Liberalism and the limits of justice.* Cambridge, UK: Cambridge University Press.

Snow, C P. (1959). *The two cultures and the scientific revolution.* Cambridge: Cambridge University Press.

Strike, K.A. (1999a). Can schools be communities? The tension between shared values and inclusion. *Educational Administration Quarterly, 35*(1), 46-70.

Strike, K.A. (1999b). Justice, caring, and universality: In defense of moral pluralism. In M. Katz, N. Noddings, & K. Strike (Eds.), *Justice and caring: The search for common ground in education* (pp. 21-36). New York: Teachers College Press.

Tonnies, F. (1988). *Community and society.* New Brunswick, NJ: Transaction Books.

Vivian, C. (2000). *The influence of school communities on student identity.* Ithaca, NY: Cornell.

Wisconsin v. Yoder (1972). 406 U.S. 205 (U.S.S.C.).

APPENDIX 1:
THREE SKETCHES OF SCHOOLS AS CONGREGATIONS

Comprehensive doctrine (religious) schools

- Ruling conception: School communities are constituted from values interpreted within a common tradition or comprehensive doctrine such as a religion. A comprehensive doctrine and the dominant goals and practices that flow from it are prior to the community. Acceptance of them is a condition of full membership. Religious schools are the most common, but not the only, examples. While one should not uncritically identify cultures with comprehensive doctrines, schools reflecting thick ethnic or national cultures may be quite similar. The idea that the state should be neutral between competing conceptions of the good is expressed through educational freedom of association and equal treatment of different traditions. The curriculum and practices of the school are organized so as to realize the distinctive goods and view of life of the tradition. "Elders" (those who exemplify the goods and virtues of the moral tradition) play a key role in the work of the school and in its governance. That is, being an exemplar of the community's values is viewed as a significant qualification for any leadership role. Governance may be hierarchical or participatory depending on the details of the tradition. Small scale and shared values often make informal, participatory, consensual decision making more likely even in schools whose comprehensive doctrine emphasizes hierarchy. (Catholic schools are the obvious example.) The school may be connected to one or more local congregations making functional communities with generation closure (Coleman & Hoffer, 1987) more likely.

- Roles:
  Teachers and administrators: Teachers and administrators occupy the role of elder. That is, they are expected to be exemplars of the goods, values, and commitments of the tradition.
  Students: Students are viewed as initiates into the tradition.
  Parents: Parents are also "congregational" members. They may be involved in the school not just as parents, but also as members of the larger congregation or group with which the school is associated. They may be direct participants in the school as need and tradition warrant.
  Community: The school community is viewed as a part of a larger, extended community. It is part of a "congregation."
  Motivation: Motivation is intrinsic, internal to the tradition, and connected to the sense of identity of members. Students are taught to want to learn for reasons internal to the values of the community and to internalize a desire for the goods that are important to the tradition. A sense of belonging (affiliation with the tradition and attachment to its members) is part of the motivation for learning.
- *Goods of community*: In addition to those goods that are internal to communities of most sorts (trust, membership, belonging, and loyalty, for example) these may include the enjoyment of the shared attainment of those goods that are distinctive to the tradition.

Deliberative democracy schools

- Ruling conception: The school community is formed around values of citizenship and thick, participatory democracy. Democracy is viewed as a way of life. The school aims to create a democratic culture and to form democratic character. While democracy is viewed as prior to the establishment of the school and acceptance of a democratic view is a condition of membership, many of the goals and practices of the school are established through democratic deliberation. Governance emphasizes inclusion, participation, reciprocity, dialogue, and consensus among community members. The curriculum emphasizes democratic and civic participation. Teaching and learning are as participatory as is consistent with competence. Small scale is important in order to permit maximum participation.

- Roles

  Teachers and Administrators: Teachers and administrators are "first among equals." That is, teachers and administrators are viewed as equal citizens in the school along with students and parents, but they also have a larger responsibility for the activities of the school, and may therefore sometimes require power and voice commensurate with greater responsibility and special competence.

  Students: Students are potential citizens, citizens in initiation. Their participation in school activities and governance may be viewed as a kind of apprenticeship or practicum for democratic participation.

  Parents: Parents may be viewed as equal citizens, but they are not first among equals.

  Community: The community is the local school, not the larger polity. The aspiration is for local participatory democracy at the school level, which may require some independence from the local or national polity and from the legislature.

  Motivation: Community members are motivated by the goods of citizenship such as civic friendship. The ownership of decisions and goals brought about through participation in decision making is also motivating.
- *Goods of community:* These include the intrinsic value of participation and self rule as well as civic friendship.

Life of the mind schools

- Ruling conception: The school community is formed around the realization of the goods internal to academic practices such as math, science and the arts. The school is viewed as a union of academic and artistic guilds. Excellence and the life of the mind are highly valued and are the uniting values of the school. Knowledge is also viewed as forming such desirable character traits as reasonableness, wisdom, and good taste. "Those who know should rule" is the central commitment of governance. Preeminence is given to those who have achieved competence in academic subject matter and who are able to exhibit its virtues and internal goods. Free and open debate are highly valued not only because open inquiry is a prerequisite of the pursuit of truth, but because engaging in inquiry is intrinsically worthwhile and generates bonds of friendship and collegiality.
- Roles

  Teachers and administrators: Teachers and administrators should be exemplars of the goods, standards, and virtues internal to academic practices. Their authority is the authority of the master in a master apprentice relationship.

  Students: Students are apprentices to academic practices and initiates into life of the mind.

  Parents: Parents are largely outsiders to the academic community excluded by their lack of mastery. They are, in effect, expected to surrender the academic care of their children to those who are initiates into the life of the mind.

Community: The community is the academic community which includes not only members of the individual school, but also members of academic guilds. Such guilds are the extended communities into which students are initiated.

Motivation: The motivation for learning is (ultimately) to achieve the goods internal to practices and the values associated with the life of the mind.

Goods of Community: These are formed by participation in the characteristic activities of intellectual guilds and include shared enjoyment of the goods internal to practices, friendship and collegiality, as well as membership and belonging.

JACQUELINE A. STEFKOVICH AND JOAN POLINER
SHAPIRO[1]

DECONSTRUCTING COMMUNITIES:
EDUCATIONAL LEADERS AND THEIR ETHICAL
DECISION-MAKING PROCESSES[2]

Abstract. In our previous writings, we discussed the important part geography played in determining
the decisions that our doctoral students in educational administration made when faced with ethical
dilemmas. Those educational leaders working in urban areas tended to make very different decisions
from those who worked in the suburbs based on how they thought the community would react to their
choices. In this chapter, we build on our past research and begin to de-construct what community really
means to educational leaders. With our current diverse doctoral cohort and with some of our former
graduates, through the use of reflective essays, journal writings, and interviews, we address questions
concerning their definitions of community and how their own community does or does not impact on
their decision making processes. We believe this study will assist in discerning at a deeper level the
multiple meanings of community and their effects on educational leaders in reaching ethical decisions.

> Even though many of us acknowledge that communities can be forces for evil,
> oppression, and corruption, our language about them suggests that we typically think
> of them as social systems in which people engage in honest reflection and critique,
> pursue justice, and care for and respect one another (Beck, 1999, p. 36).

Over the past nine years, we have been working with doctoral students in
educational administration in an ethics course. Frequently, the topic of
communities is discussed in relation to ethical dilemmas about which they are
studying and writing. The graduate students have described to us both the positive
sides and negative sides of the concept of community. They have also helped us to
clarify what is meant by the concept of community. In addition, they have
discussed and described the communities they have turned to for guidance
regarding the hard ethical decisions that they so commonly face in their work in
schools and in higher education. Beck (1999), much like our students, speaks with
some ambivalence regarding the concept of community in the above quotation.
Although she mentions the down side of this concept, she nevertheless turns to the
very positive beliefs that she thinks most people associate with community.

In this chapter, we will not only provide data associated with the concept of
community, but we will also discuss this concept within the context of ethics in
educational administration. According to John Dewey (1902), ethics is the science
that deals with conduct insofar as it is considered as right or wrong, good or bad.
Ethics is from the Greek word "ethos". Originally it meant customs, usage,
especially belonging to one group as distinguished from another. Later ethics
came to mean disposition or character -- customs, not just habit, but approved ways
of acting. However, this definition raises certain questions. One might ask: Ethics
approved by whom? Right or wrong according to whom? These questions take on
added meaning when one considers them in relation to the concept of community
and its influence on educational leaders' ethical decision making.

P.T. Begley and O. Johansson (eds.), The Ethical Dimensions of School Leadership, 89–106.
© 2003 *Kluwer Academic Publishers. Printed in the Netherlands.*

Over time, in the teaching of ethics to educational administrators, we have become especially interested in the issue of silencing (i.e., Belenky, Clinchy, Goldberger & Tarule, 1986; Collins 1990; Gilligan, 1982; Gilligan, Ward & Taylor, 1988; Noddings, 1992; Shapiro & Smith-Rosenberg, 1989; Weis & Fine, 1993) as it relates to our students and the communities in which they work. We have found that an effective way to break down this silence is by opening up university classrooms for difficult dialogues. These discussions begin to prepare educational administrators to cross the borders into their diverse communities to deal with previously taboo topics. Using student-written ethical dilemmas that describe authentic situations can be one positive approach to make certain that all students are knowledgeable about emotional and sometimes painful issues related to values prior to actually facing them in their workplace and in their community. They are prepared to confront and perhaps even break the silence and facilitate the ethical debates and discussions that should take place in their school community and in other communities that impact on their personal and professional lives. The use of authentic ethical dilemmas for decision making tends to empower students and give them their own voice.

In some of our previous work (Shapiro & Stefkovich, 1994, 1997, 1998), we touched upon the concept of community and noted the important part geography appeared to play in determining the decisions that our doctoral students in educational administration made when faced with ethical dilemmas. In this chapter, we build on that past research and go beyond it by attempting to deconstruct what community means to educational leaders. To accomplish this task, we will first give a brief overview regarding the importance of teaching ethics to educators as well as a synopsis of our multi-paradigm approach to viewing ethics. With this background in place, we will then present our methodology and discuss our findings regarding the deconstruction of community in educational ethical decision making.

A MULTI-PARADIGM APPROACH TO ETHICAL DECISION MAKING

Many professions, such as law, medicine, dentistry, and business, require their graduate students to take at least one ethics course before graduation. Such courses are thought to be essential for the socialization of an individual into the profession and important to inculcate basic professional values. While the field of educational administration lacks such a requirement, there has been a recent upsurge of interest among colleges of education in offering ethics courses to school leaders.

One reason for this interest may be that there are a number of scholars in educational administration, such as Beck (1994), Beck and Murphy (1994); Cambron-McCabe and Foster (1994), Greenfield (1993), McKinney (1994), and Starratt (1994), indicating the importance of ethics as part of the preparation of educational leaders. Another reason for this attention to ethics may be that the Interstate Leaders Licensure Consortium (ISLLC), working with the National Policy Board of Educational Administration (NPBEA), consisting of representatives from 24 U.S. states and 9 associations related to educational administration, set forth the need for the study of ethics in its standards. In fact,

Standard 5 states that: "A school administrator is an educational leader who promotes the success of all students by acting with integrity, fairness, and in an ethical manner" (ISLLC, 1996, p. 18).

To meet this standard, an administrator must (a) possess a knowledge and understanding of various ethical frameworks and perspectives on ethics; b) have a knowledge and understanding of professional codes of ethics; c) believe in, value, and be committed to bringing ethical principles to the decision-making process; and d) believe in, value, and be committed to developing a caring school community (ISLLC, 1996, p. 18). This knowledge is determined through a standardized test developed by the Educational Testing Service which various states are beginning to require.

Whether required or not for entrance into the profession, the rationale for ethical preparation extends beyond the basic assumption that an educational administrator should merely be aware of professional ethics. Instead, as Foster (1986) notes: "Each administrative decision carries with it a restructuring of human life: that is why administration at its heart is the resolution of moral dilemmas" (p. 33).

A number of educational scholars (Beck, Murphy & Associates, 1997; Starratt, 1994) have recognized at least three conceptual frameworks emanating from diverse traditions that have an impact on education. These frameworks include ethics based on justice, critique, and care. To these, we add a fourth, the ethic of the profession (Shapiro & Stefkovich, 2001; Stefkovich & Shapiro, 1999). We present these four models in a paradigm that we have developed based on the work of earlier researchers and developed as a result of our last ten years of collaborative research, writing, and teaching ethics. What follows is a brief overview of our model beginning with the ethic of justice.[3]

What has come to be known as the ethic of justice generally emanates from liberal democratic ethics derived from the work of philosophers such as Socrates, Plato, Aristotle, Locke, Hobbes, Kant, and Mills. More recently, ethical writings in education, based on the liberal democratic tradition, include works by Goodlad, Soder, and Sirotnik (1990), Sergiovanni (1992), and Strike, Haller and Soltis (1998), to name but a few. In the liberal democratic tradition as it relates to education, liberalism is defined as a "commitment to human freedom," and democracy implies "procedures for making decisions that respect the equal sovereignty of the people" (Strike, 1991, p. 415). The language of liberal democratic ethics includes concepts such as justice, rights, and law. Arguments are constructed in such as way as to be perceived as objective, remote, and impartial and a framework is usually provided that asks one to think in a logical, step by step manner.

A number of writers and activists who have gained prominence (Bakhtin, 1981; Foucault, 1983; Freire & Shor, 1987; Giroux, 1994; Greene, 1988; Grogan & Smith, 1999) are not convinced by this rational, step-by-step process or its focus on abstract justice, rights, and law. These scholars see a tension in this tradition between liberalism and democracy and focus heavily on the critique both of the laws themselves and of the process used to determine if the laws are just. Rather than accepting the ethics of those in power, they challenge the status quo by seeking an ethic that will deal with paradoxes, formulate the hard questions, and debate and challenge the issues. Their intent is to awaken us to our own stated morals and values and make us realize how frequently these values have been modified and even corrupted over time, thus forcing us to rethink important concepts such as democracy, social justice, privilege, and power.

Another group (Beck, 1994; Belenky, Clinchy, Goldberger & Tarule, 1986; Gilligan, 1982; Gilligan, Ward & Taylor, 1988; Marshall, 1995; Noddings, 1984, 1992; Shapiro & Smith-Rosenberg, 1989) challenges the patriarchal laws and dominant ethics of our society. Frequently turning to voices of care, concern, and connectedness over time, they, as do the critical thinkers, see social responsibility as a pivotal part of ethics. Their focus on relationships leads to discussions of issues such as continuity, respect, trust, and empowerment. Similar to critical theorists, feminists tend to emphasize social responsibility, frequently discussed in the light of injustice, as a pivotal concept of ethics.

Starratt (1994) postulates that the ethics of justice, care, and critique are not incompatible, but rather, complementary, the combination of which results in a richer, more complete, ethic. He visualizes these ethics as themes, interwoven much like a tapestry:

> An ethical consciousness that is not interpenetrated by each theme can be captured either by sentimentality, by rationalistic simplification, or by social naivete. The blending of each theme encourages a rich human response to the many uncertain ethical situations the school community faces every day, both in the learning tasks as well as in its attempt to govern itself (p. 57).

We agree with Starratt. But, we have also come to believe that, even taken together, the ethics of justice, care, and critique do not provide an adequate picture of the factors that must be taken into consideration as leaders strive to make ethical decisions within the context of educational settings. What is missing, that is, what these paradigms tend to ignore, is a consideration of those moral aspects unique to the profession and the questions that arise as educational leaders become more aware of both their own personal and professional codes of ethics. To fill this gap, we add a fourth to the three ethical frameworks described in this chapter, an ethic of the profession.

In the past, professional ethics has generally been viewed as a subset of the ethic of justice. This is likely the case because professional ethics is often equated with codes, rules, and principles, all of which fit neatly into traditional concepts of justice (Beauchamp & Childress, 1984). In addition, a number of education-related professional organizations have developed their own professional ethical codes. Defined by Beauchamp & Childress (1984) as "an articulated statement of role morality as seen by members of the profession" (p. 41), some of these ethical codes set forth by states and professional associations tend to be limited in their responsiveness in that they are somewhat removed from the day to day personal and professional dilemmas educational leaders face (Nash, 1996). The problem lies not so much in the codes themselves, but in the fact that we sometimes expect too much from them with regard to moral decision making (Lebacqz, 1985; Nash, 1996). Thus, recognizing the importance of standardized codes, the contributions they make, and their limitations, we believe the time has come to view professional ethics from a broader, more inclusive, and more contemporary perspective.

While the idea of professional ethics has been with us for some time, identifying the process as we do and presenting it in the form of a paradigm represents a relatively innovative way of conceptualizing this ethic. Our concept of professional ethics as an ethical paradigm includes ethical principles and codes of ethics embodied in the justice paradigm, but is much broader, taking into account other paradigms, as well as professional judgment and professional decision making. We recognize professional ethics as a dynamic process requiring that administrators develop their own personal and professional codes. We believe this process is important, and like Nash, observed a dissonance between students' own codes and those set forth by states or professional groups. Through our work, we have come to believe educational leaders should be given the opportunity to take the time to develop their own personal codes of ethics based on life stories and critical incidents and their own professional codes based on the experiences and expectations of their working lives as well as a consideration of their personal codes.

Underlying such a process is an understanding of oneself as well as others. These understandings necessitate that administrators reflect upon concepts such as: what they perceive to be right or wrong and good or bad; who they are as professionals and as human beings; how they make decisions; and why they make the decisions they do. This process recognizes that preparing students to live and work in the 21st Century requires very special administrators who have grappled with their own personal and professional codes of ethics and have reflected upon diverse forms of ethics, taking into account the differing backgrounds of the students enrolled in U.S. schools today.

By grappling, we mean that these educational leaders have struggled over issues of justice, critique, and care related to the education of children and youth, and through this process, have gained a sense of who they are and what they believe personally and professionally. It means coming to grips with clashes that may arise among ethical codes and making ethical decisions in light of their best professional judgment, a judgment which places the best interests of the student at the centre of all ethical decision making. Thus, actions by school officials are likely to be strongly influenced by personal values (Begley, 1999; Begley & Johansson, 1998; Willower & Licata, 1997) and personal codes of ethics build upon these values and experiences (Shapiro & Stefkovich, 1998). Consideration of community standards, including both the professional community and the community in which the leader lives and works, are key factors that play both into the development of educational leaders' personal and professional codes. What community means is the focus of the remainder of this chapter.

METHODOLOGY

In this research, with our current diverse doctoral cohort and with some of our former graduates, through the use of reflective essays, journal writings, and review of personal and professional codes of ethics, we address questions concerning their definitions of community and how their own community does or does not impact on their decision-making processes. In addition, we performed a content analysis of ethical dilemmas submitted by students during the nine year period that we have taught ethics as part of our doctoral cohort requirements. Since the students were asked to write about problems that were familiar to them, the written assignments were analyzed taking into account the theme of each dilemma as well as factors such as race, ethnicity, social class, gender, and what these ethical dilemmas tell us about relationships between the school and the community. We conclude our research with a discussion of how school leaders and professors of ethics might break what our students have perceived as a silence between the school and the community in order to deal with difficult ethical issues.

FINDINGS

This section of our chapter discusses the findings of this research by first looking at our students with regard to the types of communities they represent, their definitions of community, and whether and how they see communities as influencing their ethical decision making. Next, we discuss themes that emerged as a result of students' ethical dilemmas. Examples illustrative of these points are provided.

Our Students and Their Communities

Students in the class ranged in age from their mid-twenties to almost sixty. The total number of our students was evenly distributed across gender with the balance varying from year to year. Some of the students had previous training in ethics. Most had none. In addition, our students represented a wide range of communities based on characteristics such as geography, race, ethnicity, religion, and professional affiliations. In the past, our students made informal comments about communities; this year, we formalized the process. We asked our current doctoral cohort, consisting of twelve students, to put in writing their definitions of community as well as provide an idea of the communities to which they turn when they make an ethical decision. In this section, the reader will hear the voices of our current students as well as some of the voices of past cohorts threaded through the discussion.

Community as geography. If one defines community as geography, then it is clear that our students lived and worked in a wide variety of communities. Some came from large urban areas; others came from smaller cities within the state of Pennsylvania and from other neighbouring states such as Delaware, Maryland, and New Jersey. Some students commuted from very rural areas while others lived in wealthy suburbs. For example, in one class, there was a woman from Trinidad, a man from Ethiopia, a relocated New Yorker, and a student born and raised in a rural area with a substantial Amish and Mennonite population.

Considering these differences, it was not surprising that at least some of our students equated community with geography. As one student, a white male teacher, concluded: "To me community means all of the people who live in a certain place." This definition is also commensurate with those of other scholars who have pointed out the importance of demographics in defining certain types of communities (Coleman, 1985; Metz & Furman, 1997).

There were also noticeable constraints depending upon geographical locations. On the whole, those students who came from urban environments tended to describe challenging moral dilemmas in their localities, while those from rural or suburban environments seemed to be more reluctant to deal with their communities' controversial issues. In some of these communities, students indicated that there is silence and even silencing on certain topics, and it appears as if many citizens wish to keep it this way.

While some rural communities may be unwilling to tackle controversial topics, that does not mean that these communities are backwards or uncaring. As one white male administrator recalled:

> My most precious memories include community Fourth of July picnics on the beach, the gathering of neighbours around the town Christmas tree singing carols, and marching in the annual Halloween parade. Everywhere I would go I would see familiar faces and that was comforting. Most recently, a family in our community tragically lost their home in a devastating fire. On at least several occasions, the community came out in droves for the various fundraisers held to help this family. It may be interesting to some that this family is African-American. However in my town, I do not recall a time where the concept of community was ever segregated . . . . The values of this community are in my estimation, worthy values. I wish to bring my children up in a community where concern for a neighbour is a natural tendency and not the exception (Shapiro & Stefkovich, 1998).

Examined from this perspective, demographics proved to be an important part of community, both in our classes and in the various aspects of our students' personal and professional lives.

Race, ethnicity and/or religion as community. Most of our students did not restrict community to geography. For example, a female middle school computer science teacher in a city school defined community this way:

> So essentially, when I look inward to find answers, I am using the indoctrination from the culture of my community -- geographic, spiritual, educational, and familial.

Another male urban graduate student wrote:

> First reference group of community is made up of neighbourhood where I live. Second reference community is the "Black community."

A number of students saw commonality of values and beliefs as an important part of this concept. A male assistant superintendent from a suburban district saw commonality this way. He wrote:

> I envision a community as a group of people who have accepted certain common morals, ideals, and standards which guide their actions, share a basic, common, bottom line of living, share core values of responsibility, trust, integrity, etc. No laws are necessary . . . have common community goals.

This commonality, more often than not, revealed itself through issues of race, ethnicity, and/or religion. Though mostly Christian or Jewish, our students represented a variety of factions within these religions. For instance, some belonged to the city's black Baptist churches. Others were white Christian fundamentalists from a "Bible Belt" part of the state. During the course of nine years that we taught ethics, we instructed Jewish students, a Catholic nun, a

Buddhist from Vietnam, persons from a wide variety of Protestant religions, and people who never mentioned religion as part of their identity.

Professional communities. Our students' professional communities were often just as diverse. There were public school teachers and administrators, others who worked in higher education institutions, and some from business. There were counselors, psychologists, and biologists. There were English teachers and physics teachers. Most of the students worked full time, but a few others were full time graduate students.

It is interesting to note that Strike (1999) has discussed the importance of thinking of educational communities as "more like congregations than stores or banks." He thinks that schools should be "places where people unite in common projects" (p. 49). We asked our students to put in writing how they defined professional communities. One high school female administrator from a rural area said:

> It's funny that I should be asked this question because I find myself using the term on a regular basis. Creating collaborative work cultures is incredibly complex. Yet it is a large part of an agenda for an administrator. . . . Facilitating the working communities within my school requires actions that foster activity of all participants (formally and informally) that incorporates diversity and differences and a sense of individualism and empowerment among students and staff members.

We also asked students about professional decision making and asked them to discuss the communities to which they turn in this process. A female middle school teacher stated:

> Whenever the decision involves a student, I ask myself what the parent of the student would want. Does the parent need to know; should the parent be excluded because the parent is causing the dilemma? . . . I also speak to co-workers and a very close friend who is ten years older but decades wiser.

A female high school administrator responded to the same question:

> My immediate community is the administrative cabinet in my school. This group is made up of administrators, myself included, who make decisions and stay in touch throughout a regular school day. Included in this group is the Administrative Director, Supervisor of Secondary Programs, Supervisor of Pupil Personnel Services and my role as Assistant Principal. It is our commitment as a group that moves the school forward and, I would think, all our efforts branch out from our style of leadership as a team. We then involve the rest of our administrative team who include a Business Manager, Maintenance Supervisor, Technology Coordinator and Cafeteria Manager. . . . The culture of the school is the immediate focus, but part of the development of a school community reaches out to wider networks of professionals. . . . We stay in very close contact with district superintendents, principals and guidance counsellors, to mention a few. . . . It takes an entire school community to work together for the benefit of its individual stakeholders.

Personal communities/professional communities: Defining the concept of community. When our students have been asked to define the concept of community, some have tended to look at it from both a personal and professional point of view. For example, a male middle school science teacher defined community this way:

> Those people that I am in contact with on a daily basis, those people whose actions (personal and professional) that affect me, my friends, and/or my family and those people that my actions (personal or professional) may affect.

Another male special education middle school teacher said:

> All of the people who live in a certain place. . . an all-inclusive community with several sub-communities . . . can start with a global community. A person is a part of many communities at the same time. Events will cause various communities to come together.

Emergent Themes in Ethical Decision-Making Dilemmas

Focusing on the ethical dilemmas written by our students, findings reveal that there has been an increasing awareness among students to grapple with the hard dilemmas. Most of them highlighted authentic challenges that they have faced as practicing administrators and leaders in their own communities. Increasingly, over the nine year time span in which we taught the course, the dilemmas have become more and more complex and touch very personal and frequently controversial aspects of society such as AIDS, sexual harassment, pornography, censorship of books, animal research, artificial insemination, and parents' rights. A number of these dilemmas are provided in detail in our book, *Ethical Leadership and Decision Making in Education: Applying Theoretical Perspective to Complex Dilemmas* (Shapiro & Stefkovich, 2001).

Through analysis of these ethical dilemmas, a number of interesting themes emerged. They included: morality; care, concern, and connectedness; democracy; and equity/diversity issues. Another theme that emerged on its own was the tension between students' personal and professional codes. Along with the themes mentioned, the issue of community was critical. The remainder of this chapter discusses the salient themes discovered when deconstructing student dilemmas with a special emphasis on their relationship to the communities in which the dilemmas occurred.

Morality and Community Standards.[4]

> Who shall teach our children is one of the great recurring issues in education. From the trial of Socrates for corrupting the youth of ancient Athens to today, this question has been a topic of concern in America since at least the beginning of the "one best system" (DeMitchell, 1993, p. 217).

DeMitchell, in his article *Private lives: Community control v. professional autonomy*, notes that teachers have always been regarded as exemplars of moral virtue and that communities, particularly in rural areas and small towns, have exerted considerable control on the personal lives of these educators (DeMitchell, 1993). We found this same type of control prevalent in discussions with our students, many of whom indicated real differences on how this issue is addressed based on geography.

An example of community differences on issues of morality can be heard in the words of a graduate student we cited in an earlier paper (Stefkovich & Shapiro, 1996). Her impressions relate to an ethical dilemma published in a book by Strike, Haller, and Soltis (1988; 2nd ed. 1998). In this particular dilemma, a teacher who is dancing topless is doing so to make extra money for a sick mother. She is dancing in the evenings and on weekends in a different community from the one in which she is teaching. The graduate student who is also a female principal said:

> What bothers me is that a teacher who dances topless would be considered a breach of moral principle in the community where I am employed. However, in the city district where I worked in the past and perhaps in other communities, the same teacher behaviour may be viewed as nothing more than a personal choice, with no consequences to her job. Does this mean that a moral principle can be such in one community but not be a moral principle in another or are there other factors that make it appear this is so?

Thus, an important finding of our research focused on community standards and morality. Here, our graduate students' dilemmas emphasize individual rights and standards of the community and provide a forum for the discussion of the ethics of justice, critique, care, and the profession. In doing so, they consider the changing face of ethics in different communities. One example of these ethical dilemmas includes "The Adult Fantasy Centre". In this dilemma, a male teacher's job is in jeopardy because his principal has found out that he moonlights as a sex shop manager in a nearby squalid community. The principal knows that the parents in her upscale community would not be pleased to find out about his job.

The "Artificial Insemination" case addresses the plight of an unmarried female teacher in her late 30's who confides to her principal that she wants to be artificially inseminated. In this small rural community which is largely Christian fundamentalist, the principal is concerned about the teacher's personal plan as well as the community's reactions to it.

Care, concern, and connection in the community. Some dilemmas move beyond the justice-based moral development stage theory developed by Kohlberg (1981) and highlight work by Beck (1994), Gilligan (1982); Gilligan, Ward & Taylor (1988), Noddings (1984, 1992, 1996), and Shapiro and Smith-Rosenberg (1989). They tend to emphasize a feminist perspective of care and concern. For example, "The Sexual Harassment Case" highlights the problems of a well-regarded, caring, untenured female professor who has been accused of sexually harassing one of her male students. The student, who was angered because he felt that the professor had expressed an interest in him that made him feel uncomfortable, brought his grievance to the male chair of department. This student also was the son of a member of the Board of Trustees of the university. This case shows how misunderstandings can escalate if they are not recognized and dealt with in a sensitive way in a timely fashion.

In "A Home for Marlon: The Foster Child Case", a principal must decide whether to tell his friend, a teacher, about harmful information he has learned from confidential records concerning a foster child for whom this teacher is providing a home. In this case, the principal cares a great deal about the foster family as the mother is a member of his school community. But he also cares about the rights of the foster child.

"Job-Sharing: Some Real Benefits" involves a pilot job-sharing program in a small town in which the teachers' union now demands full-time benefits. This case pits the expectations of female teachers with children against the role demands of women in leadership positions. It also contrasts the desires of the community with the needs of the teachers because many taxpayers are angry about how much teachers get paid compared with other local workers.

Democracy and community. In his book, *Educational leadership and the crisis of democratic culture,* Henry Giroux emphasized that:

> The most important task facing educators is not about collecting data or managing competencies but constructing a pedagogical and political vision which recognizes that the problems with American schools lie in the realm of values, ethics, and vision. Put another way, educating for democracy begins not with test scores but with the questions: What kinds of citizens do we hope to produce through public education? What kind of society do we want to create? This involves educating students to live in a critical democracy (p. 11). (Giroux, 1992, cited in Metz & Furman, 1997, p. 43).

In many of our students' dilemmas, the concept of democracy is stressed as well as the need to create a society that is accepting of debate and criticism. Here, we drew upon work from the critical theorists studied in our course (i.e., Foster, 1986; Purpel, 1989) to set the stage for the cases our students presented.

The "Abuse of Power Case" provides one such illustration. Here, an incompetent tenured faculty member, who is a poor teacher, abuses his authority with students and junior faculty. This faculty member considers himself a standard bearer for his school as he gives many students poor grades. Unfortunately, he does not hold himself to the same high standards as he does his students. The Dean of the Business School faces the dilemma of professional concern versus academic freedom. He must think of the good of the whole university community when he makes a decision on this case.

In "Parents' Rights v. School Imperatives", a principal witnesses a father giving a spanking to his son at school. The father is working class and well-meaning, and the son has many behaviour problems. The parents are divorced and the father has custody of the son to save him from a bad situation with his mother. The principal is legally bound to report this incident as child abuse to the proper authorities and yet he questions making the report, particularly as the father has been a responsible parent who has attended school meetings and has appeared whenever his son has had problems. Where does the parent's right end and the school's rights begin?

Equity and diversity. These dilemmas emphasize the importance of knowing ourselves before we seek to know others (Shapiro, Sewell & DuCette, 1995). The students stressed the need to define diversity broadly to be inclusive. They emphasized comprehensive definitions of diversity that encompass cultural categories of race/ethnicity, religion, social class, gender, disability and sexual orientation as well as individual differences taking into account learning styles, exceptionalities, and age (Banks & Banks, 1993; Cushner, McClelland & Safford, 1992; Gollnick & Chinn, 1994; Shapiro, Sewell, & DuCette, 1995; Sleeter & Grant, 1988).

We turn to the voice of an African-American urban graduate student in our class. He puts forth a major dilemma emanating from the course. Indirectly, while reflecting upon personal liberty rather than the public good, he asks: Who is the public? Who is the majority? And how do educational administrators fit into this scheme? He says it this way:

I work with a colleague who prides himself on being able to treat all of his students the same way. Regardless of race, economic status or ability, he claims to have the means to maintain a completely unbiased view on all. After working with him for six years, I have noticed that he does not have this ability. On a regular basis, I see him playing favourites, making exceptions and generally doing the exact thing he claims he does not do. As an administrator, he cannot afford to be so rigid. There must be some room for partiality. And he shows it (though he would not admit to it) daily. It seems to me that this inability to be impartial grows out of his position and, in fact, would evolve from any position of administration when the interests of minorities and the oppressed have to be served. A 21st Century administrator must be ready to bend, adjust and, when necessary, show partiality to those he/she serves if equity and justice are to be served. (Shapiro & Stefkovich, 1998).

"Responsibility & the Organization" focuses on a Jamaican student who is in a music magnet school and is quite talented; however, he is receiving mediocre grades because he has many family commitments related to music. (This is how the family supports itself.) The father of the student is angry because George has received C's in music (primarily due to absences.) The father wants the teacher to change his son's grades because he feels it is unfair to penalize him because he is performing. Yet, would this be fair to the other students?

In "Black and White and Shades of Gray", new minority teachers are to be retrenched because of economic reasons. The old rule of last hired, first fired is presented with all of its problems. The principal is placed in a very difficult position as this one time sleepy, rural, nearly all white farming region has become a bustling, quasi-suburban, multicultural area. How can he in all good conscience reduce his minority teaching staff?

In "Access to Knowledge", a principal is approached by Latino parents who want their child to take courses in the college preparatory track. The student has been discouraged by the guidance counselor and by his teachers from taking college preparatory work. The principal finds out that the student has not been doing well in his classes. Conflicting feelings on the part of the principal in handling the situation are discussed. Most of the minority students in this suburban high school are advised to join the workforce or to apply for apprenticeship training. Now that the minority students are the majority (55%) of the school, the current advice is more worrying than ever.

The dilemma, "When All Means All", deals with problems of having an emotionally disturbed child in a regular elementary school classroom. After having tried out the child in the classroom for a time, a teacher has had enough and feels that the child is infringing upon the rights of others; however, the school and the local community have made a commitment to inclusion. The principal questions if he will be following the spirit of the school and community if he separates some from others. He wonders now if inclusion really should be for all students.

Traditional curriculum and hidden curriculum. These dilemmas move instructional issues beyond the classroom and even the school. They ask educators to consider their own values in relation to their curricular selections, and to hopefully make themselves aware of some unintended outcomes for their students, the school, and the community regarding what they choose to teach or what they must teach. Those unintended consequences, in part, make up the hidden curriculum.

Although traditionalists may make the claim that their curriculum is value-free and apolitical, this assumption can be challenged. Consistently schools have conveyed the message of "possessive individualism" and "meritocracy". Implicit in the traditional curriculum is the notion that if one does not succeed, it is one's own fault. Also, implicit is the concept that those who are not middle-class, White, male, and Eurocentric are frequently considered to be "others" (i.e., different sex, race, ethnicity, sexual orientation, and culture). How do we develop a curriculum that is appropriate for all? And if this is not possible, what can we do to design a more inclusive curriculum?

In the "Vivisection" case, some students have problems with pithing of frogs, i.e., dissecting frogs when they are unconscious but not dead. Animal rights' issues are pitted against human rights' issues and the professor is placed in a difficult situation. Ultimately, this dilemma extends beyond the walls of the biology classroom and becomes a school community concern. Similarly, "The Trouble with Daddy's Roommate" points out the problem of community values, but in this case one might ask: Is there a consensus concerning values within a suburban community? In this dilemma, a group of parents complain about a book assigned in school that deals with sexual orientation and other sensitive issues.

Parents complain about a sixth grade poster project which is part of a mandated class on AIDS education, in the case, "AIDS and Age Appropriate Education". State law requires some type of instruction. The posters are very creative and some have real condoms on them. There are pregnancy problems in the school but some parents of fourth graders complain to the principal that they do not want their young children exposed to these posters. The principal is also aware of the conservative nature of his district. Not too long ago, the School Board banned a number of library books. The principal is in a quandary as to what to do.

"There's No Place Like School" illustrates problems when regular classroom teachers are reluctant to be involved in inclusion programs requiring that students with disabilities be educated in the same classrooms as all other children. The hard decisions administrators must make in assigning teachers as well as students are addressed. The personal beliefs of teachers, that may be different from the law, are also part of this dilemma.

The professional community. A number of scholars in educational administration have recognized the importance of the professional community (Furman, 1998; Louis, Kruse & Bryk, 1995; Scribner, Cockrell, Cockrell, & Valentine, 1999). Under this theme, the students in our ethics classes explored the thorny problem of what happens when an individual's personal code of ethics differs with her or his professional code, and/or with the standards of the profession.

Through our work with these students and reflecting upon our own personal and professional experiences, we identified four possible clashes, three of which have been discussed in an earlier article (Shapiro & Stefkovich, 1998). First, there may be clashes between an individual's personal and professional code of ethics. Second, there may be clashes within professional codes. This may occur when an individual's personal ethical code conflicts with an ethical code set forth by the profession, or when the individual has been prepared in two or more professions.

Codes of one profession may be different from another. Hence, a code that serves an individual well in one career may not in another.

Third, there may be clashes of professional codes among educational leaders; what one administrator sees as ethical, another may not. Fourth, there may be clashes between a leader's personal and professional code of ethics, and custom and practices set forth by the community (i.e., either the professional community, the school community, or the community where the educational leader works). For example, a number of our students noted that some behaviour which may be considered unethical in one community might in another community merely be seen as a matter of personal choice, i.e., preference.

These clashes, particularly those related to the different concepts of community, are evident in our students' ethical dilemmas. For example, in "Drunkenness or Disease", a teacher has been convicted of drunk driving. He is an alcoholic and the community wants him fired. Legally, the principal can do this because the state law says that teachers may be fired for criminal convictions. However, the principal is ambivalent because the teacher is very effective in the classroom and also is a person suffering from a disease requiring assistance.

In a similar vein, "Rising Star or Wife Beater" focuses on a teacher who is well regarded by the current school superintendent and is in line for a new and important position. The administrator finds that the teacher has been brought up on charges of domestic abuse. Although he has had the greatest respect for the teacher professionally, the superintendent now is beginning to feel differently about the teacher on a personal level. Additionally, he is concerned about what parents will think if he promotes this teacher and they find out about his personal life.

"School Budget Blues and Copyright" focuses on a district with a shrinking school budget and a recent doubling of school population where teachers cannot order the materials they need to do their jobs well. At the same time they are unable to duplicate materials because of copyright laws. Recently the principal sent out a memo reminding teachers about the copyright legislation. In this case, an outstanding teacher is caught by the principal duplicating materials. The principal is aware of the difficulties placed on the teacher who is desirous of teaching his class, and yet she is concerned about violating the law.

CONCLUSIONS

In this chapter, we have focused primarily on our graduate students and what we have learned from them about community. Our doctoral cohort offered us a wealth of definitions of community. They also indicated the varied communities that they turned to for assistance in making important ethical decisions. We also provided brief overviews of the kinds of authentic ethical dilemmas our doctoral students had to deal with in their schools. Diverse communities and concepts were discussed in these dilemmas that spoke of the need for communities of care, concern and connectedness for others, of democratic values, of equity and diversity, of inclusive and meaningful curriculum.

Through our teaching of ethics, we have both tried to give students their own voices and to empower them to speak about their work problems and those within their communities, as recommended by writers such as Belenky, Clinchy,

Goldberger and Tarule (1986), Gilligan (1982), Gilligan, Ward, and Taylor (1988), Noddings (1984, 1992), Shapiro and Smith-Rosenberg (1989), and Weis and Fine (1993). While teaching them, we made certain that there has been time for them to meet in small groups throughout the ethics course. During small group meeting time, without the constraints of the professor, students could feel free to begin a dialogue with their peers on the hard issues. The students also made formal presentations of their ethical dilemmas and frequently were asked probing questions by peers and the professor.

Although our doctoral students have not found the one perfect definition of community, they have been given the room to reflect upon this concept. Through the definitions they provided as well as the ethical dilemmas they developed, they each were given the time to deconstruct the important concept of community. Hopefully, when faced with an ethical dilemma in the real world, they will think back to the assignments regarding community in their ethics course, take the time to reflect, and then ask the appropriate stakeholders their opinions regarding the case. It is our intent that these students will ultimately make much wiser, appropriate, and more moral decisions if they take sufficient time to think, if they also listen and speak with others, and if they take into consideration different aspects of community and how they may or may not influence their ethical decision making.

NOTES

[1] Parts of this chapter are based on a paper the authors presented at a UCEA (University Council for Educational Administration) national convention in Orlando, Florida (Shapiro & Stefkovich, 1997). This chapter was also presented in its entirety at the Conference of the UCEA Centre for the Study of Values and Leadership, Bridgetown, Barbados (Stefkovich & Shapiro, 2000).

[2] The authors wish to thank Judy Leonard at The Pennsylvania State University for her invaluable assistance in helping to organize the contents of this chapter.

[3] For a more in-depth explanation of our model, refer to Chapter 2 in: Shapiro, J.P. & Stefkovich, J.A. (2001). *Ethical leadership and decision making in education: Applying theoretical perspective to complex dilemmas.* Mahwah, NJ: Lawrence Erlbaum Associates.

[4] The authors would like to acknowledge the following graduate students who contributed ethical dilemmas: Gregory Allen, Kimberly D. Callahan, Joseph A. Castellucci, Lynn A. Cheddar, Robert L. Crawford, James C. Dyson, Patricia A. L .Ehrensal, Loree P. Guthrie, James K. Krause, Patricia A. Maloney, Beatrice H. Mickey, G. Michaele O'Brien, Leon D. Poeske, John A. Schlegel, Spencer S. Stober, David J. Traini, William W. Watts and Deborah Weaver.

REFERENCES

Bakhtin, M. (1981). *The dialogic imagination.* Austin: University of Texas Press.

Banks, J.A., & Banks, C.A. (1993). *Multicultural education: issues and perspectives, 2nd edition.* Boston: Allyn & Bacon.

Beauchamp, T.L., & Childress, J.F. (1984). Morality, ethics and ethical theories. In P. Sola (Ed.), *Ethics, education, and administrative decisions: A book of readings* (pp. 39-67). New York: Peter Lang.

Beck, L. G. (1994). *Reclaiming educational administration as a caring profession.* New York: Teachers College Press.

Beck, L.G. (1999). Metaphors of educational community: An analysis of the images that reflect and influence scholarship and practice. *Educational Administration Quarterly, 35*(1), 13-45.

Beck L.G., & Murphy, J. (1994). *Ethics in educational leadership programs: An expanding role.* Thousand Oaks, CA: Corwin Press.

Beck, L.G., Murphy, J. & Associates (1997). *Ethics in educational leadership programs: Emerging models.* Columbia, MO: The University Council for Educational Administration.

Begley, P.T. (Ed.). (1999) *Values and educational leadership.* Albany, NY: State University of New York.

Begley, P.T., & Johansson, O. (1998). The values of school administration: Preferences, ethics and conflicts. *The Journal of School Leadership, 8*(4), 399-422.

Belenky, M., Clinchy, B., Goldberger, N., & Tarule, J. (1986). *Women's ways of knowing.* New York: Basic Books.

Cambron-McCabe, N.H., & Foster, W. (1994). A paradigm shift: Implications for the preparation of school leaders. In T. Mulkeen, N.H. Cambron-McCabe and B. Anderson (Eds.) *Democratic leadership: The changing context of administrative preparation* (pp. 49-60). Norwood, NJ: Ablex Publishing Company.

Collins, P.H. (1990). *Black feminist thought: Knowledge, consciousness, and the politics of empowerment.* New York: Routledge.

Cushner, M., McClelland, A., & Safford P. (1992). *Human diversity in education: An integrative approach.* New York: McGraw Hill.

Coleman, J. S. (1985). Schools and the communities they serve. *Phi Delta Kappan, 66,* 527-532.

DeMitchell, T.A. (1993). Private lives: Community control vs. professional autonomy. *West's Education Law Quarterly, 2*(2), 218-226.

Dewey, J. (1902). *The school and society.* Chicago: University of Chicago Press.

Foster, W. (1986). *Paradigms and Promises: New Approaches to Educational Administration.* Buffalo: Prometheus Books.

Foucault, M. (1983). On the genealogy of ethics: An overview of work in progress. In H.L. Dreyfus & P. Rabinow (Eds.), *Michel Foucault: Beyond structuralism and hermeneutics, second edition* (pp. 229-252). Chicago: University of Chicago Press.

Freire, P., & Shor, I. (1987). *A pedagogy for liberation: Dialogues on transforming education.* South Hadley, MA: Bergin & Garvey.

Furman, G.C. (1998). Postmodernism and community in schools: Unravelling the paradox. *Educational Administration Quarterly, 34*(3), 298-328.

Gilligan, C. (1982). *In a different voice: Psychological theory and women's development.* Cambridge, MA: Harvard University Press.

Gilligan, C., Ward, J.V., & Taylor, J.M. (1988). *Mapping the moral domain.* Cambridge, MA: Harvard University Press.

Giroux, H. (1992). *Educational leadership and the crisis of democratic culture.* University Park, PA: University Council for Educational Administration.

Giroux, H.A. (1994). Educational leadership and school administrators: Rethinking the meaning of democratic public culture. In T. Mulkeen, N.H., Cambron-McCabe, & B. Anderson (Eds.), *Democratic leadership: The changing context of administrative preparation* (pp. 31-47). Norwood, NJ: Ablex Publishing Company.

Gollnick, D.M., & Chinn, P.C. (1994). *Multicultural education in a pluralistic society.* Columbus, OH: Merrill.

Goodlad, J.I., Soder, R., & Sirotnik, K.A. (Eds.). (1990). *The moral dimension of teaching.* San Francisco: Jossey-Bass.

Greene, M. (1988). *The dialectic of freedom.* New York: Teachers College Press.

Greenfield, W.S. (1993). Articulating values and ethics in administrator preparation. In C. Capper (Ed.), *Educational administration in a pluralistic society* (pp. 267-287). Albany, NY: SUNY Press.

Grogan, M., & Smith, F. (1999). A feminist perspective of women superintendents' approaches to moral dilemmas. In P.T. Begley (Ed.), *Values and Educational Leadership.* (pp. 273-288). Albany: State University of New York Press.

Interstate School Leaders Licensure Consortium (ISLLC). (1996). *Standards for school leaders.* Washington, DC: Author.

Kohlberg, L. (1981). *The philosophy of moral development: moral stages and the idea of justice, volume 1.* San Francisco, CA: Harper & Row Publishers.

Lebacqz, K. (1985). *Professional ethics: Power and paradox.* Nashville: Abingdon.

Louis, K.S., Kruse, S., & Bryk, A. (1995). Professionalism and community: What is it and why is it important in urban schools? In K.S. Louis & S.D. Kruse (Eds.), *Professionalism and community: perspectives on reforming urban schools* (pp. 3-22). Thousand Oaks, CA: Corwin.

Marshall, C. (1995). Imagining leadership. *Educational Administration Quarterly, 3*(3), 484-492.

McKinney, J.R. (1994). Non-traditional approaches to teaching educational leadership. *Review Journal of Philosophy & Social Science, 20*(1&2), 117-134.

Metz, C., & Furman, G. C. (1997). *Community and schools: Promise & paradox.* New York: Teachers College Press.

Nash, R.J. (1996). *Real world ethics: Frameworks for educators and human service professionals.* New York: Teachers College Press.

Noddings, N. (1984). *Caring: A feminine approach to ethics and moral education.* Berkeley, CA: University of California Press.

Noddings, N. (1992). *The challenge to care in schools: An alternative approach to education.* New York: Teachers College Press.

Noddings, N. (1996). On Community. *Educational Theory, 46*(3), 245-367.

Purpel, D.E. (1989). *The moral and spiritual crisis in education: A curriculum for justice and compassion in education.* New York: Bergin & Garvey.

Scribner, J.P., Cockrell, K.S., Cockrell, D.H., & Valentine, J.W. (1999). Creating professional communities in schools through organizational learning: An evaluation of a school improvement process. *Educational Administration Quarterly, 35*(1), 130-160.

Sergiovanni, T.J. (1992). *Moral leadership: Getting to the heart of school improvement.* San Francisco: Jossey-Bass.

Shapiro, J.P., Sewell, T.E., & DuCette, J.P. (1995). *Reframing diversity in education.* Lancaster, PA: Technomic.

Shapiro, J.P., & Smith-Rosenberg, C. (1989). The 'other voices' in contemporary ethical dilemmas: The value of the new scholarship on women in the teaching of ethics. *Women's Studies International Forum, 12*(2), 199-211.

Shapiro. J.P., & Stefkovich, J.A. (1994, October). *Towards the preparation of ethical educational administrators for diverse communities.* Paper presented at the conference of the University Council for Educational Administration, Philadelphia.

Shapiro, J.P., & Stefkovich, J.A. (1997, October). *Ethical dilemmas faced by educational administration students: Breaking the silence between the school and the community.* Paper presented at the conference of the University Council for Educational Administration, Orlando.

Shapiro, J.P., & Stefkovich, J.A. (1998). Dealing with dilemmas in a morally polarized era: The conflicting ethical codes of educational leaders. *Journal for a Just and Caring Education, 4*(2), 117-141.

Shapiro, J.P., & Stefkovich, J.A. (2001). *Ethical leadership and decision making in education: Applying theoretical perspectives to complex dilemmas.* Mahwah, NJ: Lawrence Erlbaum Associates.

Sleeter, C.E., & Grant, C.A. (1988). *Making choices for multicultural education: Five approaches to race, class, and gender.* New York: Macmillan.

Starratt, R.J. (1994). *Building an ethical school.* London: Falmer Press.

Stefkovich, J.A., & Shapiro, J.P. (1995). Personal and professional ethics for educational administrators: Non-traditional and pedagogical implications. *Review Journal of Philosophy and Social Science, 20*(1&2), 157-186.

Stefkovich, J.A., & Shapiro, J.P. (1996, April). *Preparing ethical administrators for leadership in a democratic society.* Paper presented at the annual convention of the American Educational Research Association, New York.

Stefkovich, J.A., & Shapiro, J.P. (2000, September). *Deconstructing communities: Educational leaders and their ethical decision-making processes.* Paper presented at the fifth annual conference of the UCEA Centre for the Study of Values and Leadership, Barbados.

Stefkovich, J.A., & Shapiro, J.P. (1999, October). *Individual rights, the public good, and professional expectations: A multi-paradigm approach to ethical educational leadership in caring school communities.* Paper presented at the Conference on Ethics and Leadership, UCEA Centre for Ethics and Leadership, Charlottesville.

Strike, K.A. (1991). The moral role of schooling in liberal democratic society. In G. Grant (Ed.), *Review of Research in Education* (p. 415). Washington, DC: American Educational Research Association.

Strike, K.A. (1999). Can schools be communities? *Educational Administration Quarterly, 35*(1), 46-70.

Strike, K.A., Haller, E.J., & Soltis, J.F. (1988). *The ethics of school administration, first edition.* New York: Teachers College Press.

Strike, K.A., Haller, E.J., & Soltis, J.F. (1998). *The ethics of school administration, second edition.* New York: Teachers College Press.

Weis, L., & Fine, M. (Eds.). (1993). *Beyond silenced voices: Class, race, and gender in United States schools.* Albany: State University of New York Press.

Willower, D.J., & Licata, J.W. (1997). *Values and valuation in the practice of education administration.* Thousand Oaks, CA: Corwin Press.

ELIZABETH CAMPBELL

LET RIGHT BE DONE: TRYING TO PUT ETHICAL STANDARDS INTO PRACTICE[1]

Abstract. The development of ethical standards by professional associations, boards, councils, and colleges of teachers responds in part to a moral imperative that teachers and school leaders be accountable to the wider community and in part to a desire to enhance the overall professionalism of educators' behaviour. This chapter explores the conceptual and practical complexities inherent in defining ethical standards for the teaching profession with a particular focus on their questionable capacity for implementation. In combining empirical evidence from previously reported research studies with hypothetical first person narrative responses to the evidence, the chapter seeks to illustrate the difficulty, if not the impossibility, of applying ethical standards to actual situations in any professionally and ethically satisfying way. It argues further that moral dilemmas facing teachers are potentially resolvable only by communities of educators internalizing and applying principles of ethics, not formalized codes or standards.

INTRODUCTION

In my opinion, one of the most compelling lines in English dramatic literature is found in Terence Rattigan's 1946 play entitled, *The Winslow Boy*. In this play about a private citizen petitioning the British government on a matter of individual liberty with the assistance of a prominent advocate and Honourable Member of Parliament, the following "time-honoured phrase" (Rattigan, 1946, p. 55) is repeated as a central theme of the work: "Let Right be done" (Rattigan, 1946, pp. 55, 71, 89). In its simplicity, it resonates with a certainty of conviction and a commitment to the good. In an ideal context, one could adopt Rattigan's phrase as a singular statement of professional ethics for teachers. Everyone would know instinctively what is meant by the words; nothing more would be needed—no elaborate or legalistic explanation as a point of constant referral.

One may draw a loosely metaphoric comparison between such a statement of ethical intent, whether or not it is embodied as part of a code or a set of standards, and a country's criminal code. After all, "laws are usually sanctioned on moral grounds" (Haynes, 1998, p. 4). In the case of a criminal code, most of us do not know it, how it is written, or what it says specifically; we have never seen it, and no one has ever taught it, the code itself, to us. Yet, we do know what it means to break the law and how to avoid doing so. In fact, most of us live lives in which we rarely have to stop to consider how not to break the law. We just simply don't do it, and those who do are usually aware of the fact. So should it be with a professional code of ethics or a statement of ethical standards, whether it is expressed in a prohibitive way like the criminal code or an enabling way that articulates positive ideals. It should reflect principles so deeply embedded in our personal and professional being, our practice, our culture of teaching and schooling that we actually have little need to refer to it. We would just know how to "do

107

P.T. Begley and O. Johansson (eds.), The Ethical Dimensions of School Leadership, 107–125.
© 2003 *Kluwer Academic Publishers. Printed in the Netherlands.*

right"—at least theoretically—notwithstanding the inevitable human dilemmas, tensions, and complexities that ultimately complicate the implementation of that "right".

Increasingly, professional standards boards, colleges of teachers, teaching councils, and other associated bodies have been created within North America, the United Kingdom and Australia. As part of their policy mandate, they have assumed responsibilities for drafting various versions of standards governing both teachers' professional practice and their ethical practice. In attempting to legislate such standards, these professional bodies must confront questions and concerns related to their capacity to manage the realities of teachers' work. The complexities of ethical practice, specifically, should not be minimized. As Thompson (1997, p. 1) concludes in her monograph for the General Teaching Council (England and Wales): "Professional ethics cannot be imposed, for by their nature they must be internalised to become part of the collective consciousness and the individual conscience". This chapter explores this argument and conceptually addresses the application of ethical standards to the contextual realities of teaching and working in schools. The key word in its title is "trying". Its use here should alert readers to the difficulties of implementing philosophically complex concepts and the ultimate potential for its failure.

Nonetheless, the paper has as its purposes: (1) to acknowledge the reality of differing and competing perspectives on ethics generally and professional ethics specifically; (2) to consider the use of formalized codes with an emphasis on the recently developed Ethical Standards for the Teaching Profession by the Ontario College of Teachers (Canada); and (3) to present empirical evidence of ethical dilemmas in the profession as possibly resolvable only by communities of educators applying ideals and principles of ethics, not necessarily codes or standards unless they clearly embody "fundamental values and broad ethical principles" (Thompson, 1997, p. 2). In the face of the current policy directions, it is more likely that principles, not precepts, will guide and inspire professional ethical practice.

ETHICAL CODES: SETTING THE STANDARDS

I have written elsewhere (Campbell, 2000, p. 203) that "increased awareness of the ethical dimensions and responsibilities of teaching is essential for both enhanced professionalism and, more significantly, improved practice, [and] that while a code of ethics may not advance the ultimate route to such awareness, it should be able to contribute broadly and positively to a deeper examination of ethics in teaching as long as its limitations are recognized and acknowledged". Others have similarly indicated cautionary support for ethical codes, thereby acknowledging their value in informing and guiding teachers and demonstrating "a concern for doing the 'right thing'" (Gross, 1993, p. 213), while also accepting that they are not fully adequate tools for achieving either (Bayles, 1981; Beck & Murphy, 1994; Haynes, 1998; Lovat, 1998; Macmillan, 1993; Sockett, 1990; Soltis, 1986; Strike & Ternasky, 1993; Strom, 1989; Watras, 1986). Of particular significance to this paper is Sergiovanni's (1992, pp. 54-55) claims that codes of ethics that define the moral responsibilities of teachers "can provide the basis for self-regulation and can help build confidence in teachers and sustain teachers' integrity in the eyes of the public. Professional codes of ethics are helpful and necessary, but they are not enough. Conforming to a code, without making a commitment to its ideals and values, means giving only the appearance of ethical behaviour". This distinction between the code itself and its underlying ideals, values, and ethics is particularly relevant to subsequent discussions of implementation.

A further distinction may be drawn between a code of ethics as the vehicle for presenting evaluative professional norms and ethical standards that "are often the basis for many principles of professional ethics" (Bayles, 1981, p. 22). Bayles further identifies such principles as virtues that include honesty, loyalty, discretion, diligence, and candor. While a code may prescribe professional and prohibit unprofessional behaviour, standards articulate idealized principles of ethical behaviour within the context of a profession. In many cases, the two terms, *code* and *standards*, are used synonymously (American School Counselor Association, 1998). While this is quite understandable and acceptable, as noted in discussions about implementation, there is merit in at least distinguishing between a specific aspect of normative professional behaviour outlined by a code, and the ethical principle presumably embedded in it.

The articulation and implementation of standards must fundamentally be concerned with ethics. As "the central objective of ethics is to determine what is good, or what is right, or what one ought to do" (Gross, 1993, p. 202), these processes reflect the inevitable clash of differing and competing perspectives on principles and how they should be expressed as professional ethics. Alternative philosophical and ideological orientations to questions of right and wrong invariably influence one's concept of teaching, the ethical role of teachers, and moral agency that in turn influence one's interpretation of professional ethics. For example, is the theoretical authority of moral agency grounded in ethical principles that advance definitions of core objective virtues such as honesty, justice, and fairness, courage, integrity, and kindness (Campbell, 1994, 1996a; Holmes, 1992; MacIntyre, 1981; Wynne & Ryan, 1993)? Alternatively, are ethical values seen through a lens of social justice theories that address inequities related to issues of race, class, gender (Banks, 1993; Contenta, 1993; McLaren, 1989; Oakes, 1989; Oakes et al., 2000; Weis, 1993)? Do they instead reflect what has become known as an "ethic of care" as advanced by some feminist scholars (Gilligan, 1982; Noddings, 1984, 1999, see also Chapter 7)?

Unresolved philosophical controversies stemming from these and other orientations provide conceptual frameworks for the growing body of educational literature dealing with the moral purpose and moral authority of accountable practice in education (Ball & Wilson, 1996; Grace, 1995; Hansen, 1998; Sockett, 1993; Sergiovanni, 1996; West, 1993); and the moral character of teachers, classrooms, and schools (Haynes, 1998; Jackson, Boostrom, & Hansen, 1993; Kirschenbaum, 1994; Richardson & Fenstermacher, 2000). Similarly, diverse perspectives are found within the renewed emphasis on moral education or character education (Beck, 1990; Cohen, 1995; Delattre & Russell, 1993; Jarrett, 1991; Kelsey, 1993; Lickona, 1991; Lockwood, 1997; Murphy, 1998; Ryan & Bohlin, 1999; Ryan & McLean, 1987; Smith & Standish, 1997; Wiley, 1998;

Wynne & Ryan, 1993). This area of the literature has direct relevance for concepts of ethical professionalism. As Schwarz (1998, p. 23) notes, "as concern with character education increases, teachers must understand and model ethical behaviour themselves". Thus, the focus returns to the professional ethics of educators (Campbell, 1996b, 1996c, 1997a, 1997b, 1997c, 2000; Carr, 2000; Nash, 1996; Ryan, 1993; Sockett, 1993; Starratt, 1994; Strike & Soltis, 1992; Strike & Ternasky, 1993).

This acknowledgement of differing and competing orientations to ethics and their application in practice in no way implies acceptance of moral relativism. Within schools, as elsewhere, people use different frameworks to support ethical perspectives, and it is not inconsistent to recognize this while holding to a belief in foundational ethical principles. Even among those who disagree, any lack of moral clarity may not be at the level of principle, but at the level of application of principle to practice, that is, implementation of ethics. I have written elsewhere of the futility of clinging to relativist theories while simultaneously trying to advance the notion of moral and ethical professionalism (Campbell 1996a, 1997a). Others also have observed relativism's undermining effect on the pursuit of ethical professional conduct in education (Bricker, 1993; Delattre & Russell, 1993; Haynes, 1998; Holmes, 1992; Ryan, 1993; Soltis, 1986; Strike & Soltis 1992; Ternasky, 1993; Watras, 1986). Strike and Soltis (1992, pp. 76-77) argue that, "we can be rational and objective without being certain, and we can be tolerant and open to other points of view without being relativists". In recommending the process of "reflective equilibrium", they assert that individuals who are deeply divided on matters of ethical practice may still engage in discussions that produce reasoned agreement. In a later work, Strike (1999, p. 35) defends "moral pluralism", an acceptance of a range of moral goods, as the most viable way to deal with the complexity of moral conflict. Similarly, in his broad examination of professional ethics, Bayles (1981, pp. 17-18) rejects ethical relativism as unacceptable and argues that "there is a difference between ethical relativism and the view that the same norm is applicable in all societies but may require different conduct due to different conditions or perhaps social roles . . . Thus, to hold that the same norms or values justify different actions by people in different social roles or situations is not ethical relativism".

If one were to borrow Bayles' idea about different social roles and apply it to different professional communities, one could appreciate that while teachers as professionals may agree on the objective values of fairness and honesty, for example, they may, within the context of their own individual schools and classrooms, interpret them differently in the course of their daily practice. Teachers' own philosophical orientations, conscious or not, to moral and ethical issues will ultimately determine how they interpret their professional obligations and their role as moral agents. Thus, consideration of the teacher as a moral agent may reflect not a singular metaphor, but a representation of diverse moral and ethical perspectives that parallel those of the wider society. As Starratt (1994. p. 3) notes, "teachers themselves exhibit the diversity of many positions found in public life on many important ethical issues".

One of the more discussed tensions arising from this diversity concerns the teacher's efforts to balance an ethic of justice and an ethic of care when dealing with students (Katz, 1999; Noddings, 1999; Strike, 1999; Strike & Ternasky, 1993). Other ethics are also apparent. For example, in their study of the moral influence that schools and teachers have on students, Jackson et al. (1993, pp. 286-287) offer the following observation: "It was not qualities like courage, wisdom or generosity that the teachers saw themselves as modeling. . . Indeed, some of the qualities that the teachers thought it important to exemplify could hardly be called virtues at all, at least not in the usual sense. They were more like admissions of human weaknesses". This conclusion is ethically troubling on several levels, not least of which is an apparent lack of clarity within the profession that interferes with teachers' ability to articulate with confidence their undoubted qualities and objectives as moral agents.

In the practical world of the teacher, differing orientations to the moral agency role complicate considerably any chance of developing a singular or unified conception of professional ethics. Nevertheless, there exists, at least in a broad sense, some common moral ground upon which standards or statements of ethical professionalism can build. It is both based on a shared appreciation for a wide range of commonly-accepted moral virtues and grounded in ethics reflective of the professional practice itself (Hansen, 1998; Soltis, 1986; Sockett, 1990).

In this respect, some of those writing about professional ethics raise the distinction between these particular kinds of ethics and the moral responsibilities of any citizen, professional or otherwise, to themselves and to other members of society (Bayles, 1981; Goldman, 1980; Macmillan, 1993). They conclude that professionals are "bound by a sense of the ethical dimensions of the relations among professionals and clients, the public, the employing institution, and fellow professionals . . . [based on] a conception of what constitutes the profession's purposes and characteristic activities" (Macmillan, 1993, pp. 189-190). However, these ethical obligations are in addition to, not substituted for, the expectations of moral behaviour for any private individual. Bayles (1981) refers to this distinction as the difference between professional ethical norms and ordinary ethical norms, and rightly concludes that professional norms can, in no way, be justified if they are independent of ordinary ethical norms.

Within the teaching context, Piddocke, Magsino, and Manley-Casimir (1997) assert that teachers must be accountable to community norms and expectations of the wider society, and Sockett (1993, p. 90), who equates the definition of the professional teacher with the moral teacher, claims that "professional teachers are experts because of their professional virtue". This type of virtue is indistinguishable from the basic human virtues that Bayles (1981) dubbed ordinary ethical norms. In fact, Sockett (1993, p. 62) proposes that the five virtues "central to an understanding of the practice of teaching" are honesty, courage, care, fairness, and practical wisdom. He further argues (1993, p. 13) for a rediscovery of a moral language in which such words as "courage, honesty, kindness, carefulness, patience, and compassion" are used to describe what professionals do. Others have identified these and other relevant virtues such as justice, integrity, trust, truth, respect for others, consistency of treatment, responsibility, civility, commitment, honour, and balance (Hare, 1997; Haynes, 1998; Soltis, 1986; Strike, 1999). Regardless of the differences that individuals bring to their identification of virtues, the emphasis remains firmly fixed on the concept of core or fundamental principles. In this respect, I believe Sockett's recommendations are consistent with the best kind of conceptualization of ethical codes or standards.

Despite the inevitable tensions resulting from differing perspectives on moral and ethical principles or virtues, it is essential to maintain a focus on professional ethics as rooted in these very principles. If codes of ethics become too specialized in the peculiarities of the professional's employment requirements or too bureaucratic or legalistic, they run the risk of becoming removed from core virtues. Thus, their possible implementation (if one were able to achieve it) may bear little resemblance to the moral professional endeavouring to make ethically correct choices. The potential for the utility of ethical standards, then, depends on their capacity to guide and inspire professionals to "do right" in a moral sense.

THE ONTARIO EXAMPLE

Last year, I observed a teacher education workshop in which participants were asked to draft several ethical statements that they believed to be essential to the teaching profession. For my own reference, I jotted down some of my own responses to the task and came up with the following three claims, in no particular order:

- Teachers must be aware that their actions and beliefs have a fundamentally moral and ethical influence on students and, therefore, they must be able to distinguish between good and bad effects on the basis of a sound understanding of right and wrong.
- Teachers must conduct themselves as responsible professionals at all times—with honesty, integrity, fairness, impartiality, and kindness.
- A teacher's first moral responsibility is to the students in his or her care.

I still support my initial reactions, and I am struck by the emphasis on principles and ideals. These standards are decidedly non-relativist and, granted, assume a consensual understanding of certain broad, and some may say vague, concepts that may not always be supported in reality. However, as a code, its focus is on ethics and obligations, not on regulations and considerations of accountability.

This moral emphasis has continued to be my hope for newly emerging statements of ethical standards in education, even though past experience has shown ethical codes (usually written by teacher unions, not professional colleges or associations) to be largely "inadequate, bureaucratic, and legalistic" (Watras, 1986, p. 13) or "platitudinous and perfunctory" (Strike & Ternasky, 1993, p. 2). In their strong criticism of the National Education Association's (NEA) Code of Ethics and the American Federation of Teachers' Bill of Rights, Arends, Winitzky, and Tannenbaum (1998, p. 426) recommend that the teaching profession "revisit and revise" their standards as a minimal first step "given the current call for a greater emphasis on teaching as moral action".

In partial defense of the NEA code, it does at least refer to ethical principles to some extent in its rather broad mention of human worth and dignity, the pursuit of truth, and commitment to the student, among other points. The Australian College of Education's (1987) code of ethics also refers to ideal principles such as fairness, consistency of treatment, responsibility, respect for persons, trust, honesty, integrity, freedom, equality, consideration of the common interest, commitment to reason, sympathy and forbearance. And, as a further example, the code of ethics for Latvia's teachers includes discussion of the following dual sets of ideals: truthfulness and fairness, freedom and responsibility, respect and self-esteem, delicacy and sensitivity (Burane, Milts, Rocena, & Valbis, 2000). The statement of principles as a guiding force for professionals is important. Of course, the difficulty of implementation seems to complicate what should be our basic understanding of these principles, and the codes are seen to lack precise professional direction.

This sets apart the American School Counselor Association's (1998) statement of ethical standards from many codes of ethics for teachers. In this lengthy and specific document, it asserts, for example, that the counselor's primary responsibility is to students, not to colleagues, parents, the profession as a whole, or the general public. This should eliminate at least some of the confusion over conflicting loyalties. It also instructs counselors to "consult with other professionals" without fear of breaching confidentiality norms if they are in doubt of a specific point of ethics. This is certainly more direct than vague references to fostering collegiality. In its reference to maintaining standards, it compels counselors to take action to rectify situations "when there exists serious doubt as to the ethical behaviour of colleagues, or if counselors are forced to work in situations or abide by policies which do not reflect the standards as outlined in the Ethical Standards" (American School Counselor Association, 1998). While I expect the implementation of such a code by counselors is fraught with tensions and complexities as in other professions, I speculate that such clear and direct instruction accompanied by an articulation of ethical principles is not likely the norm in many teachers' codes.

In Ontario, Canada, in 1996, *The Ontario College of Teachers Act* was legislated by the provincial government to establish the College as a self-regulating professional body. In 1998, it developed a statement of ethical standards to replace what passed as a code of ethics previously written and enforced by the teachers' union. The revised version, approved by the Council of the Ontario College of Teachers in June 2000, reads as follows:

Ethical Standards for the Teaching Profession

The teaching profession fosters the growth of dedicated and competent educators. Members of the profession uphold the dignity and honour of the profession through their practice. Members of the Ontario College of Teachers in their positions of trust and influence:

- maintain professional relationships with students
- recognize and respect the privileged nature of the relationship that teachers maintain with students
- demonstrate impartial and consistent respect for all students as individuals with distinctive and on-going learning needs and capacities

- respect confidential information about students unless disclosure is required by law or personal safety is at risk
- model respect for human dignity, spiritual values, cultural values, freedom, social justice, democracy and the environment
- work with members of the College and others to create a professional environment that supports the social, physical, intellectual, spiritual, cultural, moral and emotional development of students
- base relationships with parents or guardians in their role as partners in the education of students, on respect, trust, and communication
- co-operate with professionals from other agencies in the interest of students and as required by law
- act with integrity, honesty, fairness and dignity
- respect the confidential nature of information about members of the College obtained in the course of professional practice unless disclosure is required by law or personal safety is at risk
- comply with the Acts and regulations
- advise the appropriate people in a professional manner when policies or practices exist that should be reviewed or revised.

(Ontario College of Teachers, 2000)

While the purpose of this chapter is not to analyze and critique the above statement of standards in great depth, I offer the following initial and overall reaction to it. With the exception of the ninth standard ("act with integrity, honesty, fairness and dignity") as well as selected words (respect, trust) sprinkled throughout the document in varying contexts, the statement does not obviously highlight a sense of ethical principles and moral purpose. These elements may be there, but they are embedded in a dominant interest in procedural and legal requirements. Its lack of specificity leaves it open to the widest possible interpretation, and the use of vague phrases such as "the appropriate people", "confidential nature of information about members", "other agencies", and "professional manner", for example, stimulate more questions than answers. An attempt to accommodate a range of ideological and political perspectives ("model respect for human dignity, spiritual values, cultural values, freedom, social justice, democracy and the environment") confronts teachers with possibly conflicting obligations, in which the moral imperative may become fuzzy.

While fully accepting that a code of ethics, like a mission statement, could never and probably should never become a blueprint for action, I was hopeful that a renewed statement of ethical standards would articulate moral and ethical principles and ideals that would both inspire and guide teachers through the ethically complex realities of their daily work. In this respect, the statement would be responsive to the growing body of academic literature that addresses the need to recognize teaching as an inherently moral endeavour. Its implementation would not be so much an artificial application of the rules (as will be attempted in the next section) as it would be a means to make conscious and internalized within the profession, the ideals of best ethical practice. It would serve as a catalyst for ethical discussion among groups of teachers about the core principles that should underpin their decisions, both individual and collective. It is now difficult to envision this kind of implementation stemming directly from such formalized standards or codes.

APPLYING THE INAPPLICABLE

As implied previously, implementation of genuinely ethical principles by means of applying to specific circumstances formalized statements from a code of ethics is likely a futile pursuit. Nonetheless, in keeping with the title of this paper, I am going to "try", by way of illustrating this pursuit, to put ethical standards (in this case, the Ontario code) into practice. The practice described here represents samples of empirical evidence that are my previously published accounts of moral dilemmas that teachers faced in the course of their daily work. The intention is to explore whether and how an application of ethical standards might have helped the teachers resolve their moral quandaries.

In each of the following examples, the ethical dilemma is presented in its form as empirical evidence gathered from individual teachers. This is followed by a first person narrative comment intended to represent the teacher's possible thought processes had he or she tried to resolve the dilemma using the ethical standards. It would be helpful to refer to the previous statement of "Ethical Standards for the Teaching Profession" while reading these latter accounts, which, of course, are fabricated for the purpose of this chapter, and are meant to be illustrative, not comprehensive or conclusive.

The Stolen Examination

> There are so many grey areas, and I've been involved in so many situations involving teachers where I know I have done the wrong thing - if I had heard that someone else had done it, I would judge and say, 'you shouldn't have done that'. For example, a friend of mine (another teacher) stole an exam of mine and gave the questions to a student who was a favourite of his but who was failing my course. When I raved about what a good exam this student had written and what a surprise it was, this teacher admitted it to me. And I was absolutely unbelievably upset. I didn't know what to do. I had passed the student on the basis of this exam, and he didn't deserve it; it was a terrible situation. And I told the person off, and it's always shaded my attitude. Things have never been the same since between us. But I didn't do the right thing. I mean the right thing would have been to march him to the principal and expose this. It's bothered me ever since (Campbell, 1996c, p. 201).

Well, I know my friend was wrong - he violated several standards concerning professional relationships with students, impartial respect, honesty, and fairness. But the question is, what should I do? Piddocke et al. (1997, p. 224) claim that teachers not only have an obligation to uphold the dignity of the profession, but also have "the duty to duly criticize the profession and its members when they fail to abide by the profession's own proper standards". However, our standards aren't that explicit; the last standard says I should advise the appropriate people, I guess that's the principal here, in a professional manner when policies or practices exist that should be reviewed or revised. But, this is hardly a policy and as a practice, it can't be really reviewed or revised now. I don't think this standard could be referring to this type of problem. Also, is this confidential information about a member that I have to respect? It's certainly a secret, but not one I should protect, surely. The sixth standard says I should work with other members of the College - that's my friend and colleague - to create a professional environment. But it's too late for that, the deed is done. Now it's a matter of reporting it at my own risk of losing a friend and creating a nasty collegial atmosphere that would probably undermine our ability as a faculty to work together anyway. So maybe I'm right to keep quiet. Yet, I'm supposed to act with honesty and integrity. Well, I do - I would never have done what my friend did! I just wish he hadn't told me. But that wouldn't make things right for either the student who cheated or for all the other students who didn't have the same unfair advantage during the exam. I feel that honesty means you shouldn't lie. Well, by doing nothing, I'm not really lying. Who says honesty means telling something you know even when no one has asked you?

The Thumbnail Incident

> There was one absolutely critical and specific situation that I experienced. One teacher who was in a leadership position (as a chair/coordinator) happened to walk through my open class area, and I had kids working all over. I happened to look over as he walked by a couple of my kids who were being a little goofy, certainly nothing serious. And as I watched him walk by, he took his thumbnail and stuck it hard into the kid's side and then kept on walking. As the kid came back down from the ceiling and landed on the floor ready to go after this teacher, I grabbed him and tried to calm him down. I asked what happened, knowing full well what had happened but no one knew I knew. He said, 'he struck me ...'. And the teacher turned around and said, 'I didn't touch you'. So I kind of played dumb and said I'd handle things... Anyway I went to the principal and I said that this was off the record, and that I needed some help with this. So he said to me, 'Well, this is one where you make the decision. If you're going to deal with it, then it comes from you and you have to confront him'. I was just lost. The upshot of it was that I didn't go ahead with it. When we look back at times when we chose a path that we wish we hadn't chosen, that's when I chickened out. I kind of explored it but it was in a really wishy-washy manner. And I didn't tell the youngster I knew what had really happened. And I didn't go to the teacher and say, 'I saw what you did, it was a terrible thing to do, and not only did you lie but you abused'. If we talk about the good that came out of it, it helped crystallize my own moral framework as far as what goes and what doesn't and not being afraid to say something. It was survival, but I didn't feel good (Campbell, 1996c, pp. 201-202).

Boy, did I ever display a lack of moral courage here - of course, the standards don't say I have to model that. I sure didn't show that I recognize the privileged nature of my relationship with students or model respect for their dignity. Now, at the time, neither the students nor the chair knew I saw what happened, so by not saying anything I really didn't lie and violate the principle of honesty. However, as Piddocke et al. (1997, p. 223) said, "teachers must be the sort of people who can be trusted to act properly when no one is watching". Well, I did that in a way; I mean I did try to act with integrity when I sort of reported my chair to the principal. After all, we're told to advise the appropriate people - it's just that the appropriate person here didn't seem to want to know about it. Maybe he thought I wasn't acting in a professional manner. But what does that mean? I always thought professionalism also meant maintaining loyalty to your colleagues - so perhaps I shouldn't have told on my chair in the first place. Of course, the standards don't mention that kind of loyalty the way the old union code implied (Ontario Teachers'

Federation, 1986). However, it doesn't say my primary moral responsibility is to the students either, the way the School Counselors' code does. I wish it did say that. And, how am I supposed to continue working with other members of the College in a supportive professional environment if I'm seen as a snitch?

The Announcement of Failures

> Little things happen - occasionally decisions will be made haphazardly by a vice principal or principal who's under a lot of stress. So you just modify it because it's a problem. For example, to save time this year, instead of home form teachers phoning up students to tell them they failed courses, they set aside a day where everyone was to come in, and home form teachers would tell those students who failed that they failed and would have to register for summer school.
> Q—They were to tell them this in front of everybody else?
> Yes, right. And that was ridiculous. That was something that was not thought out. The decision lacked imagination. They didn't realize that you would be stigmatizing kids for having failed subjects in front of their peers. So what I did was I told the students that if they didn't hear from me they didn't have to come in. And I phoned kids over the weekend to let them know they had failed so it wouldn't be so embarrassing for them (Campbell, 1997c, p. 251).

I don't really think this was a dilemma. I mean, clearly I did the right thing - I tried to respect both the students and the confidential information about them, and I showed them I respected their human dignity. Of course, by not advising the appropriate people, the administrators, that their new policy needs to be revised badly, I guess I behaved somewhat sneakily - maybe I even violated honesty and integrity. But at least I was fairer to students than this policy was. Again, though, by failing to work with other members of the College to create a more professional environment that would expose and examine this matter, I may have helped my students, but it didn't result in making things better for anyone else's students, did it? Well, I guess I've always been a bit of a renegade, subversive even - is that unethical, even when you know you're right? The standards said I should comply with the Acts and regulations. If I remember my school law class, I believe that one of the regulations says teachers must fulfill assigned duties from the principal, and obey other administrative or policy instructions. Oh. Maybe I should rethink about why this might be a dilemma.

The Adjusting of Marks

> I'm a new math teacher at a school known for its low academic achievement rates. The common set of midterm exams, from which our interim report cards are issued, reflect the extremely low marks of the students; in light of this, the other math teachers agreed to alter the exam marks so the total would be out of 80, not 100, and the student's final grades would not seem as bad. This, apparently, is normative grading practice at this school and is done for reasons relating to school image and students' self-esteem. I believe this is morally wrong; it endorses dishonesty and cheating and flaunts concepts of justice. Yet, I don't want my students to suffer for lower grades if the other teachers are prepared to alter their students' marks (Campbell, 1997b, p. 260).[2]

I think I'm right to be upset by this situation; it's clearly a violation of honest, fair, and even dignified professional practice. What kind of role models are we by rigging the marks? Of course, I guess you could say we're demonstrating impartial and consistent respect for all students (we're not changing only some marks) and we certainly see the students as having distinctive and on-going learning needs and capacities (in this case, very low, I might add). Because of this, I want to be fair and not disadvantage my students just to honour a higher principle. Or do I? Maybe I should advise the appropriate person, the principal, about what's going on in this department. However, I get the feeling this practice is almost implicitly approved of - it's a school culture thing. So, if I make a fuss, I'd just be labelled and ostracized as a troublemaker or whistleblower. It's really better to work with other members of the College, my colleagues, on this; but that will likely mean going along with things. Well, if it's a question of self-esteem, maybe that will help support the emotional development of the students. But, it sure won't do much for their intellectual development.

The Caretakers' Strike

> Two years ago, we had a caretakers' strike, and our (teachers') Federation said, 'Don't you take any garbage out; you can take it out of your classroom but you're not allowed to clean the washrooms etc. That's not your business'. A couple of teachers did clean up the bathrooms - they said the kids can't go into a dirty bathroom - which started trouble on staff. Teacher versus teacher. Some felt these others were scabbing or union breaking. It got into a big fight, and those guys' emotions never healed. I went along with the Federation. I made sure my room was clean, which I do anyway, but that was all (Campbell, 1996c, p. 204).

I can't actually find an ethical standard to support what I did, or didn't do, as the case may be. I didn't model respect for the human dignity of my students by accepting that they should be forced to use dirty bathrooms; and I guess I didn't work with other members of the College and others to create a professional environment supportive of students' physical development. The other standards just don't seem relevant to this workplace issue. So, maybe it's not a matter of ethics in this particular situation if my actions reflect a sense of responsibility to the caretakers more than to the students.

The Plagiarized Essay

> I just discovered that one of my senior English students has plagiarized a major essay assignment that counts for a significant proportion of the final mark. The student has near perfect marks in his science courses and is aiming to get a scholarship that would enable him to enter the medical research field at university. He needs at least a B in English to have a chance at the scholarship, and a failure on this essay would reduce his mark to a C-. The student, a recent immigrant whose first language is not English, holds down a part-time job to support his mother since his father died last year. I know that personal circumstances have adversely affected the student's ability to improve his grades in English. However, the school policy on plagiarism leaves no doubt to its intent. The penalty is automatic failure on the assignment with no chance to make up the mark. The moral message from the school is quite clear on this issue. Other students have been punished for this kind of cheating. For all I know, they too may have been trying for scholarships and may have been affected by personal hardship. What is the right and fair thing for me to do (Campbell, 1997b, p. 260)? [2]

This is the kind of moral dilemma that breaks your heart. I really want to help this student, but how do I make an exception for him and still maintain integrity, honesty, and fairness? How can I demonstrate impartiality if I let him get away with something that others have been punished for? How do I balance my need to be humane with my need to be fair? How do I ignore my obligation to comply with regulations that make clear the expectation that I follow school policy? Maybe the policy needs to be reviewed or revised, and I should advise the appropriate people of that before I take my own individual action. This is clearly a time to work with other members of the College, my colleagues here in this school, to address openly this kind of ethical issue. Maybe then, if we discussed them, the ethical standards would seem more relevant. As they exist, I feel morally rudderless in my need to make a professional decision.

This kind of artificial application of ethical standards to specific dilemmas of practice, of course, invites criticism and alternative interpretations of which ethics truly represent the described scenarios. One could take the ethical code and apply it to the dilemmas in ways that provoke an entirely different or competing analysis. And, this is the point to be made. It underlines how minimally useful, if at all, this kind of adherence to formalized statements would be in the resolution of teachers' moral dilemmas.

Jackson et al. (1993, p. 293) assert that teachers have an obligation "to learn as much as possible about their own potency as moral agents and about the moral potency of the schools and classrooms in which they work". Strike and Ternasky (1993) similarly refer to the teacher's need to appreciate the moral and ethical dimensions of their work. They write (1993, p. 225): "As moral craft, teaching will require not just that teachers treat their students fairly and with respect. It will also require that teachers comprehend the complexity of the ethical landscape". This comprehension is unlikely to flourish if we rely solely on ethical standards to guide us.

Grant (1993, p. 135), in urging teachers to "assume and exercise moral responsibility for their profession", argues that "a school is a community that cannot disavow responsibility for either intellectual or moral virtue" (1993, pp. 138-139). As discussed in the subsequent section, it is probable that, within this concept of communities of professional teachers, the ethical principles, virtues, and ideals that are hopefully embedded in the standards will become more transparent and obvious as guidelines for behaviour in ways that the standards themselves are not.

Enabling the Applicable within the School Community

> Sir Robert Morton: 'Very well, then, if you must have it, here it is: I wept today because right had been done'.
> Miss Catherine Winslow: 'Not justice'?
> Sir Robert Morton: 'No. Not justice. Right. It is not hard to do justice - very hard to do right. Unfortunately, while the appeal of justice is intellectual, the appeal of right appears, for some odd reason, to induce tears in court'. (*The Winslow Boy*, Rattigan, 1946, p. 89)

As implied previously, there may be a place in the professional world of teachers for ethical codes or standards, as long as their limitations for implementation are acknowledged. I have stated elsewhere (Campbell, 1997b, p. 257) that "becoming familiar with the principles inherent in such (ethical) codes may have intrinsic value" even though it is not enough to prepare teachers to be ethical professionals. Similarly, Soltis (1986, p. 2) claims that formal ethical codes "provide a foundation for ethical decision-making, but they also may leave prospective teachers ill-equipped to deal with the complexities of novel or unique problem situations". Beck and Murphy (1994) are also critical of those who assume professional codes of ethics can offer educators adequate directives to guide them in troublesome ethical situations, even though they accept that codes may provide useful guidelines relating to ideals.

It is this distinction between codes, rules, and regulations and ideals, norms, and principles, as explained by Sergiovanni (1992, p. 12), that is significant to discussions about the implementation of good or right action. The underlying ideals, the core ethical principles, should guide professional decisions, rather than the formalized codes or standards that are meant to embody those principles. The ultimate value of the code or statement of standards is in its ability to elucidate such principles.

As in the above quotation from *The Winslow Boy,* justice and right, while obviously related to ethical principles, codes and standards are not the same as ethics. In further support of this analogy, one may recall Gross' (1993, p. 203) examination of the legal context of professional ethics in education in which he uses the term justice "only in the juridical sense, that is, adjudicating rights and obligations in conformity with, and as determined by, laws or administrative or contractual rules". As Strike and Soltis (1992, p. 1) note, "ethical thinking and decision making are not just following the rules". In her support for obeying basic ethical requirements, Haynes (1998, p. 40) makes a similar point by arguing that, "part of what it means to be a professional is not to be someone who follows the rules automatically, but someone who is competent and intelligent and ethical in their practice". If, in this sense, we interpret "justice" to be the following of more formalized rules, we could compare its implementation to the rather artificial application of a code or standards to ethically complex situations, as attempted previously. In doing so, we could try to act out the standards in relative isolation from each other and convince ourselves that we have satisfied the legal imperative; however, we may not have achieved in our decisions and actions the more elusive concept of "right".

If, on the other hand, we regard ethical codes or standards as potential springboards for broader school efforts to define what right is in terms of ethical practice, we can hopefully make core principles central to the professional mission and, thereby, ensure a level of guidance, support, and consistency. Since "deep-seated beliefs and attitudes . . . shape the moral climate of the school and the nature of interactions between teachers and students" (Grant, 1993, p. 135), it seems critical to build a shared sense of ethical norms within local school communities. Power (1993, p. 152) argues that it is not only a collective responsibility but also an ethical duty of teachers and administrators "to examine the moral atmosphere of their schools". He refers to this as the building of community, which itself is a kind of intensified moral experience.

Internal communities of teachers and administrators within individual school contexts are best able to translate the ethical principles and ideals embedded in codes and standards into good normative and routine daily practice. This internalization of principles would resemble Wynne and Ryan's (1997, p. 60) definition of "habituation" in which "something is learned so deeply that it becomes a habit". This learning may occur in a variety of ways, although the force of collegial and collective reflection and discussion is central to a shared understanding of ethical principles. Once this understanding is the catalyst for consistently good action, continual articulation of the school's ethical norms and their sustained acceptance, any need to refer to the actual ethical standards is diminished.

In order to develop ethical norms in ways that pervade all aspects of policy making and practice, professional communities of educators, within the context of their own schools, must come to terms with difficult questions and the need to communicate with each other openly. As Strike and Ternasky (1993, p. 222) note, "If we refuse to assess the school's decision-making hierarchy, strategies, and unspoken rules, then we can expect little more than unintended consequences from attempts at ethical reform". For example, teachers and administrators may have to declare whether they believe the students really are their first moral responsibility and what that would mean for the resolution of dilemmas involving conflicting loyalties to colleagues and competing obligations to parents and others. They may have to project the types of dilemmas mentioned earlier in this paper and work through hypothetical case studies that would test their agreement on fundamental definitions of fairness, honesty, integrity, care, and so on. They may need to ensure that procedures are in place whereby any time a new school policy is developed, it would be assessed primarily on its ethical implications. A common core of virtues may have to become the ultimate measuring stick for ethical adequacy. And, most of all, there must be an expectation among everyone that all professionals in the school community not only uphold the principles themselves, but also that they assume the responsibility of helping each other to honour the ethical norms, even if it leads to the exposure of others. In the grey areas where ethical certainty is not obvious, there must be a commitment to discussing, in open forums, the reasonable applicability of principles to particular cases. If such a renewed ethical culture were to become the norm of the school community, dilemmas such as those reported previously may be avoided. Even if such incidents themselves are not completely eliminated, perhaps the apparent moral confusion among teachers surrounding what course of action is best pursued may be eradicated.

CONCLUSION

A discussion of differing and competing perspectives on ethics generally, and professional ethics specifically, initiated this chapter on the application of ethical standards to the ethical complexities and dilemmas facing teachers in the course of their daily work. Theoretical distinctions among varying perspectives may represent diverse political or philosophical points of view; however, despite their differences, they may also reinforce a sense of collective moral purpose within defined school communities. Common support for ethical principles, despite possibly differing ideological interpretations of the principles, should signify the potential for dialogue and agreement on certain fundamental qualities among individuals and groups who may differ on other issues. As both Starratt (1994) and Strike and Soltis (1992) indicate, disagreement over ethical concerns is to be expected and need not undermine the ability of individuals within groups, organizations, or communities to address core issues in morally sensitive ways. This bodes well for the implementation of principles that hopefully are reflected in professional ethical standards.

Regardless of the conceptual orientations of its members, it is highly unlikely that any school community dedicated to enabling the implementation of ethical standards would knowingly and intentionally sanction, in the name of loyalty and collegiality, the covering up of a colleague's theft or abuse, for example. Nor would the community promote a belief that the concepts of care and compassion should enable dishonest grading or the acceptance of cheating as new ethical norms.

The key, then, is to encourage professional communities to articulate openly those daily dilemmas that challenge individuals' intuitive sense of ethical propriety. Attention to the ethical dimensions of practice, formal and informal, and policy should become a priority for these communities as they work through the development of a consensual and implicit understanding of what ethical standards look like in the reality of their schools. Teachers and administrators need to discuss processes for addressing future dilemmas if and as they arise. Furthermore, they need to reach a point where the conceptual understanding and the procedural routines for the implementation of new ethical norms are so internalized and embedded in their interpretation of professionalism that any need to refer to the actual formal codes or standards becomes irrelevant.

As an issue of policy making, those involved in the conceptualization of ethical standards need to appreciate that, as Sergiovanni (1992, p. 55) claims, "only when code-specific behaviour and underlying ideals and values are connected - only when it is accepted that what teachers do and why they do it are connected - will professional codes cease to be rules of professional etiquette and become powerful moral statements". To implement ethical standards properly, professional teachers need to live out, through their practice, core principles, not codes.

It is important for educators to feel the power of their collective will to do good things in schools. The force of shared expectations should be their guide in this respect. An individual teacher without support or assurance that his or her beliefs are consistent with the group's norms, even though the moral imperative seems clear, may hesitate to take decisive ethical action. It is the hope expressed in this chapter that ethical standards, while inadequate on their own, may provoke school communities to reflect seriously on their own norms and the implementation of ethical principles. This concentrated effort on defining appropriate ethical norms by and for professionals may be enough to instill moral clarity and courage in that lone teacher who previously grappled with dilemmas and uncertainties. It is at this point when professional teachers will know how 'right' may be done.

NOTES

[1] This chapter was published originally in the *Journal of Education Policy*, and appears with the permission of Taylor and Francis Ltd.
[2] This dilemma was originally written as a case study in the third person form. The narration has been changed here for reasons of consistency.

REFERENCES

American School Counselor Association. (1998). *Ethical standards for school counselors.* Available at http://www.schoolcounselor.org/ethics/standards.htm.

Arends, R., Winitzky, N., & Tannenbaum, M. (1998). *Exploring teaching: First edition.* Boston, MA: McGraw Hill.

Australian College of Education (1987). Code of ethics. In F. Haynes (Ed.), *The ethical school* (pp. 176-178). London: Routledge.

Ball, D., & Wilson, S. (1996). Integrity in teaching: Recognizing the fusion of the moral and the intellectual. *American Educational Research Journal, 33*(1), 155-192.

Banks, J. (1993). *Multiethnic education: Theory and practice.* New York: Allyn and Bacon.

Bayles, M. (1981). *Professional ethics.* Belmont, CA: Wadsworth Publishing Company.

Beck, C. (1990). *Better schools: A values perspective.* London: Falmer Press.

Beck, L., & Murphy, J. (1994). *Ethics in educational leadership programs: An expanding role.* Thousand Oaks, CA: Corwin Press.

Bricker, D. (1993). Character and moral reasoning: An Aristotelian perspective. In K. Strike & L. Ternasky (Eds.), *Ethics for professionals in education: Perspectives for preparation and practice* (pp. 13-26). New York: Teachers College Press.

Burane, K., Milts, A., Rocena, I., & Valbis, J. (2000). Personal, social and moral education in Latvia: Problems and prospects. In M. Leicester, C. Modgil, & S. Modgil (Eds.), *Education, culture and values, volume IV: Moral education and pluralism*(pp. 123-130). London: Falmer Press.

Campbell, E. (1994). Personal morals and organizational ethics: A synopsis. *The Canadian Administrator, 34*(2), 1-10.

Campbell, E. (1996a) Suspended morality and the denial of ethics: How value relativism muddles the distinction between right and wrong in administrative decisions. In S. Jacobson, E. Hickcox, & R. Stevenson (Eds.), *School administration: Persistent dilemmas in preparation and practice*(pp. 63-74). Westport, CT: Praeger.

Campbell, E. (1996b). The moral core of professionalism as a teachable ideal and a matter of character. *Curriculum Inquiry, 26*(1), 71-80.

Campbell, E. (1996c). Ethical implications of collegial loyalty as one view of teacher professionalism. *Teachers and Teaching: Theory and Practice, 2*(2), 191-208.

Campbell, E. (1997a). Ethical school leadership: Problems of an elusive role. *Journal of School Leadership, 7*(3), 287-300.

Campbell, E. (1997b). Connecting the ethics of teaching and moral education. *Journal of Teacher Education, 48*(4), 255-263.

Campbell, E. (1997c). Administrators' decisions and teachers' ethical dilemmas: Implications for moral agency. *Leading & Managing, 3*(4), 245-257.

Campbell, E. (2000) Professional ethics in teaching: Towards the development of a code of practice. *Cambridge Journal of Education, 30*(2), 203-221.

Carr, D. (2000). *Professionalism and ethics in teaching.* London: Routledge.

Cohen, P. (1995). The content of their character: Educators find new ways to tackle values and morality, *Curriculum Update,* Association for Supervision and Curriculum Development, 1-8.

Contenta, S. (1993). *Rituals of failure: What schools really teach.* Toronto: Between the Lines.

Delattre, E., & Russell, W. (1993). Schooling, moral principles, and the formation of character. *Journal of Education, 175*(2), 23-43.

Gilligan, C. (1982). *In a different voice: Psychological theory and women's development.* Cambridge, MA: Harvard University Press.

Goldman, A. (1980). *The moral foundations of professional ethics.* Totoma, NJ: Rowman & Littlefield.

Grace, G. (1995). *School leadership: Beyond education management.* London: Falmer Press.

Grant, G. (1993). Discovering how you really teach. In K. Strike & L. Ternasky (Eds.), *Ethics for professionals in education: Perspectives for preparation and practice* (pp. 135-147). New York: Teachers College Press.

Gross, J. (1993). The legal context of professional ethics. In K. Strike & L. Ternasky (Eds.), *Ethics for professionals in education: Perspectives for preparation and practice*(pp. 202-216). New York: Teachers College Press.

Hansen, D. (1998). The moral is in the practice. *Teaching and Teacher Education, 14*(6), 643-655.

Hare, W. (1997). Review of *Ethical judgement in teaching* by K.D. Hostetler, *Journal of Educational Administration and Foundations, 12*(2), 61-66.

Haynes, F. (1998). *The ethical school.* London: Routledge.

Holmes, M. (1992). Moral education: Emancipation and tradition. *Curriculum Inquiry, 22*(4), 339-344.

Jackson, P., Boostrom, R., & Hansen, D. (1993). *The moral life of schools.* San Francisco, CA: Jossey-Bass Publishers.

Jarrett, J. (1991). *The teaching of values: Caring and appreciation.* London: Routledge.

Katz, M. (1999). Teaching about caring and fairness: May Sarton's *The small room.* In M. Katz, N. Noddings, & K. Strike (Eds.), *Justice and caring: The search for common ground in education* (pp. 59-73). New York: Teachers College Press.

Kelsey, I. (1993). *Universal character education.* Edinburgh: The Pentland Press.

Kirschenbaum, H. (1994). *100 ways to enhance values and morality in schools and youth settings.* Boston: Allyn and Bacon.

Lickona, T. (1991). *Educating for character: How our schools can teach respect and responsibility.* New York: Bantam Books.

Lockwood, A. (1997). *Character education: Controversy and consensus.* Thousand Oaks, CA: Corwin Press.

Lovat, T. (1998) Ethics and ethics education: Professional and curricular best practice. *Curriculum Perspectives, 18*(1), 1-7.

MacIntyre, A. (1981). *After virtue: A study in moral theory.* London: Gerald Duckworth & Co. Ltd.

Macmillan, C. (1993). Ethics and teacher professionalization. In K. Strike & L. Ternasky (Eds.), *Ethics for professionals in education: Perspectives for preparation and practice*(pp. 189-201). New York: Teachers College Press.

McLaren, P. (1989). *Life in schools: An introduction to critical pedagogy in the foundations of education.* Toronto: Irwin Publishing.

Murphy, M. (1998). *Character education in America's blue ribbon schools: Best practices for meeting the challenge.* Lancaster, PA: Technomic.

Nash, R. (1996). *Real world ethics: Frameworks for educators and human service professionals.* New York: Teachers College Press.

National Education Association (1975). Code of ethics of the education profession. In K. Strike & J. Soltis (Eds.) (1992), *The ethics of teaching: Second edition* (pp. ix-xi). New York: Teachers College Press.

Noddings, N. (1984). *Caring: A feminine approach to ethics and moral education.* (Berkeley, CA: University of California Press.

Noddings, N. (1999) Care, justice, and equity. In M. Katz, N. Noddings, & K. Strike (Eds.), *Justice and caring: The search for common ground in education*(pp. 7-20). New York: Teachers College Press.

Oakes, J. (1989). What educational indicators? The case for assessing the school context. *Educational Evaluation and Policy Analysis, 11*(2), 181-199.

Oakes, J., Quartz, K., Ryan, S., & Lipton, M. (2000). *Becoming good American schools: The struggle for civic virtue in education reform.* San Francisco, CA: Jossey-Bass.

Ontario College of Teachers (2000). *Ethical standards for the teaching profession.* Toronto: OCoT.

Ontario Teachers Federation (1986). *Professional conduct and the professional teacher: A handbook on relations and discipline.* Toronto: OTF.

Piddocke, S., Magsino, R., & Manley-Casimir, M. (1997). *Teachers in trouble: An exploration of the normative character of teaching.* Toronto: University of Toronto Press.

Power, C. (1993) Just schools and moral atmosphere. In K. Strike & L. Ternasky (Eds.), *Ethics for professionals in education: Perspectives for preparation and practice* (pp. 148-161). New York: Teachers College Press.

Rattigan, T. (1946). *The Winslow boy.* New York: Dramatists Play Service, Inc.

Richardson, V., & Fenstermacher, G. (2000). The manner in teaching project. Available at http://www-personal.umich.edu/~gfenster.

Ryan, K. (1993). Why a centre for the advancement of ethics and character? *Journal of Education, 175*(2), 1-11.

Ryan, K., & Bohlin, K. (1999). *Building character in schools: Practical ways to bring moral instruction to life*. San Francisco, CA: Jossey-Bass.

Ryan, K., & McLean, G. (1987). *Character development in schools and beyond*. New York: Praeger.

Schwarz, G. (1998). Teaching as vocation: Enabling ethical practice. *The Educational Forum, 63*(1), 23-29.

Sergiovanni, T. (1992). *Moral leadership: Getting to the heart of school improvement*. San Francisco, CA: Jossey-Bass.

Sergiovanni, T. (1996). *Leadership for the schoolhouse: How is it different? Why is it important?* San Francisco, CA: Jossey-Bass.

Smith, R., & Standish, P. (1997). *Teaching right and wrong: Moral education in the balance*. Stoke-on-Trent, UK: Trentham Books Ltd.

Sockett, H. (1990) Accountability, trust, and ethical codes of practice. In J. Goodlad, R. Soder, & K. Sirotnik (Eds.), *The moral dimensions of teaching* (pp. 224-250). San Francisco, CA: Jossey-Bass.

Sockett, H. (1993). *The moral base for teacher professionalism*. New York: Teachers College Press.

Soltis, J. (1986). Teaching professional ethics. *Journal of Teacher Education, 37*(3), 2-4.

Starratt, R. (1994). *Building an ethical school: A practical response to the moral crisis in schools*. London: Falmer Press.

Strike, K. (1999). Justice, caring, and universality: In defense of moral pluralism. In M. Katz, N. Noddings, & K. Strike (Eds.), *Justice and caring: The search for common ground in education* (pp. 21-36). New York: Teachers College Press.

Strike, K., & Soltis, J. (1992). *The ethics of teaching: Second edition*. New York: Teachers College Press.

Strike, K., & Ternasky, L. (1993). *Ethics for professionals in education: Perspectives for preparation and practice*. New York: Teachers College Press.

Strom, S. (1989). The ethical dimension of teaching. In M. Reynolds (Ed.), *Knowledge base for the Beginning Teacher*(pp. 267-276). Oxford: Pergamon Press.

Ternasky, L. (1993). Coping with relativism and absolutism. In K. Strike & L. Ternasky (Eds.), *Ethics for professionals in education: Perspectives for preparation and practice*(pp. 117-131). New York: Teachers College Press.

Thompson, M. (1997). *Professional ethics and the teacher: Towards a general teaching council.* Stoke on Trent, UK: Trentham Books Limited.

Watras, J. (1986). Will teaching applied ethics improve schools of education? *Journal of Teacher Education, 37*(3), 13-16.

Weis, L. (1993). *Beyond silenced voices: Class, race, and gender in United States schools*. Albany, NY: SUNY Press.

West, S. (1993). *Educational values for school leadership*. London: Kogan Page.

Wiley, L.S. (1998). *Comprehensive character-building classrooms: A handbook for teachers*. De Barry, FL: Longwood Communications.

Wynne, E., & Ryan, K. (1993*). Reclaiming our schools: A handbook on teaching character, academics and discipline*. New York: Macmillan. Company).

Wynne, E., & Ryan, K. (1997). *Reclaiming our schools: Teaching character, academics, and discipline, second edition*. Upper Saddle River, NJ: Prentice-Hall.

LAWRENCE J. LEONARD AND PAULINE E. LEONARD

VALUING SCHOOLS AS PROFESSIONAL COMMUNITIES:
ASSESSING THE COLLABORATIVE PRESCRIPTION[1]

Abstract. If the reforms currently transforming public education are to be sustained, it is commonly believed that they must be founded in new conceptions of schooling. Compelling among them is the recurrent edict that teachers and other educators must learn to work together in ways previously considered to be discretionary and, consequently, largely a matter of personal and professional preference. Notwithstanding its rising recognition as an essential ingredient of successful schools, collaborative practice remains an erratic and elusive enterprise that is fraught with uncertainty. The authors of this chapter use the literature and their own research experiences to explore how and why the wide scale establishment and nurturance of so-called professional learning communities may continue to evade realization. Despite habitual rhetoric to the contrary, a fundamental problem may be a lack of evidence that there is strong and manifested valuing of teacher collaborative practice as an integral component of schools as morally-bound communities.

The conception of professional collaboration has become a common parlance (DiPardo, 1997; Friend & Cook, 1996, 2000; Fullan & Hargreaves, 1991; Koehler & Baxter, 1997; Telford, 1996) of perceived effective schooling. In fact, for some, the infusion of teacher collaborative practices is considered to have had an immense and unprecedented impact in the field of education. Advocates of such "joint work" (Little, 1982) claim that it is an important key to the development of so-called professional learning communities where moral interpersonal relationships, collective learning, empowerment, growth, and self-efficacy are the mainstays of school life. Indeed, the very word community, as derived from the Latin word *communis* meaning *common* or *sharing* (Welch, 1998, p. 26), is habitually used in references to collaboration.

Pugach and Johnson (1995) advance that collaborative schools are more likely to become "communities of learners" in which all participants would contribute to their own and each others' growth (p. 12). Louis, Marks, and Kruse (1994) identified collaboration as one of five important elements of practice in a professional community. Sergiovanni (1996) is persuasive in his endorsement of the school as community metaphor, as opposed to the school as an organization. He defines community as a "collection of individuals who are bonded together by natural will and who are together bound to a set of shared ideas and ideals" (p. 48). Thinking of schools as communities, Sergiovanni asserts, changes the interpersonal relationships of its members from the individualistic to the collective, and helps to create a school culture where people are morally bound to collective goals. The practice of collaboration, then, is seen as an important key to the development of schools as moral communities.

Those less enamoured with the idea of teacher collaborative practice being elemental to school success tend to view it as yet another touted remedy to the persisting problems and challenges associated with schooling -- an antidote for a

P.T. Begley and O. Johansson (eds.), The Ethical Dimensions of School Leadership, 127–142.

systemic condition that defies solution. Resisting the urge to dismiss such a disparaging perspective out-of-hand may lead one to further consider the commonly-noted barriers to teacher collaboration and to look beyond the rhetoric and the reverie. The authors of this chapter attempt to clarify understandings of collaboration and its potentialities and limitations in transforming schools from organized hierarchies to moral communities. Accordingly, the ensuing discussion is comprised of four parts:

1. a discussion of the major trends undergirding the collaborative thrust embedded in reconceptualizing schools as moral communities;
2. an overview of collaboration in terms of its various definitions, and its challenges and benefits for establishing schools as moral communities;
3. a presentation of research findings examining perceptions of school collaboration;
4. a discussion of implications for theory, research, and practice pertaining to the collaborative dimension of schools as moral communities.

THE COLLABORATIVE THRUST OF SCHOOLS AS MORAL COMMUNITIES: MAJOR TRENDS

Increasingly, school administrators and teachers are encouraged to challenge traditional ways of thinking about schools as organizations. Historically, schools have been metaphorically conceptualized as knowledge-producing factories, with teachers being the producers and students being the product. Consequently, schools have been fashioned to reflect and perpetuate cultures of individualism, competitiveness, and isolation. This organizational fragmentation pre-empts the creation of new school cultures which reflect a more covenantal dimension of schools as moral communities. Schools modelled on the qualities of community values supplant contractually-based precepts, and foster cultures of collaboration grounded in strong moral ties. The increased interest in collaboration (Friend & Cook, 1996, 2000; Jordan, 1999) is rooted in changes in thinking about what makes an organization effective and what constitutes leadership.

The foundation of current collaborative practice may be examined by applying lenses of organization and leadership theories. Traditionally, organization theory rooted in business and industry attributed the power of leadership to those assuming formal roles legitimated by hierarchical structures. For example, classical theorists, representing Taylor's (1916/1996) "principles of scientific management", Weber's (1922/1996) characteristics of the "ideal bureaucracy", and Fayol's (1916/1996) "general principles of management", relied heavily upon hierarchy, one-way command structure, top-down decision-making, compartmentalization of units, and specialization of responsibilities and tasks. In later years, in response to the changing and complex needs of contemporary society, recognition of the value of collaboration for achieving organizational goals grew (Friend & Cook, 2000, p. 14). Scepticism emerged surrounding organizational and leadership practices perceived to deny the importance of *human* resources, community building and collaboration. For example, some students of organizational behaviour began to turn their attention to the importance of participative decision making (Follet,

1926/1996) and of tapping into workers' expertise and potential (McGregor, 1957/1996). Early in the 1930s, the Hawthorne studies demonstrated that workers have strong social needs, and that they value cooperation, creative relationships, and feelings of belonging. According to Miles (1965), creating opportunities for workers to share their creativity and expertise would improve decision making and increase their participation and satisfaction. These ideas retain their currency in recent organizational literature. Senge (1994), for example, writes of learning organizations where organizational members are encouraged to channel, cultivate, and learn from each others' ideas and expertise. Leaders, therefore, have been encouraged to jettison traditional management practices for non-hierarchical ones, whereby all workers would contribute, share in the decision making, and achieve their potential in the workplace.

Non-hierarchical leadership styles are described and labelled in various ways. Alternative and more inclusive views of what constitutes a leader are given full consideration in contemporary treatises on leadership in public, private and non-profit organizations (Drucker, 1996). Reconceptualizations include, among others, notions of servant leaders (Greenleaf, 1977/1995; Pollard, 1996), transformational leaders (Burns, 1978/1995; Senge, 1990), principle-centered leaders (Covey, 1991), emotionally intelligent leaders (Goleman, 1998), and distributed leaders (Handy, 1996). These leadership concepts have their educational counterparts (see Blackbourn, 1999/2000; Greenfield, 1980; Hodgkinson, 1991, 1996; Leithwood, 1992; Sarason, 1990; Sergiovanni, 1990, 1996; Starratt, 1993, 1999), particularly in the reconceptualizations of leadership which emphasize "its connection with moral dimensions" (Telford, 1996, p. 8). The notion of collaboration is pivotal in the enactment of these leadership styles. For example, in describing facilitative leadership, Blackbourn (1999/2000) states:

> Collaboration, coordination, internal and external stakeholder feedback, change orientation, development of stakeholder leadership skills, and a democracy-based workplace are all aspects of facilitative leadership (p. 2).

Blackbourn further suggests that a facilitative leadership style is appropriate for developing collaborative partnerships.

Noneducational organizations adopted notions of collaboration primarily because a shift to shared leadership and participative decision making "increases their productivity" (Leithwood, 1992). Friend and Cook (2000) determined that as collaboration is increasingly recognized in "business, industry, and general society, we are also learning to do it in schools" (p. 15). In school organizations, "the role of the principal would remain important, but would take on an investment character aimed at purposing and capacity-building" (Sergiovanni, 1996, p. 7). In this manner, new teachers, students, parents, and other stakeholders become bound by a set of "obligations result[ing] from common commitments to shared values and beliefs" (p. 34). Increasingly, in the context of education, shared governance and democratic decision making have emerged from various studies as conditions which promote the development of a professional learning community (Horn, 1997). Consequently, hierarchy, top-down management, and control have given way to considering other ways of viewing schools as organizations, which include the practice of facilitative or transformational leadership, teacher empowerment, and shared decision making – the so-called 'moral' community. In other words, "community is ... seen as an antidote to bureaucracy, which may be efficient but depersonalizes the important developmental processes and ethical or moral dimensions of organizational life" (Kruse & Louis, 1997, p. 261).

Collaboration may be the key to this reconceptualization of schools as moral communities. DiPardo (1997), for example, suggests that collaboration "may promote the creation of school communities...places that celebrate risk-taking, that encourage teachers to assume the habits of interdependence and shared leadership" (p. 100). Research findings suggest that this is a valid assumption. For instance, the Centre on Organization and Restructuring of Schools (CORS) at the University of Wisconsin conducted a five-year study and concluded in 1996 that "the most important factor in successful school reform is the presence of a strong professional community" (as cited in Horn, 1997, p. 5). In that study, the professional community was determined to be the one where teachers: i) were clear that student learning was the priority; ii) worked collaboratively; and iii) took collective responsibility for achieving that purpose.

Reconceptualizing schools as democratic, professional, collaborative learning communities has significant implications for both the leader and the led in the school community (Horn, 1997). While there is general acknowledgement that there is no one best way to lead (Blackbourn, 1999), advocates of the school-as-community metaphor assert that professional learning communities are more likely to flourish when administrators have an affinity for a non-hierarchical leadership style (Blackbourn, 1999; Fauske, 1999; Horn, 1997; Koehler & Baxter, 1997; Leonard & Leonard, 1999). In other words, a leader can be "a principal, a teacher, a parent, a student, [and] a supporting staff member...as long as they have the capacity...to influence task objectives and strategies, influence commitment and compliance in task behaviour to achieve these objectives, influence group maintenance and identification, and influence the culture of the organization" (Telford, 1996, p. 10). The potential for leadership is distributed throughout the organization, thereby fostering empowerment and moral commitment to a collective purpose.

CONCEPTUALIZING AND CONTEXTUALIZING COLLABORATION

Although collaboration has been given much consideration in the organizational and educational literatures, there is limited consensus regarding its actual meaning in definitive terms. The following is an attempt to explore the various and often ambiguous definitions of collaboration, some of the many forms that collaboration appears to take in schools, and the challenges inherent in attempts to create a collaborative professional learning community. It is notable that the discourse about collaboration often tends to meander in the proximity of its value-laden and moral dimensions.

Defining Collaboration

Defining collaboration may be as difficult as doing it. For instance, Welch (1998) believes that "most educators neither know what collaboration is nor how to practice it" (p. 27). Indeed, at least some of the confusion may be attributed to the complex nature of collaboration itself, as delineated in Schrage's (1995) analogy. Writing from an organizational management perspective, Schrage compares the concept of collaboration with that of romance. Romantic relationships, he suggests, have no clearly defined boundaries, but rather exist on a continuum of interaction from "the simple flirtation to a deep abiding love" (p. 29). Much the same way, collaborative relationships also span a continuum of interaction, ranging from momentary cooperation to deep and abiding commitment. Unlike romance however, collaboration is a purposive relationship based on a need or desire to solve a problem, create, or discover something (p. 29). Schrage defines collaboration as "the process of *shared creation*: two or more individuals with complementary skills interacting to create a shared understanding that none had previously possessed or could have come to on their own" (p. 33). The relationship, therefore, is dynamic, creative and generative, and it may or may not be long lasting.

In the field of education, Friend and Cook (1996; 2000) suggest that collaboration is a style of interpersonal interaction which is distinct from other styles. Other styles include being directive, accommodating, compromising, and competitive. Interpersonal collaboration is "a style for direct interaction between at least two co-equal parties voluntarily engaged in shared decision making as they work toward a common goal" (2000, p. 6). Friend and Cook emphasize that authentic collaboration must be voluntary and, while you can force a group to work together, you can not force group members to adopt a particular style of interaction. Along with being voluntary, collaboration has specific defining characteristics:

- parity among participants
- mutual goal(s)
- shared responsibility for participation -- a *convenient* (not necessarily equal) division of labour
- equal participation in the decision-making
- pooling the resources
- shared accountability for outcomes - whether results are positive or negative

(Friend & Cook, 2000, pp. 6-13).

Similarly, Tiegerman-Farber and Radziewicz (1998), describe the characteristics of a collaborative style in terms of coequality and coparticipation, reciprocity, common goals, and accountability (p. 70). Along with the defining characteristics of collaboration are "emergent" ones: a *belief* in the value of collaboration, a growing *trust* among collaborative partners, and an evolving sense of *community*. These characteristics are considered to be both prerequisites and outcomes of collaboration, and while they must be there to some "discernible degree at the outset of collaborative activity, ...they typically grow and flourish from successful experience with collaboration" (Friend & Cook, 2000, p. 11). In other words, they are both the seed and the harvest of collaboration.

Other definitions are less pithy and assist to obscure our understanding of what collaboration is. This circumstance is at least partially due to the synonymous usage of terminology. For example, Smyth (as cited in Brundrett, 1998, p. 305) defined collegiality as teachers conferring with other teachers. Riordan and da Costa (1996) suggest that collaboration is an aspect or form of collegiality. Similar to Friend and Cook (2000), they assert that teacher collaboration is characterized by joint work and shared responsibility. Moreover, they emphasize the importance of high levels of trust, respect, and mutuality for fostering collaborative relationships.

Some common conceptions of teacher collaboration illustrate various component approaches. Typically included among them is the requisite that collaborative group members: maintain a clear purpose (Knop, LeMaster, Norris, Raudensky, & Tannehill, 1997); be committed (Jordan, 1999; Knop et al., 1997); be selfless (Knop et al., 1997); value diversity (Jordan, 1999; Knop et al., 1997); be both trusting and trustworthy (Jordan, 1999; Walker, 1999); and, be willing to share power (Mankoe, 1996). The moral dimensions of collaboration are evident in these characterizations. In addition, Knop et al. (1997) differentiate between collaborative structure and function, the former "represent[ing] the framework within which two groups come together to form the foundation while the latter, function, is the process connecting these groups into a cohesive, working entity" (p. 177). For Welch (1998), collaboration is "working together [and] involves nothing more than sharing or exchanging tangible and intangible resources to meet a common goal" (p. 28). This exchange of resources is a dynamic interaction which can occur across various subgroups within the school organization (e.g., grades, departments, programs). Pugach and Johnson (1995) provide a broad definition of collaboration, stating that "collaboration occurs when all members of a school's staff are working together and supporting each other to provide the highest quality of curriculum and instruction for the diverse students they serve" (p. 29).

While consensual agreement upon the precise nature of collaborative practice may be elusive, there is an apparent general accord among advocates that it has significant potential for fostering the evolution of community, connectedness, empowerment and moral obligation. Moreover, definitional ambiguity has failed to constrain discussion of the forms of successful collaboration.

Challenges/Inhibitors

There is convincing evidence that achieving measurable success through collaborative initiatives is often a demanding venture. Despite the intense interest, "collaboration is acknowledged to have been one of the most glaring, persistently absent characteristics of teachers' work and the one most in need of being implemented" (Pugach & Johnson, 1995, p. 11). Such an assertion is not particularly surprising, nor is the widely-held conviction that teacher collaboration is a challenge, for there are varying definitions and forms of collaboration. By extension, there are also attendant requisite knowledge, skills, and values that teachers, administrators, and other stakeholders must acquire in the interest of creating a collaborative culture (Brundrett, 1998; Johnston & Hedeman, 1994; Jordan, 1999; Leonard, 1999a, 1999b). Still, it is necessary to understand why collaborative practice is seemingly so difficult. Without understanding the nature of those inherent barriers, "teachers and teacher educators are doomed to failure and frustration in their efforts to promote collaboration" (Welch, 1998, p. 31).

One reason for the challenge of collaboration may be found in the teachers themselves. Sergiovanni and Starratt (as cited in Koehler & Baxter, 1997) assert that teachers may be "found on a continuum that ranges not from hierarchical to collaborative but from most hierarchical to least hierarchical" (p. 8-9). Therefore, decentralized structural arrangements implemented in schools are, in and of themselves, insufficient for fostering collaborative practice. Effective collaboration involves a "sophisticated set of skills that enable people to share ideas in accepting and nonthreatening ways, to be encouraged and cooperatively analytic, in essence to create the kind of synergy that results in increased organizational effectiveness" (Koehler & Baxter, 1997, p. 12). It is important not to underestimate the level of skill required to maintain "an autonomous identity...[while yielding] some autonomy in the pursuit of partnership goals" (Mankoe, 1996, p. 12). Without doubt, this requires considerable "micropolitical" (Riordan & da Costa, 1996) astuteness, a condition which may not always be existent in school leaders.

Leonard and Leonard (1999) reported that a majority of teachers actually considered "collaboration-by-design", which is undertaken in formal structures such as school committees, to have minimal effect in terms of promoting innovation and program improvement. Additionally, in an examination of the collaborative process in the implementation of team teaching and committees at an elementary school, Leonard (1997; 1999b) uncovered a number of inhibitors to collaboration. These inhibitors, or barriers, centered around issues of teacher efficacy, time constraints, fragmented vision, competitiveness, and conflict avoidance. Other studies of collaboration address similar findings (DiPardo, 1997; Knop et al., 1997; Kruse & Louis, 1997; Louis & Kruse, 1995; Welch, 1998). Moreover, burnout, not sharing the workload, insufficient budget allocations, and limited resources (Knop et al., 1997), feeling threatened and reluctant to open up one's classrooms (Allen & Calhoun, 1998), and lack of support from administration (Lehr, 1999) all constitute potential barriers to collaboration. The variety of barriers reported in the research into collaboration underscore the range and intensity of problems teachers face when confronted with collaborative initiatives.

Another aspect, which to this point has only been addressed in terms of being a prerequisite and emergent characteristic (Friend & Cook, 2000) but is instrumental to successful collaborative practice, is the magnitude of the role trust plays in such human relationships. As Short and Greer (1997) caution, however, its incorporation is not a simple task:

> Trust building is a slow process that requires disclosure, authenticity of work and action, following through with meeting the needs of each other, respect for diversity, enabling teachers to take action in a risk-taking environment without fear of reprisal, and basic ethical actions that demonstrate a concern for the well-being of others (p. 145).

Short and Greer further contend that it is the school principal who plays a key role in building a trusting environment, and that administrators have to "walk the talk" by encouraging teachers to be risk-takers, by being genuine in their belief in participatory decision making, and by actively working alongside the others as true colleagues. Principals with such a leadership style "trusted others and earned reciprocal trust" (p. 53).

THE ROLE OF THE TEACHER IN ESTABLISHING CULTURES OF COLLABORATION AND COMMUNITY

Emerging from the literature is the recognition of teachers' vital role in achieving and maintaining a collaborative school culture. As noted earlier, traditional teacher practice has been characterized more by individualism and isolationism than it has been by collaborative orientations. There is also an accompanying widespread recognition that when teachers have common educational goals and hold similar beliefs and values about education, there are greater tendencies to move collaborative practices (for example, see Hord, 1997; Louis, 1994; Midley & Wood, 1993; Mitchell, 1995; Odden & Wohlstetter, 1995; O'Neill, 1995). Consequently, careful consideration needs to be given to the nature and extent of teachers' fidelity and commitment to a collaborative professional culture. Although numerous studies and ruminations have addressed the apparent benefits of professional sharing - in terms of organizational improvement, professional development, and student outcomes - there seems to have been limited inquiry into how teachers themselves perceive the power of collaboration for establishing a culture of community, connectedness, and moral commitment. This gap in the literature was the impetus for the authors' most recent research, reported in detail elsewhere (see Leonard & Leonard, 2001), which focused on teacher beliefs and practices pertaining to the collaborative dimensions of school culture.

Central to the premise of the Leonard and Leonard (2001) research into teachers' collaborative beliefs and practices is the pivotal role of values in the lives and interactions of educational stakeholders (Beck, 1996; Begley, 1996; Campbell-Evans, 1993; Greenfield, 1986; Hodgkinson, 1996; Roche, 1997). Moreover, these values are considered to be manifested in both tangible and as well intangible ways (Caldwell & Spinks, 1992; Schein, 1990) and, conceivably, beliefs and values pertaining to the benefits of collaboration may differ widely among members of a school community. Additionally, respective beliefs may not only differ, but may be incompatible with establishing a collaborative culture. Teachers who espouse a commitment to collaboration may merely, in Senge's (1990) and Fullan's (1992) terms, be compliant. Therefore, in order to etch a clearer picture of how to arrive at a *culture* of collaboration, the authors deemed it important to better understand if teachers actually *value* the collaborative process. An initial step in understanding the nature and function of values in the success or failure of collaborative initiatives is to examine how and to what extent those beliefs are reflected in actual, common practice in the workplace. Consequently, the aforementioned study of 565 teachers in a Western Canadian setting was guided by two main questions:

1. To what extent do teachers value collaborative practices in schools?
2. To what extent do teachers perceive collaborative processes are actually occurring in their schools?

Schein's (1984, 1990, 1992) framework for understanding the underlying dimensions of organizational culture was considered to be a useful tool for structuring this study into teachers' value orientations toward collaboration. Using Schein's framework, the researchers developed a 55-item survey questionnaire which contained Likert-scale items addressing four major dimensions of collaborative culture. Paired questions addressed teachers' beliefs and practices pertaining to collaboration in terms of these four dimensions: the nature of teacher activity, the nature of teacher relationships, the nature of decision making and conflict resolution, and the nature of teacher time.

The investigation was designed to provide a vehicle for teachers to voice their perspectives both in terms of what they believed about professional collaboration, as well as the extent to which they considered it to be an actual factor evident in their schools. Comparisons of espoused beliefs to teacher perceptions of actual conditions in their schools re-affirmed some popular conceptions, but also revealed a number of disturbing factors and circumstances which may act to severely curtail the realization of intentions. An analysis of the emergent data allowed the researchers to identify four essential findings pertaining to the selected collaborative dimensions:

1. Teachers perceived less collaboration occurring in their schools than they considered desirable.
2. Teachers espoused the desire for expanded roles and professional relationships in terms of decision-making and collaborative practice, but felt that current school circumstances were curtailing such developments.
3. With the possible exception of sensitivity to individual student needs and interests, the teachers felt that inadequate worth was given to school diversity in terms of values, beliefs, conflict resolution processes, and consensus building.
4. Although teachers demonstrated strong convictions that professional collaboration was an appropriate use of their time, they felt that they were unable to partake in such processes to the extent desirable and necessary.

Participants in this study professed robust support for the overriding concept that professional practice and teacher activity *should* be highly collaborative. This is an important revelation. Articulating a belief in the value of collaboration is at least a good starting point from which to establish a collaborative culture. Arguably, collaboration would be less likely to occur if teachers did not desire to collaborate. In terms of teachers' beliefs about the nature of professional relationships, teachers in this study believed that teaching should be based upon co-operation and teamwork; however, they perceived their schools to be characterized by competition and individualism to greater degrees than desirable. Teachers also saw the condition of people "liking" each other as being important to collaborative ventures. Accordingly, they felt that professional collaboration would be enhanced if there was a greater affinity among teachers. Yet, they were less inclined to see evidence of that in their own schools. Moreover, the data suggested that the respondents' schools were not characterized by the kind of trusting, caring environments deemed conducive for collaborative activities.

The findings in this study regarding teachers' beliefs about decision making and conflict resolution suggested that, while they believed that schools function better when teachers share common values and beliefs, they also agreed that divergent opinions and practices were indicative of a healthy organization. Moreover, there was substantially low inclination that the wishes of the majority should be imposed upon the individual. The implication embedded in this finding is significant: While teachers believed it was desirable to hold common beliefs, the importance of which is supported elsewhere in the literature (Hord, 1997; Louis, 1994; Midley & Wood, 1993; Mitchell, 1995; Odden & Wohlsetter, 1995; O'Neill, 1995), they did not express agreement that majority beliefs should be imposed. This would indicate that respondents in general believed in a democratic process for negotiating and reconciling conflicting beliefs and values that may be reflected in diverse groups.

Furthermore, there was strong support for the notion that expending time on collaborative practices was appropriate. Not surprisingly, in light of findings from previous studies, there was also emphatic recognition that teachers were not allotted sufficient time to partake in collaboration. Teachers believed that they were not expected to use their time in collaborative ventures to the extent most regarded to be desirable.

IMPLICATIONS OF FINDINGS FOR THEORY, RESEARCH, AND PRACTICE

Inasmuch as theory, research, and practice inform one other in complex and dynamic ways, the following implications of the reported cumulative research findings and consequent deliberations are also interrelated. This synthesis and evaluation have significance for those interested in creating collaborative school communities, suggesting that we need to focus on the following: i) increasing our *knowledge* of collaboration - what it is and what it looks like; ii) articulating our understanding of collaboration *skills* - what they are and how to develop them; and iii) uncovering our *values* and *beliefs* about collaboration - what they are and how they influence the collaborative process.

Knowledge of Collaboration

A review of the literature on collaboration highlights the varying and often ambiguous definitions of collaboration. It is important for advocates of collaboration to continually clarify, define, and refine the concept on the basis of theoretical discussions, research findings, and informed practice. A working conceptualization or definition of collaboration is necessary for focusing our continued research efforts. We know from previous studies of schools that norms of collaboration need to be encouraged by site principals (Rosenholtz, 1989) and that principals are deemed pivotal for influencing a school's culture (Deal & Peterson, 1991). Additionally, the implications of the findings suggest that additional research is needed in terms of addressing the role of principal in setting expectations for creating collaborative cultures and facilitating teacher commitment, as opposed to teacher compliance to organizational goals (Senge, 1990). Furthermore, if schools are to emerge as truly moral communities of mutual commitment and democratic principles, it is those in administrative standing who must provide the thrust toward the institutional vision founded in member empowerment.

Increasing demands for heightened teacher involvement in decision-making and its attendant acceptance of both the inherent obligations and responsibilities necessitate consideration of applicable skills which would prepare practitioners with limited related experience to assume these emerging roles. Horn (1997), for example, suggests that the "transformation of teaching from an occupation into a profession creates new leadership roles for teachers who wish to stay in the classroom but are willing to take on additional assignments" (p. 4). Horn recommends that teachers be provided with necessary leadership development opportunities, and that they be compensated for their extra work and responsibilities. Moreover, creative structural and operational policies, which promote and support such high density involvement and the development of schools as professional communities, need to be adopted. It is also necessary to increase understanding and knowledge of how to address the ubiquitous issue of time, or the lack thereof. It is important to seriously consider ways to counteract the microsystemic influences, such as the highly bureaucratic structure of schools (Welch, 1998), which result in rigid scheduling of timetables and insufficient time for teachers to collaborate. If, as the authors' research suggests, teachers have the *will*, there remains the necessity to further explore the *means* and to customize it for maximum local potential.

Skills of Collaboration

Effective collaboration requires sophisticated skills which do not simply materialize when teachers come together, either voluntarily or otherwise. Collaborative skills need development. If collaborative endeavours are to meet with any degree of success, then teachers need to develop proficiency in consensus building, decision making, and the processes of conflict resolution, whereby the means become as important as the ends. How teachers interact with each other to resolve differences, to arrive at consensus and to share visions, has significant implications for the endurance of collaborative relationships. In the effort to collaborate, principals *and* teachers must work together to clarify their vision, to intensify efforts to be reflective, to develop problem solving skills, and to concentrate on improving their conflict resolution strategies (Fullan, 1992).

It is important to persist in the development of theory and to conduct research designed to improve our knowledge and understanding of collaboration, but it is also imperative to continue to examine current practice, particularly in teacher preparation programs. Although it is commonly felt that college and university pre-service programs have made notable strides in providing opportunities for students to become immersed in teaching, it remains to be determined how effectively they are being prepared to collaborate with other practitioners. The manner and extent to which opportunities are provided for prospective teachers to balance the largely autonomous goals of empowerment and self-efficacy with community goals of joint work and collaboration may yet be largely undefined. Such considerations remain largely in the domain of how schools are perceived in terms of actor relationships, the nature of the roles individuals assume, and the extent to which schools are valued as professional communities.

Values of Collaboration

The reported survey research (Leonard & Leonard, 2001) into teachers' espoused beliefs about collaboration and their perceptions of practice may be an initial step in understanding the nature and function of values in the success or failure of collaborative initiatives. The findings suggested that teachers, in general, espoused beliefs that are deemed conducive to the development of a collaborative culture; however, the findings also suggested that teachers, in general, did not perceive their schools to be characterized by collaborative practice. This may be because teachers' espoused values are in conflict with their basic assumptions about collaboration, or perhaps the barriers to collaboration may have inhibited collaborative practice. Further research is required to better understand the relationship between espoused values and basic assumptions, and their influence on collaborative practice and the development of schools as moral communities.

Moreover, the relationship between establishing a climate of trust and creating a culture of collaboration also needs researcher attention. If trust is indeed "the foundation for shared governance and teacher empowerment" (Blase & Blase, 1994, p. 18), then we need to focus our attention on how trust may help overcome many of the previously described barriers to collaboration, particularly those issues related to self-efficacy, conflict avoidance, and competitiveness. The implications of the significance of trust for dismantling barriers to collaboration are fairly obvious for exploring ways to engender trust in collaborative partnerships.

Teachers play an important role in the gradual development of trusting, collaborative relationships (daCosta & Riordan, 1996). Maintaining one's personal integrity in interacting with colleagues spawns trust. Demonstrating loyalty to colleagues does not have to be at the expense of sacrificing or compromising one's pedagogical beliefs. When teachers are collegial and loyal, they will more likely trust each other to disagree on the basis of ideology and pedagogy, not personal characteristics. Moreover, as Fullan and Hargreaves (1991) suggest, teachers need to cultivate their sensitivity to others' perspectives and circumstances.

CONCLUSION: THE CREDIBILITY FACTOR

It is said that the best leaders lead by example (Kouzes & Posner, 1987). When people act upon the values they espouse, they lead by example, and they are credible. Credible leaders are able to engender "trust and commitment" in others (Ulrich, 1996, p. 215). Accordingly, in order to realize schools as moral communities and collections of individuals bonded together by "natural will" (Sergiovanni, 1996, p. 48) and shared knowledge, skills, and values, all members -- and particularly principals -- will need to practice their espoused beliefs about collaboration. Principals will need to engender trust, be facilitators of decision making, and provide support in the interest of developing a safe environment where members are encouraged to take responsibility and to be accountable. Teachers will need to do the same if they are to gain credibility for the values they espouse or try to impart to their students. How to arrive at this collective goal requires continued deliberations about, and research into, collaboration as key to the development of a professional learning community.

In conclusion, and in consideration of the preceding discussions, we offer a provisional prescription for school success through collaborative practice that may allow us to move past the *reverie* and further into the realm of *remedy*. The prescription is in three parts; but only together can they comprise a cogent whole. First of all, decide what professional collaborative practice is in its most basic and its most sophisticated forms. Then, strive for only the latter. Second, make collaborative practice in schools a genuine priority, not an add-on. Provide teachers with substantial and ongoing development in the conceptions of shared professional work, as well as substantial opportunities for meaningful application. Third, strongly believe that professional learning communities can only exist in an environment that not only espouses values of collaborative practice, but which is also committed to cultivating a climate of trust founded in professional regard, personal respect, and shared commitment to common goals. Without freedom from fear of failure and retribution, without assurance that support and encouragement are implicit and explicit, without confidence that what teachers are doing through collaborative practice is both admired and beneficial, sustained teacher collaboration as a norm of behaviour -- not just normative behaviour -- is doubtful. The emergent effect may be the sustenance of schools that are characterized less by true elements of the moral community than they are by those that reflect a desire to create the image of being so.

NOTES

[1] This chapter is a revised and updated version of a paper previously published as an article in a special issue (Vol. 4, No. 4, 353-365) of the *International Journal of Leadership in Education* (2001).

REFERENCES

Allen, L., & Calhoun, E.F. (1998). Schoolwide action research: Findings from six years of study. *Phi Delta Kappan, 79*(9), 706-710.

Beck, C. (1996, September). *Values, school renewal and educational leadership.* Paper presented at the Toronto Conference on Values and Educational Leadership, Toronto.

Begley, P.T. (1996). Cognitive perspectives on values in administration: A quest for coherence and relevance. *Educational Administration Quarterly, 32*(3), 403-426.

Blackbourn, J.M. (1999). *Leadership for the new millennium: Lessons from Deming, Glasser, and Graves, Volume 17E, No. 4* Available at http://www.nationalforum.com/15blackbourn.htm

Blase, J., & Blase, J.R. (1994). *Empowering teachers.* Thousand Oaks, CA: Corwin Press.

Burns, J.M. (1978/1995). Transactional and transformational leaders. In J.T. Wren (Ed.), *The leader companion: Insights on leadership through the ages* (pp. 100-101). New York: The Free Press.

Brundrett, M. (1998). What lies beyond collegiality, legitimation or control? An analysis of the purported benefits of collegial management in education. *Educational Management & Administration, 26*(3), 305-316.

Caldwell, B.J., & Spinks, J.M. (1992). *Leading the self-managing school.* London: Falmer Press.

Campbell-Evans, G. (1993). A values perspective on school-based management. In C. Dimmock (Ed.), *School-based management and school effectiveness* (pp. 92-113). London, Routledge.

Covey, S.R. (1991). *Principle-centered leadership*. New York: Summit Books.

da Costa, J. L., & Riordan, G. (1996, June) *Teacher collaboration: Developing a trusting relationship*. Paper presented at the annual meeting of the Canadian Society for the Study of Education, St. Catharines.

Deal, T.E., & Peterson, K.D. (1991). *The principal's role in shaping school culture*. Washington, DC: US Department of Education.

DiPardo, A. (1997). Of war, doom, and laughter: Images of collaboration in the public-school workplace. *Teacher Education Quarterly, 24*(1), 89-104.

Drucker, P.F. (1996). Not enough generals were killed. In F. Hesselbein, M. Goldsmith, & R. Beckhard (Eds.), *The leader of the future*(pp. xi-xv). San Francisco, CA: Jossey-Bass.

Fauske, J.R. (1999, November). *Organizational conditions that sustain collaboration and encourage trust*. Paper presented at the University Council of Educational Administration Convention, Minneapolis.

Fayol, H. (1916/1996). General principles of management. In J. M. Shafritz & J. S. Ott (Eds.), *Classics of organization theory, fourth edition* (pp. 52-65). Albany, NY: Wadsworth Publishing Company.

Follet, M.P. (1926/1996). The giving of orders. In J. M. Shafritz & J. S. Ott (Eds.), *Classics of organization theory, fourth edition* (pp. 156-162). Albany, NY: Wadsworth Publishing Company.

Friend, M., & Cook, L. (1996). *Interactions: Collaboration skills for school professionals, second edition*. White Plains: Longman.

Friend, M., & Cook, L. (2000). *Interactions: Collaboration skills for school professionals, third edition*. New York: Longman.

Fullan, M. (1992). Visions that blind. *Educational Leadership, 49*(5), 19-20.

Fullan, M., & Hargreaves, A. (1991). *What's worth fighting for? Working together for your school*. Toronto: Ontario Public School Teachers Federation.

Goleman, D. (1998). What makes a leader? *Harvard Business Review, 76*(6), 93-102.

Greenfield, T.B. (1986). The decline and fall of science in educational administration. *Interchange, 17*(2), 57-80.

Greenfield, T.B. (1980). The man who comes back through the door in the wall: Discovering the truth, discovering self, discovering organizations. *Educational Administration Quarterly, 16* (3), 26-59.

Greenleaf, R. (1977/1995). Servant leadership. In T.J. Wren (Ed.), *The leader's companion: Insights on leadership through the ages* (pp. 18-23). New York: The Free Press.

Handy, C. (1996). The new language of organizing and its implications for leaders. In F. Hesselbein, M. Goldsmith, & R. Beckhard (Eds.), *The leader of the future*(pp. 3-9). San Francisco, CA: Jossey-Bass.

Hodgkinson, C. (1991). *Educational leadership: The moral art*. Albany, NY: SUNY Press.

Hodgkinson, C. (1996). *Administrative philosophy: Values and motivations in administrative life*. New York: Pergamon.

Hord, S. (1997). *Professional learning communities: Communities of continuous inquiry and improvement*. Austin, TX: Southwest Educational Development Laboratory.

Horn, C. (1997). *Teacher professionalism and leadership-catalysts of school reform*. Available at http://www.teachnet.org/docs/Network/PolicyInstitute/Research/Leadership/Horn/html

Johnston, S., & Hedeman, M. (1994). With devolution comes collaboration, but it's easier said than done. *School Organization, 14* (2), 195-207.

Jordan, C. F. (1999). Using collaborative action teams to create community schools. *NASSP Bulletin, 83*(611), 48-56.

Knop, N., LeMaster, K., Norris, M., Raudensky, J., & Tannehill, D. (1997). What we have learned through collaboration: A summary report from a National Teacher Education Conference. *The Physical Educator, 54* (4), 170-179.

Koehler, M., & Baxter, J. C. (1997). *Leadership through collaboration: Alternatives to the hierarchy*. Larchmont, NY: Eye on Education.

Kouzes, J., & Posner, B. (1987). *The leadership challenge*. San Francisco, CA: Jossey-Bass.

Kruse, S. D., & Louis, K. S. (1997). Teacher teaming in middle schools: Dilemmas for a schoolwide community. *Educational Administration Quarterly, 33* (3), 261-289.

Lehr, A. E. (1999). The administrative role in collaborative teaching. *NASSP Bulletin, 83*(611), 105-111.

Leithwood, K. (1992). The move toward transformational leadership. *Educational Leadership, 49* (5), 8-12.

Leonard, P.E. (1997). *Understanding the dimensions of school culture: An investigation into educators' value orientations and value conflicts.* OISE/University of Toronto: Unpublished doctoral dissertation.

Leonard, P.E. (1999a). Understanding the dimensions of school culture: Value orientations and value conflicts. *Journal of Educational Administration and Foundations, 13*(2), 27-53.

Leonard, P.E. (1999b). Inhibitors to collaboration. In P.T. Begley & P. E. Leonard (Eds.), *The values of educational administration* (pp. 84-105). London: Falmer Press.

Leonard, L.J., & Leonard, P.E. (1999). Reculturing for collaboration and leadership. *Journal of Educational Research, 92*(4), 237-242.

Leonard, P.E., & Leonard, L.J. (2001). Assessing aspects of collaboration in schools: Beliefs versus practices. *Alberta Journal of Educational Research, 47*(1), 4-23.

Little, J. (1982). Norms of collegiality and experimentation. *American Educational Research Journal, 19*(3), 325-340.

Louis, K.S. (1994). Beyond managed change: Rethinking how schools improve. *School Effectiveness and School Improvement, 5*(1), 2-24.

Louis, K.S., & Kruse, S.D. (1995). *Professionalism and community: Perspectives on reforming urban schools.* Thousand Oaks, CA: Corwin Press.

Louis, K.S., Marks, H., & Kruse, S.D. (1994, April). *Teachers; professional community in restructuring schools.* Paper presented at the annual meeting of the American Educational Research Association, New Orleans.

Mankoe, J.O. (1996, June). *Building partnerships: A strategy in resource mobilization for public education.* Paper presented at the annual meeting of the Canadian Society for the Study of Education, St. Catharines.

McGregor, D.M. (1957/1996). The human side of enterprise. In J. M. Shafritz & J. S. Ott (Eds.), *Classics of organization theory, fourth edition* (pp. 176-182). Albany, NY: Wadsworth Publishing Company.

Midley, C., & Wood, S. (1993). Beyond site-based management: Empowering teachers to reform schools. *Phi Delta Kappan, 75*(3), 245-252.

Miles, R.E. (1965). Human relations or human resources? *Harvard Business Review, 43*(4), 149-156.

Mitchell, C. (1995, June). *Teachers learning together: Organizational learning in an elementary school.* Paper presented at the annual meeting of the Canadian Society for Studies in Education, Montreal.

Odden, E.R., & Wohlstetter, P. (1995). Making school-based management work. *Educational Leadership, 52*(5), 32-36.

O'Neill, J. (1995). On schools as learning organizations: A conversation with Peter Senge. *Educational Leadership, 52* (7), 20-23.

Pollard, C.W. (1996). The leader who serves. In F. Hesselbein, M. Goldsmith, & R. Beckhard (Eds.), *The leader of the future* (pp. 241-248). San Francisco, CA: Jossey-Bass.

Pugach, M.C., & Johnson, L.J. (1995). *Collaborative practitioners: Collaborative schools.* Denver, CO: Love Publishing Company.

Riordan, G.P., & da Costa, J.L. (1996, June). *The development, purposes, and features of voluntary collaboration among high school teachers.* Paper presented at the annual meeting of the Canadian Society for Studies in Education, St. Catherines.

Roche, K.W. (1997). *Principals' responses to moral and ethical dilemmas in Catholic school settings.* University of Toronto: Unpublished doctoral dissertation.

Rosenholtz, S.J. (1989). *Teachers' workplace: The social organization of schools.* New York: Longman.

Sarason, S. (1990). *The predictable failure of educational reform.* San Francisco, CA: Jossey- Bass.

Schein, E.H. (1984). Coming to a new awareness of organizational culture. *Sloan Management Review, 25*(2), 1-15.

Schein, E.H. (1990). Organizational culture. *American Psychologist, 45*(2), 109-119.

Schein, E.H. (1992). *Organizational culture and leadership, second edition.* San Francisco, CA: Jossey-Bass.

Schrage, M. (1995). *No more teams! Mastering the dynamics of creative collaboration.* New York: Doubleday.

Senge, P.M. (1990). The leader's new work: Building learning organizations. *Sloan Management Review, 32*(1), 7-23.

Senge, P. (1994). *The fifth discipline: The art and practice of the learning organization.* New York: Currency/Doubleday.

Sergiovanni, T.J. (1990). Adding value to leadership gets extraordinary results. *Educational Leadership, 47*(8), 23-27.

Sergiovanni, T. (1996). *Leadership for the school house*. San Francisco, CA: Jossey-Bass.

Short, P.M., & Greer, J.T. (1997). *Leadership in empowered schools*. Upper Saddle River, NJ: Merrill.

Starratt, R.J. (1993). *The drama of leadership*. London: Falmer Press.

Starratt, R.J. (1999). Moral dimensions of leadership. In P.T. Begley & P.E. Leonard (Eds.), *The values of educational administration* (pp. 22-35). London: Falmer Press.

Taylor, F.W. (1916/1996). The principles of scientific management. In J. M. Shafritz & J. S. Ott (Eds.), *Classics of organization theory, fourth edition* (pp. 66-79). Albany, NY: Wadsworth Publishing Company.

Telford, H. (1996). *Transforming schools through collaborative leadership*. London: Falmer Press.

Tiegerman-Farber, E., & Radziewicz, C. (1998). *Collaborative decision making: The pathway to inclusion*. Upper Saddle River, NJ: Merrill.

Ulrich, D. (1996). Credibility x capability. In F. Hesselbein, M. Goldsmith, & R. Beckhard (Eds.), *The leader of the future* (pp. 209-220). San Francisco, CA: Jossey-Bass.

Walker, K. (1999, October). *The foundations and fragility of trust in school leadership: A symposium overview*. Paper presented at the Convention '99 Contradictions in Accountability University Council for Educational Administration, Minneapolis.

Weber, M. (1922/1996). Bureaucracy. In J. M. Shafritz & J. S. Ott (Eds.), *Classics of organization theory, fourth edition* (pp. 80-85). Albany, NY: Wadsworth Publishing Company.

Welch, M. (1998). Collaboration: Staying on the bandwagon. *Journal of Teacher Education, 49*(1), 26-37.

PART 3:

**CROSS-CULTURAL PERSPECTIVES ON
EDUCATIONAL COMMUNITIES**

ALLAN D. WALKER

DEVELOPING CROSS-CULTURAL PERSPECTIVES ON EDUCATION AND COMMUNITY[1]

Abstract. Anglo-American English-speaking perspectives generally dominate the field of educational administration. Most 'international' studies have tended to skirt the reality that practice and theory are socially constructed and manifestly influenced by the values, beliefs and assumptions school leaders in different cultural contexts carry into their schools. This chapter argues that if educational administration is to be more relevant both within countries and internationally it must take greater notice of how it is conceptualized and practiced in a broader range of cultural settings. The chapter has two major aims. The first argues that the near exclusive grounding of educational administration theory in Anglo-American values and understandings impedes theory development, restricts understandings of practice both between and within different societies and can lead to the cloning of inappropriate policies in some educational systems. The second discusses some key issues to be carefully considered if understanding and research is to proceed in a meaningful manner. The area presents abundant pathways for developing more inclusive understandings of how societal culture influences policy implementation, the practice of educational administration and the micro-relationships and processes within schools.

With few exceptions, perspectives developed predominantly in Anglo-American English-speaking Western societies[2] have long dominated the field of educational administration. Over the last decade, calls have emerged for greater understanding of the field from a cross-cultural perspective (Begley, 2000; Cheng, 1995a; Hallinger & Leithwood, 1996a, 1998; Walker & Dimmock, 2000a). To date, most 'international' studies of educational administration have tended toward somewhat narrow descriptions and analysis of systems, policies and practices in different societies without developing depth understandings of the contexts and cultures within which they reside. Although such studies are useful for fracturing education systems into their constituent elements (structures), their explanatory power is limited as to how processes, or why various elements, interact. They have tended to ignore that practice and theory are socially constructed and manifestly influenced by the values, beliefs and assumptions school leaders in different cultural contexts carry into their schools (Dimmock & Walker, 2000a; Southworth, 2000).

The central theme of this chapter concerns the extent to which the field of educational administration is internationally relevant. It is argued that if the field is to be more relevant it must take greater cognizance of how it is conceptualized and practiced in a broader range of cultural settings. While arguing for a cross-cultural approach to educational administration, the pitfalls of operationalizing such an agenda are acknowledged. The chapter therefore has two general aims. The first is to summarize some of the key components of the case for increasing understanding of the influence of societal culture on educational administration. The guiding argument is that the field of educational administration is largely grounded in Anglo-American values and understandings; this impedes and constrains theory development, restricts understandings of practice both between and within different societies, and can lead to the cloning of inappropriate policies in some

145

P.T. Begley and O. Johansson (eds.), The Ethical Dimensions of School Leadership, 145–160.
© 2003 *Kluwer Academic Publishers. Printed in the Netherlands.*

educational systems. The second aim is to explore a number of conceptual and methodological issues which need to be addressed if such understanding is to progress. These issues include difficulties in defining culture, the dangers of cultural stereotyping and the shifting nature of cultures.

EDUCATIONAL ADMINISTRATION FROM A CROSS CULTURAL PERSPECTIVE

The field of educational administration has traditionally been dominated by Anglo-American theories that have largely ignored indigenous perspectives. Few would argue the ethnocentricity underlying theory development, empirical research and prescriptive argument in the field. While considerable research has been devoted to understanding organizational culture, and to areas such as, cross-cultural learning, international management, and cross-cultural psychology, little attention has been paid to understanding the influence of societal culture on school administration. This is somewhat surprising, given the increasing political and economic interdependence of societies at a global level. Neglecting how educational administration is socially constructed in different cultures denies the reality that much can be learned from contextualizing both its theory and practice in non-Western societies. Indeed, indigenous perspectives may broaden the knowledge base of the field to the benefit of scholars and practitioners alike. Wider exposure to non-Western knowledge and practices can add richness to our knowledge base through exposing alternative ways of thinking and working. As Hallinger and Kantamara (2000) state: "We can only understand the nature of leadership by exposing the hidden assumptions of the cultural context. This will open new windows through which to view educational leadership" (p. 202).

Anglo-American scholars exert a disproportionate influence on theory, development and its subsequent dissemination. Thus, a relatively small number of scholars representing less than eight percent of the world's population purport to represent the rest. Although the knowledge base underpinning educational administration has strengthened in recent years, it remains vulnerable. Theory is generally tentative and needs to be heavily qualified, and much that is written in the field is prescriptive, being reliant on personal judgment and subjective opinion. Empirical studies are rarely cumulative, making it difficult to build systematic bodies of knowledge. Yet despite these serious limitations, rarely do scholars explicitly bound their findings within geo-cultural limits (Dimmock & Walker, 2000b). Claims to knowledge are made on the basis of limited samples as though they have universal application. A convincing case can be mounted for developing middle range theory applying to, and differentiating between, different geo-cultural areas or regions. Such contextually bounded theories may allow us to distinguish, for example, how Chinese or Russian school administration differs from say, American or British.

The hegemony of Anglo-American thinking in educational administration is apparent in standard texts in the field – texts that tend to have an increasing international audience. Almost without exception, such texts are framed by research, theory and practice drawn exclusively from Western English-speaking contexts. Consequently, two adverse effects result from the state of the field as reflected in this Western literature. First, there is an over-reliance on a mono-cultural perspective, which may limit conceptualization and understanding in both Western and non-Western societies alike, through presenting restricted and decontextualized views of educational administration. As noted earlier, there is almost an inherent assumption that worthwhile theory and practice can only emanate from an Anglo-American perspective. Secondly, when this literature is commonly used, for example, in Asian settings to inform administrative theories and practices, academics and practitioners whose societies and cultures bear little similarity to those in which the theories originated often adopt it uncritically. Consequently, such perspectives become the dominant benchmarks for both theory and practice, and are subsequently used to frame research through assumptive bases that may be inappropriate for a given context. Cheng (1995b, p. 2) exemplifies the danger of basing understandings on culturally conceived assumptions when discussing some basic differences between Western and East Asian education systems:

> In typical "Western" systems of education, although practices vary, there is a common core in the philosophy of education that individuals should be developed to the fullest of their capacity. In the individual-community dichotomy, there is a fundamental assumption that the ultimate goal of a nation is no more than serving and satisfying its individual members. Such an assumption is taken for granted in the West, to the extent that alternatives are almost inconceivable.

> In East Asia, the fundamental assumption is almost diametrically different. There, education has always been seen as a national endeavour. Although the "individuals' fullest development" argument appears in most of the stated goals of education, there is always a further goal for individual development, and that is national development. This is equally true in both economically underdeveloped socialist Chinese Mainland and in highly developed capitalist Japan.

The enduring mono-cultural influence on educational administration theory so evident in its major texts also spills over into many university courses in the area, and into leadership preparation and training programs. Such programs throughout the world are often founded on the assumption that management theories can be automatically transferred from one system to another using the same values, theories and learning approaches, regardless of indigenous cultural influences and imperatives. The situation of monocultural understandings driving the field and subsequent training is further compounded by the fact that many Western theories and perspectives were originally generated in the business sector, and then automatically applied to education. Consequently, a further complication arises concerning the cultures of the commercial world and education. The argument can be made that deeper understanding of cultural differences in administrator training (Lomotey, 1995), and indeed for the success of schools in multi-cultural societies, is just as important to increasingly multi-cultural and diverse Western societies as it is to non-Western cultures.

Relying exclusively on theories built in the Western societies, then, not only denies the traditions and understandings of the field in 'far-away' countries, but also those existent within the multi-cultural milieu of Western societies themselves. As Hallinger and Leithwood (1996b) note: "(The) trend towards multiculturalism has implications for the management of schools and for the knowledge base underlying school leadership. It is crucial to understand better how schools can productively accommodate such diversity and the forms of leadership likely to assist such accommodation" (p. 6). In this regard, a cross-cultural approach to educational administration that adopts an international perspective may, in turn, contribute to an understanding of culturally related educational issues in 'home' cultures. Such understanding appears imperative, given the growing global trend towards multi-cultural societies. As such, societies (including the US, Canada, the UK, much of Europe and Australia and an increasing number of societies in Asia, including Hong Kong and Singapore) become more multicultural, demographics change, as do the racial and ethnic compositions of populations. These changes, in turn, are reflected in more culturally diverse school communities and, in some cases, more culturally diverse staff. Children and teachers with widely different cultural backgrounds attend the same schools, sit in the same classes, and experience the same curricula, posing challenges for teachers and school leaders alike. Yet, this important phenomenon, although quite widely discussed in other educational fields, has not attracted sufficient attention among scholars in the field of educational administration.

The exploration of educational administration has, to a large extent, been based on the tendency for policy makers in different societies to ignore the significance of culture in the formulation and adoption of educational policy and its implementation in practice. Policies mandating increased accountability, for example, have permeated strategic and operational policy and planning across the globe. Although the importation of policies and approaches has long existed under the pretence of colonization, in many ways, the trend has become more pronounced, and more subtly inculcated, as a result of globalization. Hallinger and Leithwood (1998) make a strong case for considering the influence of globalization and the easy availability and transferability of knowledge on the practice and understanding of educational administration. They rightly point out that concepts and practices which once held influence within relatively localized domains, now evoke a 'global response' and confront educational administrators in very different settings. In educational terms, one has only to look at the current push toward school-based management throughout a number of Asian societies (Walker & Dimmock, 2000b).

Although there are certainly advantages associated with the wider dissemination of ideas and practices, there often seems an untested assumption that what is developed and thought of as 'good' and 'working' in one setting, will automatically have similar effects in another. As Steingard and Fitzgibbons (1995) note: "Despite its unchallenged and unfettered expansionism, globalization is *not* a value free, natural phenomenon catapulting the world into a pristine state of progress" (p. 31, emphasis in original). Whitty, Power and Halpin (1998) point out that adopting policy across cultures without recognizing their distinctive historical and cultural dimensions risks 'false universalism' (Rose, 1991). In other words, unthinking importation too often concentrates on identifying 'surface' similarities, but does so without reference to the cultures in which the policies or practices were conceived. It should also be noted that the risks of "cross-cultural cloning" (Dimmock & Walker, 1998a) may apply equally between and within apparently similar societies as they do between more obviously diverse cultures. For example,

Seddon (1994, cited in Whitty, Power, & Halpin, 1998) argues that Australia has displayed "a dependent and subservient preoccupation with development in the UK and USA" (p. 4). In short, with the growing internationalization of education policy and practice, it may be considered naive to continue to ignore the significance of non-Western perspectives in the adoption and implementation of educational policy and practice in diverse school contexts.

A tentative move toward greater international understanding of education has stemmed from interest in large-scale comparative studies such as The Third International Mathematics and Science Study (TIMMS) or the numerous studies conducted by the International Association for the Education of Evaluation Achievement (IEA). Such studies normally take the form of separate country studies and the most recent include a number of international surveys conducted on national differences in student achievement (see Reynolds, 2000, for summary of the most influential of these). The focus of these studies has been the extent to which "effective" practices at school and classroom level are the same or are different in different countries. It is clear from these studies that the Pacific Rim societies such as Taiwan, Korea, Japan and Singapore are superior in their education achievement (according to the criteria set by the research). While such studies provide important comparisons, the cultural and cross-cultural explanations remain highly speculative. For example, reasons postulated for superior performance of Pacific Rim countries include the high status given to teachers, the value placed on learning and education, the cultural stress reflecting 'Confucian' beliefs about the role of effort and the high parental aspirations for their children. However, these explanations remain speculative, and much more needs to be done on connecting these characteristics to school performance and indeed to school leadership.

The findings of recent international comparative studies have induced an interesting 'reverse' trend - one that advocates the adoption of "effective" practices from, particularly, the Pacific Rim countries to English-speaking western countries. On the grounds of school improvement this tendency is understandable and even laudable; however, such 'reverse cloning' is fraught with the same hazards as those accompanying the unthinking importation of Western policies and practices. It raises problems with regard to the extent to which "effective" practices are culture based. If they are culture sensitive, then recommendations that a particular policy or practice be transposed from one society to another must surely take into account the full cultural and contextual conditions of both host and adopting systems. A further concern relates to which of the school improvement factors mentioned in the cross-national studies are in fact related to culture. For example, is the fact that Korean and Taiwanese students spend 222 days in school a year (Reynolds, 2000), compared to 192 days for students in England, a cultural or an institutional phenomenon? Furthermore, even if it is an institutional factor, may that not ultimately reduce to being cultural? Such complex questions provide support for expanding the exploration of educational administration from a cross-cultural perspective.

In conclusion, it is important to conceptualize educational administration more broadly through recognizing that it is practiced throughout the world, not just in countries dominated by Judaeo-Christian traditions and values. It is restrictive and perhaps arrogant to assume that worthwhile theory and practice can only flow 'one-way'. There is a need to gear analysis to pluralistic rather than singular perspectives and to dig "deeper" into organizational phenomena in different contexts, in order to distinguish phenomena which are disguised or hidden by apparent surface similarities. Schools in different countries, for example, seem to be similarly organized. This similarity of appearance, however, often disguises subtle differences of purpose, meaning, process, effect and outcome. Begley (2000) labels this phenomenon as 'cultural isomorphs', which he defines as "social positions or value postures that appear to share the same shape or meaning in different countries but actually consist of quite different elements" (p. 23). An examination of educational administration in a broader array of cultural contexts can help expose the more intimate aspects of school organization and leadership.

Among the reasons why a stronger cross-cultural emphasis has not taken root in educational administration is the area is fraught with challenges and pitfalls. For example, the very nature of culture itself, at whatever level it is discussed, makes it open to debate and laden with difficulty. After explaining briefly why societal culture is a useful concept for exploring educational administration in diverse contexts, the following section discusses a number of the issues and pitfalls that need to be addressed by scholars interested in the area.

ISSUES FOR CONSIDERATION ABOUT CULTURE

Organizational culture has become widely recognized and an increasingly studied concept in educational administration. Culture at the societal level, however, has not received similar attention. Cheng (1995) challenges this neglect and bemoans the fact that most research in the field makes little reference to larger macro-societal, or national cultural configurations. Since culture is reflected in all aspects of school life, and people, organizations and societies share differences and similarities in terms of their cultures, it appears a useful concept with universal application - one appropriate for exploring influences and practices endemic to educational administration. Since culture exists at multiple levels (school and sub-school, local, regional and societal) it provides rich opportunities for exploring their interrelationships, such as between schools and their micro-and macro-environments. It also helps identify characteristics across organizations that have surface similarity but are quite different in *modus operandi.*

Understanding educational administration through a cross-cultural guise, however, is easier said than done. The concept of culture itself, for example, has generated multiple definitions and ambiguities. Alone, it does not have the explanatory power to account for all of the differences between schools in different societies or regions. Economic, political, geographic religious and demographic factors, for example, may play a key role. Cultures more often than not do not equate with national boundaries. These and a number of other issues cloud its utility and form a basis for ongoing debate. Many of these issues result from the fact that culture is difficult to handle both politically and emotionally. "It (culture) is also difficult to deal with intellectually because there are problems of definition and measurement and because cause and effect relationships between culture and other variables like policies, institutions....run in both directions" (Harrison, 2000, p. xxxii).

The Definition of Culture

The concept of culture itself is nebulous (Brislin, 1993). There appears to be only general agreement in the literature on a definition of culture. Perhaps the most widely adopted definition comes from anthropology and holds that culture consists of the ideals, values and assumptions that are widely shared among people that guide specific behaviour. This or similar definitions are most commonly used in cross-cultural studies in the field of international management and cross-cultural psychology. Others endorse more expansive definitions. Lewellen (1992, as cited in Heck, 1998) suggests two ways of conceiving culture. The first is in line with the definition provided above - emphasizing more traditional and enduring characteristics - whereas the second conceptualizes culture as an adaptive system where, "...groups adapt to the challenges of their particular environment" (Heck, 1998, p. 61). Sharp and Gopinathan (2000) adopt a socio-political perspective of societal culture. They argue, for example, that societal culture, "...can be understood as an evolving mix of what we term 'traditional' and 'modernizing' cultures, which are in turn complexly related to dominant political and economic processes" (p. 88). This perspective embraces a 'middle' view of culture – one that takes a position between culturalists and modernists (the latter including many economists and 'rational choice' political scientists).

In general terms, culturalists (such as Fukuyama) hold that "contemporary societies are characterized by distinctive cultural traits that have endured over long periods of time" (Inglehart, 2000, p. 81) – and that these traits have an important impact on all aspects of society. Modernists, on the other hand, hold that the world is changing in ways that erode traditional values, and that globalization will inevitably minimize cultural differences. Daniel Patrick Moynihan captured the debate between these two positions (cited in Harrison, 2000, p. xiv) when he stated: "The central conservative truth is that it is culture, not politics, that determines the success of a society. The central liberal truth is that politics can change a culture and save it from itself".

While it would be foolhardy to suggest that culture is the only influence on people or organizations, it may be equally hazardous when searching for cultural influence on school administration to adopt too broad a definition of culture. The question then becomes one of which definition of culture to adopt. While not discounting broader definitions, much initial work in the area has opted for the traditional anthropological definition prevalent in the literature (Walker & Dimmock, 2000c; Hallinger & Leithwood 1998, Cheng & Wong, 1996). This appears in line with conceptions of culture used to guide organizational culture studies in the field. For example, Mitchell and Willower (1992) define culture as "the way of life of a given collectivity (or organization) particularly as reflected in shared values, norms, symbols and traditions" (p. 6). And Tierney (1996, p. 372) sees culture as "those informal codes and shared assumptions of individuals who participate in an organization. All of an organization's members shape and are shaped by the symbols and rituals of the organization." Arguments for using a more focused definition have also been made outside of education. For example, the argument is made eloquently by cultural pluralist Shweder (2000, p. 164) who describes himself as a confusionist. "A "confusionist" believes that the knowledge world is incomplete if seen from any one point of view, incoherent if seen from all points of view at once, and empty if seen from "nowhere in particular". Shweder (2000) continues: "Given the choice between incompleteness, incoherence and emptiness, I opt for incompleteness while staying on the move between different ways of seeing and valuing the world" (p. 164).

In the field of international and cross-cultural business management, Hofstede (1991) also supports the notion of beginning with a more focused, anthropological definition of culture when he addresses the concept specifically from a national or societal perspective. Hofstede defines culture as, "patterns of thinking, feeling and acting" underpinning "the collective programming of the mind which distinguishes the members of one group or category of people from another" (pp. 4-5). The "patterns of thinking, feeling and acting" included in this definition raise the likelihood that culture will simultaneously influence, and be influenced by, organizational structures and processes, since both are subject to people's thoughts and actions (Lau, McMahon, & Woodman, 1996). The "collective programming of the mind" refers to the shared beliefs, values, and practices of a group of people, whether that group is a society, nation state, or organization. Building on the work of Hofstede, Trompenaars and Hampden-Turner (1997) suggest, "culture is the way in which a group of people solves problems and reconciles dilemmas" (p. 6). These authors suggest that cultures distinguish themselves from others in how different groups of people approach and solve problems.

CULTURAL DIVERGENCE OR CONVERGENCE

Taken to the level of the individual school, the debate over how culture should be defined raises the question of whether culture on its own is sufficient to explain differences between school administrators, teachers and schools as organizations in different societies. Stated another way, the question is whether organizations, such as schools, are culture bound or culture free (Trice & Beyer, 1993). The main debate in the literature at the organizational level is between proponents of either convergence or divergence. Mirroring the wider debate, proponents of convergence believe that organizations are largely culture-free and therefore similar across societal cultures. In short, the processes of organizing and using technologies make certain universal requirements on organizations, thereby inducing the cultures themselves to become more similar over time. Conversely, the reasons why organizations may be thought to be culture bound, and therefore divergent (as espoused by culturalists), are that their internal cultures and formal structures reflect their external environmental cultures. In this event, differences persist because of unique histories, traditions, expectations, resources, demography, stage of development, and cultural inertia (Trice & Beyer, 1993).

'Culturalists', Wilkinson (1996) claims, have a tendency to attribute rather simplistically any residual unexplained phenomena to culture and to ignore 'institutionalist' arguments that it is primarily historical and political conditions that shape organizations. The argument may not be as dichotomous as some claim and an exclusive concentration on either perspective may risk constructing an incomplete picture. Culture interacts with economic, political and sociological factors to shape organizations such as schools. The separation and search, therefore, for any type of causality may, in itself, be too facile given the synchronous relationships between culture and other societal influences. Hofstede (1996) makes this very case when challenging the common sociological-institutionalist argument. He states:

> Institutions do differ. By why do they differ? In attempting to understand institutional differences, one needs history, and in understanding history one needs culture. Culture is at the root of institutional arrangements, and even if the sociologist does not dare to venture historical/cultural explanations, cultural differences appear as a consequence of institutional differences.....thinking is affected by the kind of family they grew up in, the kind of school they went to, the kind of authorities and legal system they are accustomed to. The causality between institutions and culture is circular: they cannot be separated (p. 531).

Specificity of Definition

At a less theoretical and macro level, the methodological conundrum that emerges from problems with defining culture exposes a tension between taking a fragmented or a monolithic view of culture. The monolithic view assumes culture to be ubiquitous, thereby elevating a particular conception of culture and creating a risk of over-generalization, making comparisons precarious. As Harrison (2000, p. xv) warns, "If culture includes everything, it explains nothing". A fragmented and localized interpretation of culture, on the other hand, through recognizing multiple sub-cultures and failing to draw any form of generalization, may equally fail to provide valid comparison. The problem here is to seek generalization while at the same time taking into account the specificity of cultural conditions. Research adopting an either/or view, on the one hand, risks conclusions made at too high a level of generality, or, on the other hand, conclusions so micro-specific that they offer no opportunity for generalization.

One response to problems such as this has been to make a distinction between culture-common and culture-specific concepts (Brislin, 1993). Culture-common concepts (etics) can be found among people from different societies and cultures; for example, all societies seek to socialize children, or to build harmonious relationships in an effort to prevent violence. Culture-specific (emics) concepts are additions or variants on culture-common concepts and tend to deal, for example, with *how* different cultures socialize children. As Brislin (1993, p. 71) explains: "...culture specific concepts represent different ways that people deal with culture-general demands". Cross-cultural researchers in other fields have tended to focus on a combination of culture-common and –specific concepts, "both of which are necessary for an understanding of culture and cultural differences" (p. 71).

Cultural Baselines

A related difficulty when using culture as a basis for increasing understanding of education administration is to assume that culture has to be interpreted using a baseline culture for comparison. However, the problem then becomes deciding whose culture provides that baseline. For American or British researchers, for example, to automatically assume that their culture should form the baseline for comparison only serves to reinforce, rather than question, the dominance of Anglo-American theory and practice. A common error in cross-cultural study is made by researchers believing that their own etic-emic combination is true of all cultures (Brislin, 1993). Moreover, research based on overly simplistic dichotomies can lead to false stereotyping and hidden forms of discrimination. While it is true that some forms of stereotyping may be useful to researchers for purposes of categorization and labeling, the danger is that all individuals and groups within a society are assumed to think and behave in the same way – as discussed in further detail below. Equally, without 'deeper' exploration, there may exist an even greater danger - that national cultural stereotypes are used as surface generalizations and that the processes operating below the surface are ignored.

Clearly, research into cross-cultural aspects of educational leadership and administration while using some type of baseline must avoid discriminatory stereotyping. Shaw and Welton (1996) argue that this is beginning to happen, as the discipline of cross-cultural research is moving from "the direct comparison of nation states with each other, identifying characteristics of the indigenous peoples using complex Western research tools, towards a more sensitive and organizationally-focused approach, using research tools elaborated in mixed-culture teams" (p.3). The latter point is worth reinforcing. The conceptualization and application of any approach, but particularly one purporting to explore cross-cultural issues, is unavoidably influenced by the researchers' own inherent cultural bias (Ronan, 1986). For English-speaking Western, or other homogeneous groups of researchers, to embark separately on cultural inquiry could be counterproductive and might well restrict the validity of such research. Equally, researchers from within a certain culture may find it difficult to explore their own cultures as, within themselves, cultures tend not to be widely discussed because they simply represent "the way we do things around here". In fact Brislin (1993) suggests that in many situations 'outside' researchers can provide insightful analysis because they do not hold the same 'taken for granted' values, norms and behaviours as those who live the culture on a day-to-day basis. In short, a collaborative mix of researchers from within and without particular cultures under investigation may well yield more robust understandings and comparative insights.

STEREOTYPING CULTURES

Cross-cultural research in educational administration may be skewed by a tendency to assume that cultures are homogeneous within national boundaries, or even within larger groups of countries such as 'Asia' or 'Europe' (Walker & Dimmock, 2000d). For example, within national boundaries, one only has to look at the complex cultural composition of societies such as the United States, Australia or Malaysia to see that such perspectives ignore the fact that cultures differ as much within as they do between nations (Redding, 1994). As Leung and Tjosvold (1998) note: "In Malaysia, Malay, Chinese and Indian managers have their own values systems" (p. 336). Misconceptions also occur through the unwarranted grouping of countries into some homogenized, identical collective. A common example of this inaccuracy is the grouping of Asian countries into an undifferentiated 'Confucian' mass. As Rizvi (1997, p. 21) notes: "More collectivism modes of social organization are portrayed as Asian compared to the liberal individualism that is believed to be so dominant in the West." Leung and Tjosvold (1998) for example, concluded that even though different societies in South and East Asia generally value relationships over a focus on task, they approach conflict management in different ways.

INDIVIDUALS AND CULTURE

A further issue confounding the search for the influence of culture on educational administration is the relationship between individual personality and culture. Arguments downplaying the role of culture claim that individuals will behave in line with their own beliefs or mental models regardless of cultural background. As explained above, in terms of organizations, this may be a circular argument. As Lindsay (2000, p. 284) explains: "Mental models apply to individuals and groups of individuals – and are identifiable and changeable. Culture reflects the aggregation of individual mental models and in turn influences the types of mental models that individuals have. The two are linked in a perpetually evolving system."

Culture has the capacity to influence and explain the behaviours of individuals and groups of all sizes and complexities (Schneider, 1991). It can be observed as an influence at the macro (societal culture) level, at the organizational (school culture) level, and at individual level, since individual behaviour is the product of the interaction between individual personality and both societal and organizational cultures. Indeed, Hofstede (1991) claims that organizational behaviour is resultant from a complex interplay between the personality and motives of individuals, the cultures of society and organization in which individuals live and work respectively, and generic characteristics of human nature. Hofstede (1991) remarks that every individual is born with, and therefore inherits, universal and generic characteristics of human nature. The individual's personality, however, is formed from both inherited and learned characteristics. Culture, at its different levels, acts as a mediating influence to affect the learned part of behaviour and personality (Hofstede, 1991). The concept of culture then captures reality by enabling explanations of human and organizational behaviour to be expressed in terms of interactions between individuals (their personalities), the organizations and institutions in which they live and work, and the larger environments which circumscribe both. To reaffirm, the concept of culture is particularly appropriate for studying the relationships between schools and their micro- and macro-environments (Dimmock & Walker, 1998b).

CULTURAL HYBRIDITY

Issues of cultural definition and shape are further complicated by the fact that firstly, cultures are constantly shifting and, secondly, that cultural values seem to produce different effects at different times. Cultures are not static, moribund entities; rather, they are dynamic and invariably changing (Trice & Beyer, 1993).

As Rizvi (1997) notes, with increasing globalization and population mobility, cultures can best be described as hybrids, constantly shifting, growing and developing as they encounter different ideas, new knowledge and changing circumstances. Following this assertion, Rizvi (1997, p. 22) claims: "(We) cannot know cultures in their pristine and authentic form. Instead, our focus must shift to the ways in which culture forms become separated and recombine with new forms in new practices in their local contexts." One increasingly important manifestation of the developing hybridity of cultures results from their changing multicultural nature, often caused by migration. Societies such as the US, UK and Australia are now truly multicultural and, their cultures constantly evolving. The shifting composition of cultures makes investigation more troublesome, but does not negate the importance of identifying how they influence organizational behaviour in schools. As has been argued elsewhere, a deeper understanding of the influence of culture is predicated on the need to develop cross-cultural models, frameworks and taxonomies by which to compare schools within the same, and across different, systems (Dimmock & Walker, 1998a; Hallinger & Leithwood, 1996; Walker & Dimmock 1999). The use of frameworks utilizing broad dimensions and common elements for analysis may, in fact, allow room for cultural forms to shift and develop, even though they unavoidably capture only a snapshot of cultural influences at a certain point in time.

Researching culture is difficult because, at different times, the same values seem to produce different effects. Pye (2000) shows this clearly using the example of 'Asian' values; values which have been used over the last decade to explain both the rapid economic rise of many Southeast Asian economies and, conversely, the fragility and vulnerability of these very same economies. An example of this phenomenon is apparent in discussions of the merits and otherwise of education systems and methods in Southeast and East Asian countries. When seeking explanations for why countries such as Taiwan, Singapore and Korea consistently outperform countries like Canada and Australia in international math and science tests, the values of discipline, hard work and respect are often credited. Conversely, when trying to account for the lack of creativity in the same Asian educational contexts, the same values are 'blamed'.

Pye uses two general hypotheses in an attempt to explain such phenomenon, both of which indicate cultural hybridity. The first states that the same values operating in different contexts will produce different outcomes. "That is, the values of the Asian cultures have remained the same but the contexts have changed, and hence what had been positive outcomes become negative ones" (p. 245). His second explanation is that cultural values clusters can be combined at different times, in different ways, to produce differing effects. Pye concludes that it is impossible to establish any cause-and-effect relationship because of the number and complexity of variables involved and warns that cross-cultural researchers take great care when ascribing weights to specific cultural variables. His parting words signal caution to all cross-cultural researchers, especially in times of rapid change. "We know that they (cultural variables) are important, but how important at any particular time is hard to judge. We are dealing with clouds, not clocks, with general approximations, not precise cause-and-effect relationships" (p. 254).

Methodologies for Cross-Cultural Exploration

The conceptual issues discussed above have implications for the type of methodology that may guide cross cultural exploration in the field. Given the underdeveloped state of cross-cultural research in educational administration, it may be that guidance can be drawn from disciplines such as cross-cultural psychology and international business management, anthropology, sociology and culture studies (see Brislin, 1993) that have relatively established methodological traditions. Researchers in these fields have faced and addressed, to varying degrees, many of the problems now facing cross-cultural researchers in educational administration. For example, in an expansive review of the field of comparative management theory, Redding (1994) concluded that although the plethora of research in the area remained remarkably confused, there was agreement that research needed to move away from positivism (descriptive) toward ethnoscience (interpretative) and from ideographic micro-analytic theory toward more nomothetic theory-building approaches.

An over-reliance on methodology from other fields, however, should be tempered by the fact that they may not be suitable to education or to all cultures. Besides issues of methodological validity, the appropriateness and respective merits of qualitative and quantitative methods to research cultural matters need to be considered. Although most cross-cultural studies in international business and psychology are purely quantitative, there are promising avenues to be explored within the qualitative paradigm through the use of narrative, case studies and interviews, and, more generally, through symbolic interactionist perspectives emphasizing the perspectives and meanings attributed to school leader's actions in different cultures. In regard to quantitative approaches, more sophisticated statistical methods developed recently open up the possibility of new insights into cross-cultural studies of educational administration. Structural equation modeling, for example, as Heck (1998) notes, seems ideally suited to capture data on key interrelationships found between the societal culture, sub-cultural (regional/local) and organizational levels.

CONCLUSION

The purpose of this chapter was to recognize the possibilities, prospects and problems of developing research in the field of cross-cultural educational administration. The area is replete with opportunities to develop more inclusive understandings of how societal culture influences the practice of educational administration. Such opportunities include discovering how and in what ways societal cultures and sub-cultures influence the practice of school leadership. Such research could include, for example, how culture influences relationships and processes within the school, such as teacher evaluation and shared leadership? It would also be interesting to explore how the sets of dominant values and practices associated with cultures and sub-cultures affect the meanings attributed to the implementation of change in schools and school systems, and the meanings that key concepts such as 'collaboration' and 'school-based management' have in different cultural settings. At a policy level, it would be useful to better understand the influence of globalization and its relationship to policy formation, adoption, implementation and evaluation in different cultural contexts (Walker & Dimmock, in press). The list could easily continue - the bottom line is that leadership cannot be fully understood without considering its socio-cultural context. A greater understanding of this context and how it influences educational administration can only benefit scholars, practitioners and policy makers as they work toward improving schools.

NOTES

[1] The work described in this paper was partially supported by a grant from the Research Grants Council of the Hong Kong Special Administrative Region. (Project No. CUHK 4327/98H/1998/Education and Social Sciences).
[2] For ease of understanding, I use the term Anglo-American to refer to Anglo-American English-speaking Western societies, and Non-Western to refer to societies outside these countries. Anglo-American refers to predominantly English-speaking societies which include the United States, United Kingdom, Australia, Canada and New Zealand. The US and UK are seen producing much of literature in the field of educational administration. I also recognize that other influential but less accessible literature has been and is generated in the non-English-speaking Western societies of Continental Europe such as Germany and France. For our purposes here, non-Western societies include societies in Asia, Africa and Central and South America. It is recognized that man y of the countries in the latter two categories are at least bilingual societies. I prefer to use the term societies rather than countries in recognition that, within national boundaries, multiple cultures co-exist.

REFERENCES

Begley, P. (2000). Cultural isomorphs of educational administration: Reflections on western-centric approaches to values and leadership. *Asia Pacific Journal of Education, 20*(2), 23-33.

Brislin, R. (1993). *Understanding culture's influence on behaviour.* Orlando, FL: Harcourt-Brace.

Cheng, K.M. (1995a). The neglected dimension: Cultural comparison in educational administration. In K.C. Wong & K.M. Cheng (Eds.), *Educational leadership and change: An international perspective* (pp. 87-102). Hong Kong: Hong Kong University Press.

Cheng, K.M. (1995b). *Excellence in education: is it culture-free?* Keynote address presented at the 9th annual meeting of the Educational Research Association, November, 22-24, Singapore.

Cheng, K.M., & Wong, K.C. (1996). School effectiveness in East Asia: Concepts, origins and implications. *Journal of Educational Administration, 34*(5), 32-49.

Dimmock, C., & Walker, A (2000a). Developing comparative and international educational leadership and management: a cross-cultural model, *School Leadership and Management, 20*(2), 143-160.

Dimmock, C., & Walker, A. (1998a). Comparative educational administration: Developing a cross-cultural comparative framework. *Educational Administration Quarterly, 34*(4), 558-595.

Dimmock, C., & Walker, A. (1998b). Towards comparative educational administration: Building the case for a cross-cultural, school-based approach. *Journal of Educational Administration, 36*(4), 379-401.

Dimmock, C., & Walker, A. (2000b). Globalization and societal culture: Redefining schooling and school leadership in the 21st century. *COMPARE, 30*(3), 303-312.

Hallinger, P., & Kantamara, P. (2000). Educational change in Thailand: Opening a window into leadership as a cultural process. *School Leadership and Management, 20*(2), 189-206.

Hallinger, P., & Leithwood, K. (1996a). Culture and educational administration: A case of finding out what you don't know you don't know. *Journal of Educational Administration, 34*(5), 98-116.

Hallinger, P., & Leithwood, K. (1998). Editors' introduction. *Peabody Journal of Education, 73*(2), 1-10.

Hallinger, P., & Leithwood, K., (1996b), Editorial. *Journal of Educational Administration, 34*(5), 4-11.

Harrison, L. (2000). Why culture matters. In L. Harrison & S. Huntington (Eds.), *Culture matters: how values shape human progress* (pp. xvii-xxxiv). New York: Basic Books.

Heck, R. (1998). Conceptual and methodological issues in investigating principal leadership across cultures. *Peabody Journal of Education, 73*(2), 51-80.

Hofstede, G.H. (1991). *Cultures and organizations: Software of the mind.* London: McGraw Hill.

Hofstede, G.H. (1996). An American in Paris: The influence of nationality on organizational theories. *Organization Studies, 17*(3), 525-537.

Inglehart, R. (2000). Culture and Democracy, In L. Harrison & S. Huntington (Eds.), *Culture matters: how values shape human progress* (pp. 80-97), New York: Basic Books.

Lau, C.M., McMahon, G., & Woodman, R. (1996). An international comparison of organizational development practice in the USA and Hong Kong. *Journal of Organizational Change, 5*(2), 4-19.

Leung, K., & Tjosvold, D. (1998). (Eds.) *Conflict management in the Asia Pacific: Assumptions and approaches in diverse cultures.* Singapore: John Wiley & Sons.

Lewellen, T. (1992). *Political anthropology: An introduction (second edition).* Westport, CT: Bergin & Garvey.

Lindsay, S. (2000). Culture, mental models, and national prosperity. In L. Harrison & S. Huntington (Eds.), *Culture matters: How values shape human progress* (pp. 268-281). New York: Basic Books.

Lomotey, K. (1995). Social and cultural influences on schooling: A commentary on the UCEA knowledge base project, domain 1. *Educational Administration Quarterly, 31*(2), 295-303.

Mitchell, J.T., & Willower, D.J. (1992). Organizational culture in a good high school. *Journal of Educational Administration, 30*(6), 6-16.

Pye, L. (2000). "Asian values": From dynamos to dominoes? In L. Harrison & S. Huntington (Eds.), *Culture matters: How values shape human progress* (pp. 244-255). New York: Basic Books.

Redding, S.G. (1994). Comparative management theory: Jungle, zoo or fossil bed? *Organization Studies, 15*(3), 323-359.

Reynolds, D. (2000). School effectiveness: the international dimension. In C. Teddlie & D. Reynolds (Eds.), *The international handbook of school effectiveness research* (pp. 232-256). London: Falmer.

Rizvi, F. (1997). Beyond the East-West divide: Education and the dynamics of Australia-Asia relations. In J. Blackmore & K.A. Toh (Eds.), *Educational research: Building new partnerships* (pp. 13-26). Singapore: Singapore Educational Research Association.

Ronan, S. (1986). *Comparative and multinational management.* New York: Wiley.

Rose, R. (1991). Comparing forms of comparative analysis. *Political Studies, XXXIX*, 446-462.

Schneider, S. (1991). Strategy formulation: The impact of national culture. *Organizational Studies, 10*(2), 149-168.

Seddon, T. (1994, August). *Decentralization and democracy.* Paper presented at the Teachers and Decentralization Seminar, National Industry Education Forum, Melbourne.

Sharp, L., & Gopinathan, S. (2000). Leadership in high achieving schools in Singapore: The influence of societal culture. *Asia-Pacific Journal of Education, 20*(2), 99-109.

Shaw, M., & Welton, J. (1996, August). *The application of education management models and theories to the processes of education policy making and management: A case of compound cross-cultural confusion.* Paper presented at the Eighth International Conference of the Commonwealth Council for Educational Administration, Kuala Lumpur.

Shweder, T. (2000). Moral maps, "First world" conceits and the new evangelists. In L. Harrison & S. Huntington (Eds.), *Culture matters: how values shape human progress* (pp. 158 177). New York: Basic Books..

Southworth, G. (2000). *School leadership in English schools at the close of the 20th Century: Puzzles, problems and cultural insights.* Paper presented at the annual meeting of the American Educational Research Association, New Orleans.

Steingard, D., & Fitzgibbons, D. (1995). Challenging the juggernaut of globalization: A manifesto for academic praxis. *Journal of Organizational Change Management, 8*(4), 30-54.

Tierney, W. (1996). Leadership and postmodernism: On voice and qualitative method. *Leadership Studies, 7*(3), 371-383.

Trice, H., & Beyer, J. (1993). *The cultures of work organizations.* Englewood Cliffs, NJ: Prentice-Hall.

Trompenaars, F., & Hampden-Turner, C. (1997). *Riding the waves of culture (second edition).* London: Nicholas Brealey.

Walker, A., & Dimmock, C. (1999). A cross-cultural approach to the study of educational leadership: An emerging framework. *Journal of School Leadership, 9*(4), 321-348.

Walker, A., & Dimmock, C. (2000a). Developing educational administration: The impact of societal culture on theory and practice. In C. Dimmock & A. Walker (Eds.), *Future school administration: Western and Asian perspectives* (pp. 3-24). Hong Kong: Chinese University of Hong Kong Press.

Walker, A., & Dimmock, C. (2000b). Insights into educational administration: the need for a comparative cross-cultural perspective. *Asia-Pacific Journal of Education, 20*(2), 11-22.

Walker, A., & Dimmock, C. (2000c). Leadership dilemmas of Hong Kong principals: Sources, perceptions and outcomes. *Australian Journal of Education, 44*(1) 5-25.

Walker, A., & Dimmock, C. (2000d). One size fits all? teacher appraisal in a Chinese culture. *Journal of Personnel Evaluation in Education, 14*(2), 155-178.

Walker, A., & Dimmock, C. (in press). Moving school leadership beyond its narrow boundaries: developing a cross-cultural approach. In K. Leithwood & P. Hallinger (Eds.), *Second International Handbook of Educational Leadership and Administration*. The Netherlands: Kluwer Academic Publishers.

Whitty, G., Power, S., & Halpin, D. (1998). *Devolution and choice in education*. Melbourne: Australian Council for Educational Research.

Wilkinson, B. (1996). Culture, institutions and business in East Asia. *Organization Studies, 17*(3), 421-447.

ISAAC A. FRIEDMAN

SCHOOL ORGANIZATIONAL VALUES: THE DRIVING FORCE FOR EFFECTIVENESS AND CHANGE

Abstract. Analysis of the major classical, neo-classical and modern organizational theories reveals that these theories are founded on eight primary values: Task-orientation, Elitism, Innovation, Consideration, Egalitarianism, Conservatism, Conformity, and Self-direction. A study was conducted to test for the empirical structure of the inter-relationships among these values, based on the premise that the relations among these values may align along four axes: Egalitarianism–Elitism; Consideration–Task-orientation; Conservatism–Innovation; Conformity–Self-direction. Thirty elementary and secondary schools in Israel participated in this study. Small Space Analysis (SSA) generated a unique concentric pattern of relations, different from what might have been expected. The findings of this study suggest that school cultures do not usually differ from one another in terms of the Consideration, Task-orientation, Innovation values, and that the variations among school cultures can be accommodated by the remaining values. A new theory of the unique structure of school organizational values is proposed based on the importance they attribute to each of these values. This theory may be helpful in classifying school cultures.

This chapter shows that, to a great extent, the values shared by an organization's administration and most of its active individuals will determine its culture and image, orient the behaviour of the people within it, and predict the organization success in achieving its goals[1]. In addition to being a place where social and educational processes take place, a school is also an administrative organization. An administrative organization is defined as a system of roles and an arrangement of activities designed to achieve common, agreed goals (Robey, 1986). For the purposes of this chapter, the term "system of roles" refers to the organizational structure while "activities" relates to the processes that take place within the organization. These three combined elements -- roles, activities, and goals – form the essence of an organization, and in this respect, there are no significant differences between different public and private types of organizations – whether industrial organizations, social organizations or administrative organizations. In schools the roles include those of the principal, teachers, teaching subject coordinators, and of course, the students. All are linked in a system of defined relationships. The activities that take place in school include school-based educational and social activities, and activities that involve and benefit the environment outside the school.

Also implied in the definition of an organization proposed above is that an organization requires a set of common, consensual goals, followed by goal-oriented processes, reflecting particular values. These values, some of which are conspicuous, while others are less so, are important for understanding the organization's modus operandi and culture. Where the organization is a school, the values pertain to its educational, social and political roles, and to its educational and social activities.

161

P.T. Begley and O. Johansson (eds.), The Ethical Dimensions of School Leadership, 161–179.

According to Rokeach (1973, p. 5), values are "enduring beliefs concerning a particular behaviour, outcome or end situation which individuals or society prefer to another behaviour". Values represent personal preferences regarding desirable situations and suitable ways of achieving them. They are also described as "perceptions of the desirable associated with the choice of patterns of human behaviour and action, or special cases of attitudes serving as standards, against which alternative ways of acting are examined and evaluated" (Smith, 1963). Values are ideals and ways of relating, and are the standards by which we test the nature of our actions, goals and experiences.

Theorists have offered a variety of taxonomies of values. For example, Alport, Vernon, and Lindzey (1951) identified six basic values: theoretical, economic, aesthetic, social, political, and religious. They also devised a questionnaire for measuring the relative strength of these values. Super (1962) developed a scheme for analyzing job-related values which were characterized as either intrinsic or extrinsic. Intrinsic values focus on altruism, creativity, autonomy, intellectual stimulation, aesthetics, achievement, and management. Extrinsic values focus on the ends that work is instrumental in providing: life style, pleasant surroundings, congenial associates, security, status, and purchasing power. Max Weber (1904) argued that Protestant values were responsible for the rise of industrial capitalism in Europe. The Protestant Ethic may be viewed as a cluster of values that motivate people to work and to subscribe to the tenet that honest work is work's own reward. The Protestant ethic notion of work values spawned several studies (e.g., Cherrington, 1997; Greenberg, 1977) which investigated the association between job-related values, satisfaction at work, and self-esteem. In recent years, studies have been conducted by various researchers who explored the impact of values on the educational systems in different cultures (Gardner, 2001).

The work of Hofstede (1980) is notable for encouraging interest in the impact of individual and cultural values on organizational dynamics. Hofstede identified four dimensions of organizational values: Power distance, Uncertainty avoidance, Individualism-Collectivism and Masculinity-Femininity. Later, Hofstede and Bond (1988) suggested an additional value, which they named Confucian dynamism. According to Hofstede (1990), an organization's culture (or that of an entire country) can be described these five value dimensions.

Schwartz (1992), suggested that values may be classified according to their contents. He proposed a set of ten categories of value-types, which he claimed were responsible for motivating human behaviour: (1) *Self Direction*: to actualize this value, the individual must achieve, or try to achieve, independent thought and action, including choice, creativity and investigation; (2) *Stimulation:* boldness, diversification, and sensitivity; (3) *Hedonism:* pleasure from satisfying of needs; (4) *Achievement:* excellence, competence, success and survival; (5) *Power:* status, social kudos, wealth, authority, public image and social acknowledgement; (6) *Stability:* personal and social harmony and stability; (7) *Conformity:* constraining any actions, propensities and impulses which have the potential to annoy or harm others; (8) *Traditionalism:* beliefs and norms which acknowledge, respect and preserve a common social background; (9) *Humanism:* promotion and conservation of human values, e.g., the welfare of individuals and society; (10) *Universalism:* understanding, respect, tolerance and protection for humans and nature. For these values to be realized, the individual must behave in a certain way, and therefore, these values may be called 'motivating values'. Schwartz further demonstrated the existence of a dynamic structure linking the various motivating values. Within the dynamic structure, values of the same type are usually located closer to one another, while conflicting values are remote from one another, or located in opposition to one another. With this dynamic structure as a basis, Schwartz (1999) propounded a theory of values which makes it possible to compare national cultures, on the basis of three polarized dimensions: Conservatism versus Intellectual and Emotional Autonomy, Hierarchy versus Equality, and Power versus Harmony.

According to Hodgkinson (1999), values are neither unitary nor homogeneous, but rather hierarchical and with different levels of motivating force. For example, values can be classified as "core" or "peripheral": core values are those that define the essence of any culture; peripheral values are not universally accepted by a culture. They may be regarded as core values by some groups, but are not by everyone. Radical change in core values will dramatically affect social norms, structures and individual belief systems (Johansson & Bredson, 1999).

ORGANIZATIONAL THEORIES AND THEIR UNDERLYING VALUES

Organizational values, either directly or indirectly, form the basis of organizational theories. A survey and analysis of the major classical, neo-classical and modern organizational theories shows that these are based on seven primary values:

a) *Task-Orientation*. The value at the heart of many, if not all, organizational theories, is Task-Orientation. Task-Orientation involves defining those goals in the pursuit of which organization members dedicate their personal and professional capabilities. In order to achieve its goal(s), an organization allocates tasks to individuals and units, makes intelligent use of personnel, time and resources, selects and trains professional staff and ensures that staff employ scientific procedures in their work (Taylor, 1911).

b) *Elitism*. This value means that people at different echelons of the organization have the power and authority to act, instruct lower level employees to act, supervise work, introduce change, maintain discipline, reward and penalize staff. This concept serves as the basis to other concepts such as centralization, order, levels of authority, hierarchical chain, etc. (Fayol, 1949; Lawrence & Lorsch, 1969; Merton, 1940; Mooney, 1930; Weber, 1946).

c) *Innovation*. Innovation is the force which motivates the organization to adopt measures that will foster change, lead to alternate means of achieving goals, and to proposing and cultivating new ideas (Fayol, 1949; Milgrom & Roberts, 1992). Innovation is linked to a faith in personal ability and willingness to cut through the accepted limits of thinking and behaviour.

d) *Consideration*. The value of Consideration calls for the recognition of each individual's worth, needs and uniqueness, while rigorously encouraging a healthy relationship between the individual and his or her environment (Etzioni, 1988; Follett, 1926). This value also concerns showing optimal regard toward the employee as a person, and might therefore conflict with Task-

Orientation, since the latter's main aim is to accomplish the organization's objectives and demands subordination of the wishes and wills of the organization's members to attaining the organization's objectives.

e) *Egalitarianism.* This value combines justice, courtesy and empathy. It seeks to narrow the gap between the wielders of great power and those with little power. In organizational terms, Egalitarianism means greater closeness between management echelons and rank and file staff (Baum & Oliver, 1991; Fayol, 1949; Salancik & Pfeffer, 1978).

f) *Conservatism.* In its narrowest sense, this value concerns the stability and permanence of the organization's human resources (Fayol, 1949; Mooney, 1930). In its broadest sense, this value within the organization is about reluctance to change, the preservation of procedures, routines, attitudes and discipline, respect for authority and a clear-cut division of labour and authority (Gulick, 1937). This value is associated with the more modern concepts of organizational theory, e.g., certainty versus uncertainty, stability versus change (Lawrence & Lorsch, 1969).

g) *Autonomy: Self-direction–Conformity.* The locus of decision-making in organizations can either be internal or external. There is an external locus of decision-making when an organization normatively follows clear instructions dictated by an outside authority. In such cases, the organization has a clear code of orders and discipline which its members cannot alter (Weber, 1946). Here, the employees seek to conform to the organization's norms, rules and environmental demands. In contrast, an organization is said to have an internal locus of decision-making when individuals are encouraged to make independent decisions, effect change and act as a consequence of self-direction. The external locus of decision-making expresses the value of Conformity, the internal locus of decision-making expresses the value of Self-Direction.

The values underlying organizational theories relate to motivating certain behaviours in the organization and therefore may be termed 'motivating values'. A motivating value will spur the individual to action, and to successfully implementing the actions which actualize the motivating factor.

A HYPOTHESIZED STRUCTURE OF ORGANIZATIONAL VALUES

The degree of importance ascribed to a value by individuals is a significant basic attribute. Members of organizations ascribe different levels of importance to different values and tend to prioritize their values. The tendency to prioritize values is embedded in human nature since people reject values that oppose human nature and adopt values that are consonant with human nature. Organization members tend to prioritize values depending on the extent to which the values help support their group or organization: the more a value advances the organization's goals, the greater the importance ascribed to it.

According to Schwartz (1992), depending on the weight ascribed to the value, it is possible for two values to clash, support, or provide closure with one another. For example, we can find a negative correlation between two values if one value is considered 'important' and 'desirable', while the other is seen as 'unimportant', 'undesirable' or even 'objectionable'. Values are positively correlated when both are regarded as 'important' and 'desirable', or when both are thought of as 'unimportant' or 'objectionable'. These values complement one another.

Applying Schwartz's (1992) principles to organizational values, Figure 1 gives examples of positive and negative correlations for pairs of motivating organizational values. The four pairs of negatively correlated values are (see Fig. 1):

a) *Innovation* and *Conservatism*. The value of Innovation encourages people to dare to change, to abandon the tried and tested and aim for fresh ground. Organizations that place great emphasis on this value are known as 'ground breaking' organizations. They develop new, sometimes courageous ideas. This behaviour stands in opposition to behaviour that is typically conservative, acquiescent, and interested in personal and organizational assurance and stability, in other words behaviour driven by the value of Conservatism. Both values coincide with Hofstede's (1980) Uncertainty Avoidance.

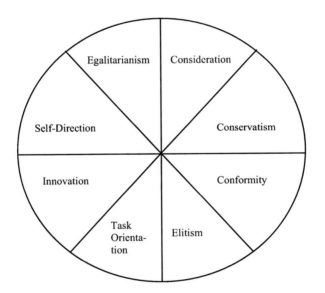

Figure 1. A Hypothetical Structure of Negative and Positive Correlations Among Organizational Values.

b) *Self-.... ....j........ ....*ith the desire for independent action and thought found in decision-making. In the education system, this value is reflected in the desire for autonomously functioning schools. Schools which ascribe significance to the value of self-direction, undertake important decisions themselves, manage their resources independently and aspire to keep themselves up to date without pressure or influence from outside. Schools with a strong emphasis on the value of Conformity are typically obedient, stability-oriented, unadventurous, and generally dependent on external resources – the state or another agency.

Furthermore, such schools also typically seek to achieve harmony and fit between internal ideas (school-arising) and external ideas (stemming from the outside environment, both near and far).

c) *Egalitarianism-Elitism.* The value of Egalitarianism moves people and organizations to maintain standards of social justice, egalitarian principles, belief in people and the human ability to realize potential – even if latent. Schools that ascribe importance to this value will accept any student, without screening or selection. They aim to achieve a heterogeneous social synthesis, reflecting the social structure of the community outside the school. They offer everyone the same curriculum and strive toward goals accepted by society at large (universal goals). Elitism, on the other hand, occurs when individuals and organizations seek high social status, professional authority, together with power and control over people and resources. Status-seeking schools are selective. They are unwilling to accept all-comers, they apply external (pre-acceptance) and internal (post-acceptance) selection procedures even at the cost of injustice, and may demonstrate a lack of generosity and broadmindedness. In conceptual terms, Elitism and Egalitarianism are mutually exclusive, and it is doubtful whether in practice similar emphasis can be ascribed to both within a single organizational framework.

d) *Consideration - Task-Orientation.* Task-Orientation means seeking excellence that conforms to accepted social standards, high performance levels, meticulousness, accuracy, and constant personal and professional progress. Often, the drive toward persistently high Task-Orientation places pressure on students and staff (teachers and school faculty in schools, employees in other types of organizations). These pressures are accompanied by a lack of consideration for personal problems and individual limitations, and lead to sanctions being applied where people have difficulty in meeting required standards. In this sense, the value of Task-Orientation opposes the value of Consideration, the latter expressing the wish to advance the values of love of fellow people, fairness, honesty and loyalty. In extreme cases, these two values conflict with one another. Some argue that it is possible to appreciate both these values highly at the same time, especially in educational settings.

The following values are positively correlated (see Figure 1): Self-Direction (independent thought and action with the purpose of achieving, making decisions, etc.) and Innovation (the Task-Orientation of excellence in conformance with accepted standards, highly skilled performance); Task-Orientation and Elitism (social status, status of authority with recognition of that authority, control over people and resources); Elitism and Conformity (obedience, achieving a fit between the organization's opinions and prevailing opinions); Conformity and Conservatism (internal harmony, sociability, decency, love of others); Conservatism and Consideration (Consideration may require a lesser drive for achievement and lead to stability and preservation of the status quo). Consideration and Egalitarianism (promoting sense of Egalitarianism, social justice, generosity and broadmindedness).

AN EMPIRICALLY BASED STRUCTURE OF SCHOOL MOTIVATING VALUES

The main goal of the study reported here was to test a hypothesis that the empirical structure of values in schools resembles the pattern shown in Figure 1. The pattern indicates that certain values clash while others dovetail positively. To test the assumption, Facet Theory (Guttman, 1968) was chosen as the methodological approach due to its advantages in conceptualizing complex constructs and theory. Facet Theory is a research methodology integrating concrete tools and procedures for analyzing and structuring research contents with procedures for processing multivariate data (Shye, Elizur, & Hoffman, 1994). In Facet Theory, the observations of a study, i.e., the main content domain of the research issue, is broken down into components, which represent the chief general properties of the domain of inquiry. Each component is termed a Facet. A Facet, in other words, is a classification of elements of a study domain with various significant and exclusive properties (Tziner, 1987).

The main tool of Facet Theory is the mapping sentence, which links the "population facet" (i.e., the subjects of the study -- teachers in our case), the "content facets" and the "range facet" (i.e., the importance ascribed to different values), classifies the research observations, and constitutes a basis for hypotheses regarding the observations. According to Levy & Guttman (1976), a Facet Theory approach to defining "social value" is as follows:

An item pertaining to social values belongs to the universe of value items if and only if its domain requires a (cognitive) assessment of the importance of a

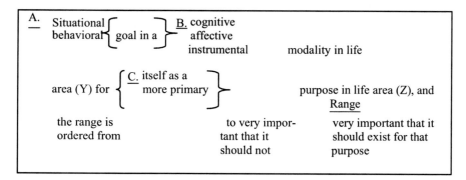

The above definition of social values specifies that the assessment of importance can be regarded as cognitive behaviour. Therefore, of the three possible modalities of behaviour, values are restricted to the cognitive. The situational or behavioural goal (Facet A), whose importance is being assessed may be of any of the three modalities (Facet B). The importance of the situation or behaviour can be assessed as an end in itself or as a means to a more primary end (Facet C: Response).

For example, Elizur (1984) divided the contents domain for work values into two facets: Facet A *modality of outcomes*, which is concerned with the "materiality" of work outcomes or results, i.e., whether they are concrete and practical; "affective", in the sense of influencing others (i.e., a social relations outcome) or "psychological" in the sense of reflecting enjoyment or interest in the work itself. The second facet (Facet B) is *relation to task performance*, which depends on whether the rewards of work depend on the quality of the job, or whether reward stems simply from membership in the organization regardless of the employee's performance.

Facet theory employs smallest space analysis (SSA), a statistical model in which distances in a multidimensional space represent similar coefficients among sets of objects. For example, given a correlation matrix of item scores, SSA displays these items as points in a Euclidean plane such that the higher the correlation between items, the closer the points are to one another. The item deployment picture (map) derived from an SSA often reveals patterns in the data that would otherwise remain obscure, and is far easier to interpret than a table of coefficients.

Three main item deployment patterns are of some importance to this study and will therefore be described briefly. The three patterns are the *axial*, the *radial* and the *angular* partitions of the SSA map. With an *axial* partitioning, parallel lines divide the space into simply arranged stripes. *Radial* partitioning forms a pattern resembling a set of concentric bands. *Angular* partitioning cuts the space into sectors with rays emanating from a common origin – resembling a pie cut into slices. Facet Theory argues that the inner contextual structure of the facets determines the empirical deployment of items in the SSA map. Thus, each facet has a certain "role" in the partitioning of the SSA map. In a case where a specific order of the facet elements is hypothesized (order of importance, hierarchy, or any other order), this facet is known as an "ordered facet". An ordered facet, it is said, has an ordering role in the partitioning of the SSA map, since an order similar to that of the facet is expected to appear in the map, forming contiguous regions in the geometric configuration. An angular pattern in the SSA map is usually attributed to a facet's polarizing role. A facet is designated "polar" when three or more lines originating at the same pole (centre), divide the space by radiating out in different directions, with each slice of the "pie" formed corresponding to one of the facet's elements. A "polar" facet usually contains unordered elements. Hence, when there is no order between the facet elements, i.e., when none of the facet elements are necessarily more important than the others, that facet can be hypothesized to play a polar (or polarizing) role (Tziner, 1987). When an order does exist between the elements of a facet, in the sense that some elements are likely to be more closely related to one another than others, that facet plays a modulating role. The corresponding partitioning of the geometric space appears in the form of concentric circles surrounding a common origin, so that the closer one moves to the centre, the more interrelated the variables comprising the respective facet element are.

Items can be arranged in an SSA map on the basis of more than one facet. For example, a combination of ordered and unordered facets can provide a special pattern called a "*radex*". Geometrically, a radex is a combination of circular and angular lines which partition the SSA map.

In the present study, no formal mapping sentence was proposed, since the idea was to determine whether or not the wheel-shaped structure (see Figure 1) could be substantiated empirically.

Sample

Thirty schools were sampled out of Israel's 2,000 Jewish and Arab state elementary and high schools. Four or five teachers were sampled in each school and asked to complete a questionnaire. One hundred and twenty nine teachers completed the forms (96% return rate). These teachers were employed in various teaching positions and taught different class levels.

Instruments

The instrument, entitled "Process and Organizational Behaviour Patterns in the School", contained 51 items. The items related to the eight motivating values as shown below (see Table 1).

Table 1. Items in the "Processes and Organizational Patterns in the School" Questionnaire.

Item No.	Item Contents
	Innovation
48	Teachers often introduce new ideas for school improvement and change.
52	The school administration encourages teachers to seek new directions and challenges in teaching.
60	Parents are encouraged to suggest new, innovative ideas.
43	Ideas for change are carefully scrutinized before being introduced.*
	Conservatism
57	The school is very cautious about introducing radical changes (to the curriculum, school rules, etc.).
63	The school strongly favours maintaining the current status quo.
27	Social and recreational activities are organized for teachers and other staff members.
	Self-Direction
31	Organizational and educational plans are developed without outside intervention.
15	Teachers are involved in school decision-making and policy decisions.
47	Staffing and financial decisions are made autonomously.
50	Teachers have freedom in curriculum design and implementation.
59	The school is more likely to accept ideas from inside the school than from outside the school.
	Conformity
64	The school does not favour divergent modes of behaviour or activities.
17	Students are under great pressure to perform well academically.
44	The school introduces new ideas that may clash with accepted educational values*

36 The school organizes activities that may not conform to parents'
expectations *

Egalitarianism

49 Students may enter the teacher's staff room whenever they feel like.
51 Students with problems are free to enter the teachers' offices to speak to
teachers.
55 Educators are invited to attend social activities organized by students.
54 We believe in egalitarian student-teacher relations.
37 The school admits equal numbers of high and low achieving students.
65 Teachers and students are expected to obey the same rules.
58 Students address teachers by their first names.
45 The school accepts students with learning difficulties and behaviour
problems.

Elitism

56 The school carefully screens and selects student applicants.
18 The school publicizes its academic and social achievements.
28 Students are expected to be familiar with and adhere to the school's ethos.
26 The school wishes to project a positive public image.
62 The school actively seeks to acquire a prominent position in its social and
educational.
42 The school accepts low achieving students *
21The school contributes to the local community with services and activities
20 There is careful monitoring to ensure that the school curriculum conforms
to official Ministry
    of Education policy
29 Students take part in community volunteering programs.
34 The school receives social recognition from parents and the community.
61 The school is reasonably successful academically and socially.

Consideration

22 Students receive individual support and personal attention as required.
30 The curriculum is examined carefully to ensure that agreed humanistic
values are upheld
    and fostered.
19 There are regular activities to promote student group cohesiveness.
40 Experts are brought into the school to help teachers with teaching and
evaluation.
16 The school introduces varied new curricula, which are customized to
individual student needs.
38 Humanistic ideas and messages are integrated in the observable and hidden
curriculum.

Task-Orientation

39 Teachers, students and members of the community all collaborate to
achieve school goals.
53 There is an effective feedback system, which constantly monitors student
progress.
23 Teachers are actively involved in pinpointing and solving problems.

41Regular meetings are held to discuss student progress and achievements.
32 Teachers and staff at the school receive regular in-service training and
enrichment programs.
46 Teachers and students hold personal talks even after school hours.
24 The school is going through a clear process of change and renovation.
25 Careful efforts are made to monitor teacher punctuality and absences.
33 Careful efforts are made to monitor student punctuality and absences.
35 Organizational and academic changes have transformed the school.
* Item scores were reversed (recoded)

1. *Innovation* (4 items): "Teachers often introduce new ideas for school improvement and change".
2. *Conservatism* (3 items): "The school strongly favours its current status quo".
3. *Self-direction* (5 items): "The school is more likely to accept ideas from inside the school than from outside the school".
4. *Conformity* (4 items): "Our school does not favour divergent modes of behaviour.
5. *Egalitarianism* (8 items): "We believe in egalitarian student-teacher relations"; "The school admits equal numbers of high- and low-achieving students".
6. *Elitism* (11 items): "The school carefully screens and selects student applicants"; "The school seeks to project a positive public image".
7. *Consideration* (6 items): "Students receive individual support and personal attention where needed".
8. *Task-Orientation* (10 items). "Teachers, students and members of the community collaborate to reach school goals"; "Teachers are actively involved in identifying and solving problems".

Items were rated on a five-option range, from 1 (not at all true), through 5 (very true). In the introductory note to the questionnaire, participants were asked to describe what was happening at their school, based on the item statements.

RESULTS

The first step in data processing was to calculate correlations (monotony coefficients) for the scale item scores. The second step involved a small space analysis (SSA) using the Hudap (Hebrew University Data Analysis Package) computer program. The SSA solution for the scale item scores yielded a coefficient of alienation[2] of .27 in a two-dimensional space.

Figure 2 shows the deployment of variables (see Table 1) in a two-dimensional space. It presents the empirical structure of the school organizational values domain. Observing Figure 2, we find that each of the basic components defined (values) has a distinct region in the conceptual space. There is, however, a remarkable deviation from the expected structure shown in Figure 1. Some of the components (Innovation, Task-orientation, and Consideration) occupy a circular region in the centre of the map. Items comprising these values represent the school's pedagogical policies regarding the curriculum, teaching, and concern for students and their academic progress (see Table 1). The remaining components are dispersed about the periphery. The outer circle contains four regions hosting the following values: Conservatism, Conformity, Elitism, Self-direction and Egalitarianism. Items in the outer circle represent administrative and social policies, including school managerial strategies.

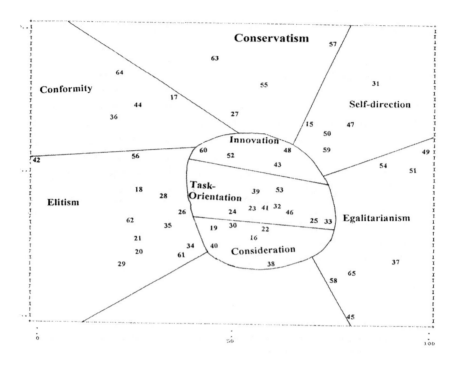

*Figure 2. Smallest Space Analysis of School Monitoring Values:
A Two-dimensional Space.*

It is interesting (and perhaps not too surprising) to note in Figure 2 that: (a) Task-orientation values (e.g., "Teachers, students and members of the community all collaborate to achieve school goals" - Item 39; "Teachers are actively involved in pinpointing and solving problems - Item 23) are located in the centre of the map, and more importantly, (b) Task-orientation values are not antagonistic to Consideration values.

In Facet Theory nomenclature, Figure 2 is a radex composed of two concentric circles (as the result of a facet's modular role), and an angular division (as a result of an unordered facet). The inner circle contains those values which pertain to the pedagogical aspect of school work: Teaching students and handling their learning, emotional and personal matters, as well as helping teachers achieve their educational goals. These values are, naturally, more central to school work, and are highly interrelated. They are most likely to be classified as the school's "core values". The outer circle contains values relating to the school's operational mode:

social policy (integration vs. segregation; community-school relations), and managerial modes (self-management vs. conformity). According to Facet Theory, the inner circle items in a radex are less differentiated and more related to one another than outer circle items, which are more differentiated, less related to one another, or even contrasting and opposing to one another.

It is also interesting to note that the region opposite Conservatism in the SSA map (bottom of the map) is empty. While this is obviously due to nature of the items selected, it nevertheless has important implications for the study. The question we need to ask here is what should, or could, have filled this empty space? Based on the contents of the outer circle values and on Facet Theory principles, the space might have been occupied by items representing the semantic opposite to those that make up Conservatism in the operational mode of the school as an organization. This suggests that another (organizational) value (or values), which may be tentatively termed "Change", could be added. Change in this context refers to the position adopted by organization members regarding organizational, administrative or managerial policies, strategic approaches, or in general - attitudes towards the need for "overhauling" the school. A value of this kind would belong in the outer circle, since it deals directly with the administrative and social domain of the school's strategic functioning policies.

A PROPOSED THEORY OF SCHOOL ORGANIZATIONAL VALUES

The first underlying assumption of the new theory is that schools are similar and different from other social organizations with regard to value structure in different aspects. Like other organizations, schools assign differing levels of importance to organizational values. However, in contradistinction to other organizations, schools seek to integrate the extreme poles of Task-Orientation and Consideration and this "combined" dimension, Task-Orientation-Consideration, together with the inclination towards educational innovation, may be identified as the school's "core" values. As we have noted, the core values are the values most emphasized by the organization, and regarding whose importance most organizational members concur. The second underlying assumption is that the remaining values (those pertaining to the school's operational mode) may be regarded as peripheral values. Peripheral values are those which the organization may or may not emphasize strongly, and the importance attributed to such values is usually not unanimously agreed upon by all its members.

The third underlying assumption is that we can describe school operating policies (peripheral values) in terms of three polarized orientations:

1. *Decision-Making Orientation:* Internal (Self-management) vs. external (Conformity).
2. *Social Relations Orientation:* Egalitarianism vs. Elitism. This orientation is congruent with Hofstede's (1980) power-distance conception.
3. *Change Orientation:* Especially changes in administrative and managerial policies and practices --Conservatism vs. Change. This orientation coincides with Hofstede's (1980) uncertainty avoidance values.

The three underlying assumptions point to the suggestion that schools have a complex value structure, compared to other types of administrative organizations whose value structure is shown schematically in Figure 1. School value structures are complex since schools are motivated by two hierarchically ordered groups of values, namely Pedagogical, and Operational values, where the Pedagogical values are core values and the Operational values are peripheral. Pedagogical values are the basic, generally agreed upon values at the centre of the school's activities, or the main purpose underpinning its existence, namely teaching, class management, student education, instilling knowledge and humanistic care. To these ends schools harness all the power and resources at their disposal.

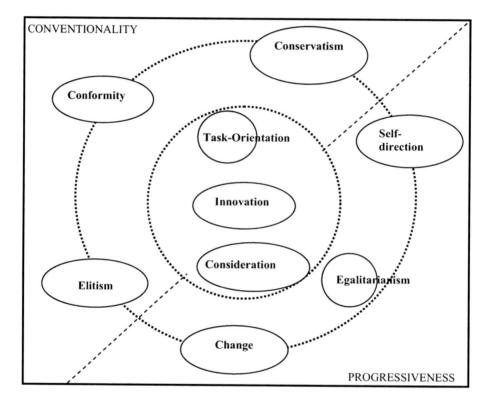

Figure 3. A Model of School Organizational Values.

The common relations pattern among school motivating values is in the form of two concentric circles. The inner circle contains the chief ('core') values, whose position reflects both their ascribed significance and the degree of consensus among school staff regarding their importance. The other ('peripheral') values appear in the outer circle.

The theoretical model is shown in Figure 3. In the centre of the model we find the core values: *Task-Orientation, Innovation* (mostly pedagogical), and *Consideration*. In the second circle, peripheral values appear as contrasting concepts in the following order: *Conformity* vs. *Self-Direction* (Decision-making orientation); *Elitism* vs. *Egalitarianism* (Social relations orientation); and *Change* vs. *Conservatism* (Change orientation). Schools that strongly emphasize values like *Conservatism, Conformity* and *Elitism* will most likely lean towards Conventionality and preservation, whereas those that place high value on *Self-direction, Egalitarianism* and *Change* will most likely value progressiveness and change.

APPLICATION OF THE SCHOOL ORGANIZATIONAL VALUES THEORY: CLASSIFICATION OF SCHOOLS ACCORDING TO THEIR PERIPHERAL VALUES

Differences in emphasis of the peripheral values (see Figure 3) can result in different types of schools. The four major types are: 1. The Conservative-Traditional School; 2. The Conservative Self-Managed School. 3. The Traditional-Reform Seeking School; 4. The Self-Managed Self-Reforming School.

Conservative-Traditional School

The conservative-traditional school is a school whose organizational culture espouses low level self-management and insularity with strict adherence to prevailing educational, social and religious traditions. Such schools tend to introduce neither internally originating change (prompted by teachers, staff or students) nor externally originating change (stemming from parents and the community). They do, however, accept and implement (submissively) change dictated by recognized authorities (the Schools Inspectorate and Ministry of Education).

Characteristic high values of such schools are:

1. *Conservatism* - conservative, thorough investigation of each step before taking a decision to act. Little interest in change, which if introduced, is implemented with great caution.
2. *Conformity* - avoids actions or trends, which may irritate or harm others, or which might fail to meet social norms. Accepts cultural and religious norms and outlooks.
3. *Elitism* (high or low) – tries to exert an influence, maintain its public image and to achieve social recognition and kudos.

Conservative-Self-Managed School

The self-managed conservative school is an autonomous community school. Such schools proceed with extreme caution when introducing change of modus operandi, school programs or the character of the school. School staff share a conservative and very cautious attitude to change with the school's environment (the parents and the community). If the environment places a high premium on the value of change, serious conflict may erupt between the school and its environment.

Characteristic high values of such schools are:

1. *Conservatism* - thoroughly explores each step before deciding to act. Seeks little change, which if introduced, is introduced very cautiously, perhaps even reluctantly.
2. *Self-Direction* - encourages independent thinking and action where choice, decision-making, investigation and seeking new routes are concerned.
3. *Egalitarianism* – interested in interacting harmoniously with its environment, shows consideration, respect, tolerance and cooperation. No desire to stand out from its environment and certainly no wish to alienate it. No desire to control people or funding within its environment.

Traditional, Reform-Seeking School

The traditional, reform seeking school presents a closed facade to the environment, wishes to be noticed and be a community power. Such schools are willing to experiment with new ideas, while endeavouring not to be too "different" or unusual. They therefore submit to recognized authorities. These schools can experience considerable internal conflict since their propensity towards change may clash with their inclination toward conformity and submission to authority. Due to their change-oriented thrust, these schools may resemble the self-managing conservative school, and indeed, the traditional, self-reforming school may essentially be in transition to becoming a self-managing school.
Characteristic high values of such schools are:

1. *Change* - seeks challenge, espouses daring approaches and diversity. Does not devote much energy and effort to considering the risks versus the probabilities of success.
2. *Conformity* - avoids actions or trends that may annoy or harm others, or fail to meet social norms. Accepts cultural and religious norms and outlooks.
3. *Elitism (high or low)* - Seeks to influence, maintain a public image and achieve social recognition and prestige.

Self-Managed-Self-Reforming School

The self-reforming self-managed school is an autonomous community school whose culture diametrically oppose the culture of conservative-traditional schools. Self-reforming self-managed schools are keen and open to accepting and adopting fresh ideas (though they may not investigate them thoroughly), regardless of whether they originate within the school, with the teachers, staff, or perhaps students, or outside the school, with the parents, community or professional bodies. Such schools most probably have an effervescent style as a result of constant innovation and great "openness" and willingness to take risks and involve any other willing parties in that risk.
Characteristic high values of such schools are:

1. *Change* - seeks challenges, espouses daring and diversity. Does not devote much energy or effort to considering risks versus the probability of success.
2. *Self-Direction* - encourages independent thinking and action wherever choice, decision-making, investigation and seeking new routes are concerned.
3. *Egalitarianism* - keen on functioning harmoniously with its environment, demonstrates consideration, respect, tolerance and cooperation. No desire to stand out from its environment and certainly no wish to alienate it. No desire to control people or funding within its environment.

Just as the traditional-conservative school and the reformative self-managed school are opposed in terms of style, the conservative self-managed school and the traditional, reformation-seeking school represent another pair of opposites. Many schools in Israel and around the world conform to the four types of school described above.

CONCLUSION

Based on the issues presented in this chapter, I would like to recommend that organizational evaluations should estimate the importance ascribed by the organization's incumbents to the principle organizational values. It is especially effective to try to discover a fit (or lack of fit) between the importance ascribed by officials within the organization to the different values, and the members of the organization and the organizational environment. A lack of fit may provide very fertile ground for conflict and contention, and in extreme cases may result in the organization's collapse and ruin. In other words, we might say that an organization would lack harmony unless it enjoys consensus with respect to its driving organizational values.

The current trend in many jurisdictions is to urge organizations, schools included, to strive toward constant change. The conservative-traditional type of school represents, therefore, great cause for concern for educational policy makers and those who make up the school environment. According to the school organization values theory, the conservative-traditional school places great emphasis on uncertainty avoidance, which is paramount in generating the conservative policy that these schools display. I would therefore strongly recommend to try to expose the relevant parties to this value and its implications, urging a reassessment of their beliefs and attitudes towards uncertainty, security and the question of loss associated with relinquishing familiar work or behaviour patterns. By effectively addressing these values and preferring the value of *Change* to *Conservatism*, we can help propel these organizations toward change. The trend toward increased self-management in schools, now in full swing in many Western countries, would receive additional impetus from added recognition of the importance of *Self-direction* and a choice of *Self-direction* and *Egalitarianism* rather than *Conformity* and *Elitism*. It may well be that an appreciation of the importance of these values will help to increase schools' capacity and willingness for self-management.

NOTES

[1] The author would like to express his appreciation to Prof. Christopher Hodgkinson for his very helpful comments on an earlier version of this chapter.
[2] Coefficient of alienation is a measure of goodness of fit between the correlation matrix and the spatial deployment of the items in the SSA map. The coefficient of alienation ranges from 0.00 to 1.00, where the highest value indicates worst match between the initial correlation matrix and the SSA map. A coefficient of .27 is a borderline coefficient of goodness of fit, considering the number of items (51) in the questionnaire.

REFERENCES

Alport, G.W., Vernon, P.E., & Lindzey, G. (1951). *Study of values*. Boston: Houghton Mifflin.
Baum, J.A.C., & Oliver, C. (1991). Institutional linkages and organizational mortality. *Administrative Science Quarterly, 36*(1), 187-218.
Cherrington, D. (1997). The values of younger workers. *Business Horizons, 20*(6), 18-20.
Elizur, D. (1984). Facets of work values: A structural analysis of work outcomes. *Journal of Applied Psychology, 69*(3), 379-389.
Etzioni, A. (1988). *The moral dimensions: Toward a new economics*. New York: The Free Press.
Fayol, H. (1949). *General and industrial management*. London: Pitman.
Follett, M.P. (1926). *The new state: Group organization, the solution of popular government*. London: Longmans, Green.
Gardner, R. (2001). Mapping patterns of change in cultures and schools. In J. Cairns, D. Lawton, & R. Gardner (Eds.), *Values, culture and education* (pp. 107-121). London, UK: Kogan-Page.
Greenberg, J. (1977). The Protestant work ethic and reactions to negative performance evaluation on a laboratory task. *Journal of Applied Psychology, 62*(6), 682-690.
Gulick, L. (1937). Notes on the theory of organization. In L. Gulick & L. Urwick (Eds.), *Papers on the science of administration* (pp. 3-13). New York: Institute of Public Administration.
Guttman, L. (1968). A general non-metric technique for finding the smallest coordinate space for a configuration of points. *Psychometrika, 33*, 469-506.
Hodgkinson, C. (1999). The will to power. In P.T. Begley (Ed.), *Values and educational leadership* (pp. 139-150). Albany, NY: State University of New York Press.
Hofstede, G. (1980). *Culture's consequences: International differences in work-related values*. Beverly Hills, CA: Sage.
Hofstede, G. (1990). *Cultures and organizations: Software of the mind*. London: McGraw-Hill.
Hofstede, G., & Bond, M.H. (1988). The Confucius connection: From cultural roots to economic growth. *Organizational Dynamics, 14*(2), 5-39.
Johansson, O., & Bredson, P.V. (1999). Value orchestration by the policy community for the learning community: Reality or myth. In P.T. Begley (Ed.), *Values and educational leadership* (pp. 51-72). Albany, NY: State University of New York Press.
Lawrence, P.R., & Lorsch, J.W. (1969). *Organizations environment*. Boston, MA: Harvard University Press.
Levy, S., & Guttman, L. (1976). *Values and attitudes of Israeli high school youth*. Jerusalem: The Jerusalem Institute of Applied Social Research (Hebrew with a summary in English).
Merton, R. (1940). Bureaucratic structure and personality. *Social Forces 18*(5), 560-568.
Milgrom, P., & Roberts, J. (1992). *Economics, organization, and management*. Englewood Cliffs, NJ: Prentice-Hall.
Mooney, J.D. (1930). *The principles of organization*. New York: Harper & Row.
Robey, D. (1986). *Designing organizations*. New York: Irwin.
Rokeach, M. (1973). *The nature of human values*. New York: The Free Press.
Salanick, G.R., & Pfeffer, J. (1978). A social information processing approach to job attitudes and task design. *Administrative Science Quarterly, 23*(1), 224-253.
Schwartz, S.H. (1992). Universals in the content and structure of values: Theoretical advances and empirical tests in 20 countries. In M. Zanna (Ed.), *Advances in Experimental Social Psychology, 25* (pp. 1-65). New York: Academic Press.
Schwartz, S.H. (1999). A theory of cultural values and some implications for work. *Applied psychology: An International Review, 48*, 23-47.
Shye, S., Elizur, D., & Hoffman, M. (1994). *Introduction to facet theory*. Newbury Park, CA: Sage.

Smith, M.B. (1963). Personal values in the study of lives. In R.W. White (Ed.), *The study of lives* (pp. 324-347). Englewood Cliffs, NJ: Prentice-Hall.

Super, D.E. (1962). The structure of work values in relation to status, achievement, interests and adjustment. *Journal of Applied Psychology, 46*(?), 231-239.

Taylor, F.W. (1911). *The principles of scientific management.* New York: Harper & Row.

Tziner, A.E. (1987). *The facet analytic approach to research and data processing.* New York: Peter Lang.

Weber, M. (1904). *The Protestant ethic and the spirit of Capitalism.* Translated by T. Parsons (1930). New York: Scribner.

Weber, M. (1946). *The theory of social and economic organization* (Translation). New York: Free Press.

JOHN L. COLLARD

THE RELATIONSHIP OF GENDER AND CONTEXT TO LEADERSHIP IN AUSTRALIAN SCHOOLS

Abstract. This chapter focuses upon the interactions between core components of the organizational culture of Australian schools (level and size of schools, sectorial identity, and student gender) and the beliefs of a balanced sample of male and female principals. The findings qualify previous discourse about leadership and gender by suggesting that organizational variables generate significant variations both within and between genders. Some factors draw men and women towards shared belief platforms; others lead to highly significant differences within each gender. The findings thereby question essentialist typecasts which portray men as naturally bureaucratic and instrumental and women as collaborative and nurturing. The concept of "multiple masculinities and femininities" (Connell, 1995), is advanced as a more useful theoretical construct.

Australia replicates the pattern of advanced western democracies where schools are highly feminized workplaces but disproportionate percentages of principalships are held by men. This mirrors broader patterns in the workforce where men hold 70% to 80% of administrative, executive and managerial roles. The 1996 census indicated that although 69% of teachers in Australia were women, only a third of school principals in Australia were female (ABS Census, 1998; Connell, 1987). In the state of Victoria, where this study was conducted, 67% were males and 37% were females. Observations that Canadian and English schools are institutions where "men manage and women teach" (Ozga, 1993; Reynolds, 1995) would appear to be equally applicable to Australia.

PREVIOUS INTERPRETATIONS

Explanations for the low proportions of women in the principalship in Western democracies include cultural and historical theses, which argue that such patterns reflect traditional gender roles sanctioning teaching as an appropriate sphere for "the emotional labour of women but precluding them from school leadership (Blackmore, 1993, 1999; Reynolds, 1995). Other theorists have argued that men dominate the principalship because of the patriarchal traditions of public leadership (Hearn, 1993; Seidler, 1994). Feminist critiques have defined educational administration as "gender blind" and a "masculinist enterprise" which consistently marginalizes women (Blackmore, 1993, 1999; Rusch & Marshall, 1995; Shakeshaft, 1987, 1989). Other explanations related to women's career choices and reluctance to apply for leadership positions frequently claim that they are restricted to roles in schools which are compatible with other life-roles as wives and nurturers (Acker, 1989; Antonucci, 1980; Darley & Lomax, 1995). It is usually assumed that men are not inhibited by similar restraints. Organizational theorists have pointed to the cultures and structures of the workplace as forces which systematically marginalize women from promotional tracks whilst male networks advantage men (Connell, 1987; Kanter, 1977, 1993; Russell, 1995). The culture of educational administration itself, especially the limited nature and sexist assumptions that infuse the dominant journals and university coursework, has also been identified as a contributing factor (Rusch & Marshall, 1995).

There is also evidence of essentialism and typecasting in much of the existing leadership discourse. It is frequently assumed that there are pervasive differences

P.T. Begley and O. Johansson (eds.), The Ethical Dimensions of School Leadership, 181–199.
© 2003 *Kluwer Academic Publishers. Printed in the Netherlands.*

between men and women. Unitary stereotypes depict men as "directive, bureaucratic and instrumental" and women as "collaborative, relational and organic" (Adler, Laney, & Packer, 1993; Ferguson, 1984). Claims that men operate from a values base of "abstract principle" and women from a "relational focus" when confronting intensely personal issues are assumed to apply to the realms of school leadership (Gilligan, 1982). Gray's (1989) gender paradigms in schools are a classic example of such typologies. He linked a feminine paradigm to primary schools and the masculine with secondary schools:

NURTUANT/FEMININE PARADIGM	MASCULINE/AGGRESSIVE PARADIGM
Caring	Highly Regulated
Creative	Conformist
Intuitive	Disciplined
Aware of Individual Differences	Normative
Non-competitive	Competitive
Tolerant	Evaluative
Subjective	Objective

Figure 1. Gray's Gender Paradigms in Schools 1989, p. 111.

The field of gender studies itself has moved beyond essentialist typecasting in recent years and developed more fine-tuned theories based upon the interactions of both genders with specific and diverse social contexts. Connell's concept of "multiple forms of masculinity and femininity" reflects this increased sophistication. He argues that various cultures generate diverse forms of masculinity within Australia and illustrates this through case studies of working class, environmental, gay and corporate men. He also alerts us to different forms of femininity ranging from compliance with patriarchal regimes to active contestation of them (Connell, 1995). Critical feminist writers have also stressed the interaction of gender with other variables such as culture, class and race (Blackmore, 1999). It is also logical to argue that the characteristics, cultures and histories of particular schools and sectors generate diverse forms of masculine and female leadership. Indeed, there is a rich heritage of contingency theory in educational administration which argues that organizational context is a key influence upon leader behaviour (Bass & Stogdill, 1970; Greenfield, 1975). It is therefore possible that different environments may promote varied perceptions and beliefs amongst male and female leaders and even generate differences within each gender. Conversely, similar contexts may ameliorate differences between men and women and draw them towards a consensus which belies oppositional typecasts.

Another problem in the field of leadership and gender has been the tendency for theorists to base claims on limited case studies and narrative accounts which cannot provide a representative basis upon which to mount generic claims (Adler et al., 1993; Fennell, 1999; Hall, 1996; Hurty, 1995; Limerick & Anderson, 1999; Ozga, 1993). The rare studies which have made some attempt at representative sampling have all disputed the validity of gender typecasts (Court, 1998; Coleman, 1998; Evetts, 1994; Kruger, 1996; Shum & Cheng, 1997). Critical feminists have also become sceptical about "women's ways of leading" without recognition of "structural constraints and discourses" which shape leadership styles (Blackmore, 1999, p. 156). The status of gender typologies in the field is therefore questionable simply because the evidence to sustain them is inadequate. They cannot be regarded as incontrovertible foundations upon which to build theory and practice and we are well advised to heed recent advice to question romanticized claims about the leadership style of women in populist discourses (Blackmore, 1999; Grogan, 2000). There is a need for broad-scale studies to test the claims of qualitative research if we are to advance our understanding of the role of gender in school leadership.

This study explored the interactions of principal gender with the key contextual variables of schools. Recent UK research has identified level of schooling as a factor which differentiates principals (Hall, 1996; Pascall & Ribbins, 1998). It was assumed that this factor may have similar valence in Victoria. As the majority of primary schools in the state contained less than 600 pupils, whereas secondary sites ranged between 600 and 1000+ pupils, school size was also included as an important variable. Over a third of Victorian students are in non-government schools (Australian Bureau of Statistics, 1998) and sectorial identity was also considered to be a likely source of differences between principals. Many of the non-government schools are also segregated according to student gender whereas almost all Government sites are co-educational. Student gender was therefore also considered another potential source of differentiation between the beliefs of principals.

THE RESEARCH PROJECT

In June 1996, there were 2259 principals in Victoria. Of these, 76% were in primary sites and 24% in secondary sites. The proportion of females was much higher at primary than secondary levels (62% compared to 25%). There was also great variation according to sector.

The disparity in the proportions of males and females was most marked in the Government sector whereas in Catholic schools, the proportion of females was marginally higher than the males[1]. Girls' only schools were more likely to be led by women, whereas the overwhelming majority of principals in boys' only sites were men.

In 1997, a questionnaire was administered to a stratified sample of principals from all three sectors and both levels of schooling. Subjects were asked to respond to items according to a five-point scale, ranging from strong disagreement to strong agreement. The constellations included:

- perceptions and beliefs about student abilities
- perceptions and beliefs about curriculum goals and pedagogy
- perceptions and beliefs about working with teachers
- perceptions and beliefs about the roles of parent and community members

- perceptions and beliefs about the nature of principalship
- perceptions and beliefs about personal and professional wellbeing.

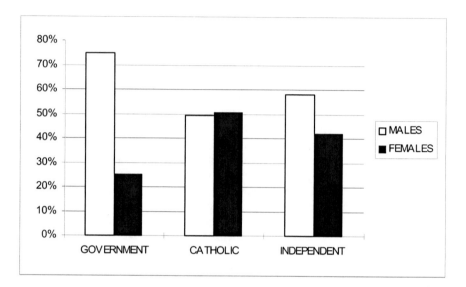

Figure 2. Distribution of Principals According to Gender and Sector, Curriculum Corporation Database 1996.

Each section explored a continuum, ranging from hierarchical and bureaucratic to relational and collaborative concepts and, in this respect, sought to test beliefs and values which previous theorists have stereotyped as masculine and feminine. The sections on teacher and parent roles and on the principalship itself juxtaposed directive and exclusive stances with collaborative and participatory approaches.

Respondents had the option of volunteering for a confidential follow up interview. Interview questions were linked to key concepts in the questionnaire, but also provided opportunities to question or qualify the questionnaire items. The interview responses were compared to patterns which emerged from the questionnaire. Although six months separated the two processes, there was a high degree of consistency in responses.

A total of 371 questionnaires were returned, establishing a response rate of 73.4%. Of these, 51.1% were male principals and 49.9% female[2]. Women from Government secondary schools provided a particularly low response rate. Bivariate analysis was utilized to explore associations between variables. Responses were tabulated according to frequencies and then cross-tabulated according to the variables of gender, school level, sectoral identity, student gender and school size. The cross tabulations were analyzed using the Pearson Test of Statistical Significance. Associations at the .05, .01, and .001 levels were considered significant and unlikely to be a function of sampling error. This method enabled analysis of data in the form of paired observations on two variables, such as principal gender and school sector. The findings indicated the presence or absence of a relationship between the two variables, and also permitted a second level of analysis to determine whether the pattern according to principal gender as a solitary variable remained stable when organizational factors were considered.

Equal numbers of males and females were interviewed, and the data was analyzed to confirm, supplement and expand understandings based upon the quantitative data. As such, it was akin to a validation exercise, in that the knowledge claims which had emerged from the quantitative research were tested through a dialogue between researcher and a representative sample of the population who completed the questionnaire (Evers & Lakomski, 1996a, 1996b; Kvale, 1996). Responses which contradicted or qualified the questionnaire data and new emergent themes were also noted.

Perceptions of Students

The findings confirmed many previous claims about leader gender but also indicated significant and previously unacknowledged variations in the perceptions and beliefs of Victorian principals. Gray's claim that women are more aware of individual differences than men was confirmed. They were more sensitive to the difficulties of individuals and groups and also had higher expectations of student abilities. Over two-thirds (67%) believed their schools contained many "high achievers" but only 59% of men shared this perception. This was, in turn, allied to a higher commitment to more diverse forms of curriculum provision, whereas men were more satisfied if generic programs were in place. Leaders from secondary sites (65%) were significantly more optimistic than their primary counterparts (55%). This may well reflect the possibility that the smaller scale of primary sites means that principals have more intimate knowledge of students and are consequently more aware of learning difficulties.

Highly significant differences emerged when sector was taken into consideration. Whereas 94% of leaders from Independent schools believed there were many "high achievers" in their care, the corresponding proportions for Government (48%) and Catholic schools (54%) were remarkably lower.

This suggests that the more selective nature of the student intake and traditions of high academic achievement in the Independent sector actively shape the perceptions of school leaders. There was also evidence that sector can exaggerate gender patterns, for in this sector, 76% of the women held this perception compared to only 52% of the men. Conversely, in the Government sector, women were less optimistic than the men (12% compared to 16%). The lower optimism of Catholic leaders may well reflect the place of Catholic schools in the educational market place. They provide a broad public education like Government schools, but a minority of secondary colleges promote themselves as providers of high academic attainment for a privileged elite in a similar manner to Independent schools[3]. Ambivalence amongst leaders from this sector was reflected in high proportions of uncertainty on this item: males 30%, females 27%. The findings clearly suggest that the perceptions of both genders are highly influenced by the cultures of the schools they lead.

The pattern was also amplified by student gender. Women from girls' schools were most likely to believe their sites contained many "high achievers" (77%) and to disagree that there were large numbers "who find learning difficult" (90%). The vast majority of these women came from Independent girls' schools. Conversely, 50% to 60% of leaders from co-educational and boys' schools believed they led schools with large numbers of students who struggle. When viewed in tandem, the findings indicate the existence of a distinctive, optimistic and achievement-oriented leadership culture amongst the female leaders of Independent girls' schools. This was a recurrent pattern throughout the study and may be directly related to current trends, which indicate that girls from such sites are the most likely of all Victorian students to achieve high levels of academic success (Teese, 2000). The findings, with regard to perceptions of student populations, also clearly indicate that generalized claims about male and female belief systems are too simplistic to capture the diversity amongst Victorian school principals. The reality is much more complex than unitary stereotypes suggest.

Curriculum Goals

Repetitive claims that men are more aligned to "instrumental and technical values" than women (Adler et al., 1993; Craib, 1987; Ferguson, 1984; Parsons & Bales, 1956) gain some support from this study. They were slightly more predisposed to support "utilitarian curriculum goals" and women were more oriented towards "personal-developmental" objectives. When the two types of goals were juxtaposed, the women were more adamant and unified about their beliefs than the men who expressed greater uncertainty; however, this apparent conformity to gender stereotypes was qualified by interview responses from both groups. Many argued that a polarization between personal-developmental and utilitarian goals was too arbitrary and that the two were interdependent. A comment by a principal from a school with both primary and secondary classes illustrates this:

> One of my priorities is the development of self esteem because it helps the development of skills such as numeracy and social skills in the Junior School whereas at the other end, the Senior School, the academic bit must come first but is supported by the pastoral.

The comment indicates that school level can be a consistent source of differences about curriculum goals. Primary school leaders were significantly more supportive of "self esteem" than their secondary counterparts (90% compared to 67%). Both genders were in relative correspondence at both levels and this points to the power of the respective developmental stages of students to draw men and women towards consensus. At the primary level, where young children are moving from familial dependence and developing foundational skills, there was agreement about the need for a supportive environment which nurtures self esteem. At the secondary level students are moving towards independence and there was less emphasis upon developing positive self images. The pattern recurred with regard to viewing "learning as a search for personal meaning" (58% compared to 54%); however, men at the secondary level were significantly less supportive of personal-developmental goals than their female counterparts (48% compared to 60%). The

ITEM: THIS IS A SCHOOL WHICH HAS MANY STUDENTS WHO ARE HIGH
ACHIEVERS

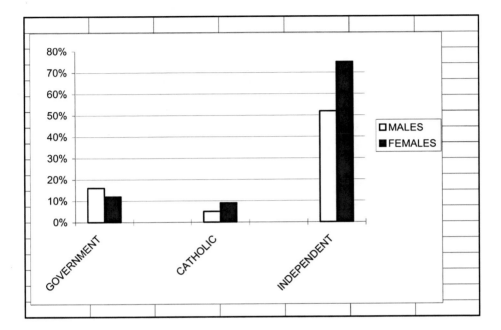

(Statistical Significance .01, 6df)

Figure 3. Proportions of Overall Agreement by Principal Gender and Sector.

gap was much less pronounced at the primary level (women 59%, men 57%). It
suggests that direct exposure to the learning needs of students draws men into
alignment with their female colleagues at the primary level, whereas they become
more differentiated in secondary schools.

The patterns of response were again complicated by sector. The strongest
support for personal-developmental goals came from men and women from
Independent schools. The lowest came from Government school leaders. Women
from this sector were notably less enthusiastic than other females. The proportion
who supported personal-developmental goals was actually below that for men in
the non-government sectors.

ITEM: THIS IS A SCHOOL WHICH ENCOURAGES LEARNING AS A
SEARCH FOR PERSONAL MEANING

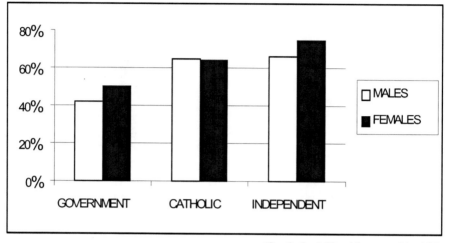

(Statistical Significance .01, 6df)

Figure 4. Proportion of Overall Agreement by Principal Gender and Sector.

This suggests the existence of different cultural values in the various sectors and
these appear to be more powerful influences upon curriculum beliefs than principal
gender. Explanations for this are undoubtedly related to the heritage of religious
traditions, with associated emphasis upon personal formation, in non-government
schools. Buntine's address about Christian values at Camberwell Grammar in 1927
is a famous example:

> We endeavour to cultivate all round boys and men, with every side of their natures
> developed to the fullest possible extent. It is the duty of the school to train its pupils
> for life, and not merely for living…not only mental, but physical, social, devotional
> or spiritual (Hansen, 1986, p. 126).

Such pronouncements differ markedly from the "free, secular and compulsory"
rhetoric associated with the establishment of the Government school system in the
1870s. The founders of this sector placed stronger emphasis upon social and
vocational skills for an industrial workforce and a democratic citizenry (Austin,
1977; Barcan, 1980; Evans, Murray, & Evans, 1995; Vlahogiannis, 1989). It
would appear that different cultural heritages continue to influence the values of
leaders in the 1990s and a consequence of this is that women from Government
schools differ significantly from their female counterparts in other sectors. It
indicates that sectorial cultures can lead to substantial differences within a gender
on some issues and these may be more substantial than variations between the
genders.

Pedagogy

Another recurrent claim has been that women are more oriented to the ethics of care and service than men. The converse, that men are more autonomous, rational and analytical than women has also been frequently asserted (Craib, 1987; Gilligan, 1982; Hall, 1996; Noddings, 1984; Shakeshaft, 1987; Seidler, 1994; Steinberg, 1993). Evidence from this study both supports and qualifies such claims. The more collaborative stereotypes of women would suggest that they would be less sympathetic to competitive and individualistic pedagogies than men. This was the case. They were more likely to disagree that their schools encourage "students to be winners in a competitive world". The pattern was common to both levels of schooling although it should be noted that primary leaders were more opposed to a "competitive ethic" than their secondary counterparts (55% compared to 37%); however, a significant variation emerged when sector was taken into account. In both the Government and Independent sectors, women were more opposed to competition than men. The reverse was true in the Catholic sector. Although both men and women from Catholic schools were the most opposed to competition, the men were more inclined than the women (57% compared to 54%). The statistics suggest the influence of strong sectorial, values which ensure relative correspondence amongst the two genders, but also lead men to deviate from the dominant pattern for men in the study.

This was a recurrent pattern throughout the study and indicates that men from the Catholic sector were more ideologically committed to collaborative values than men from Government and Independent schools. It undermines claims that all male leaders are committed to competitive values in the manner asserted by much previous discourse in the field.

Conversely, both genders from Independent sites were the least opposed to competition. The fact that women from the sector were less opposed to competition than women from Government and Catholic schools again suggests that sectorial culture can be a more compelling influence than principal gender. The findings thereby provide two clear examples of how specific groups of leaders, men from Catholic schools and women from Independent sites, contradict stereotypes of gendered values. In both instances, the values which inform the institutional cultures appear more powerful than gender.

Working with Teachers

Claims that women wish to work in more relational ways than men were confirmed by this study. They were much more committed to collegiality and teamwork. They were more willing to foster a consultative climate within the school and allow staff to participate in decision making. They were more receptive to advice and demonstrated greater tolerance for debate about goals and policies. They believed teachers want collaborative leadership and favoured collective responsibility rather than frameworks for accountability. The women also held more active conceptions of teachers as "continuing learners", placed greater value upon teacher autonomy and were more prepared to grant space for innovation and adaptation of sectorial policies to local realities. They were also more inclined to believe that teachers would question unilateral decisions, whereas men were more likely to expect them to implement system mandates without dissent. This was

ITEM: THIS IS A SCHOOL WHICH ENCOURAGES
STUDENTS TO BE WINNERS IN A COMPETITIVE WORLD

		MALES	FEMALES			
GOVERNMENT		33	53			
CATHOLIC		57	54			
INDEPENDENT		21	26			

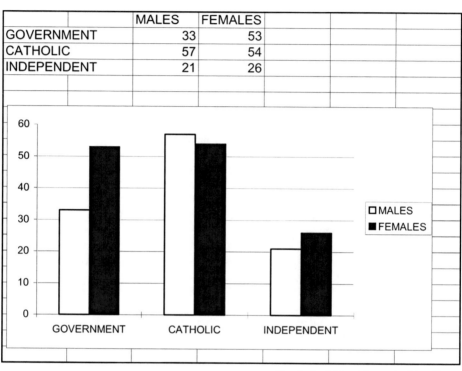

(Statistical Significance .02 6df)

Figure 5. Proportions of Disagreement by Principal Gender and School Level.

not to say that women lacked strong leadership vision. Indeed, they were more confident that they held an appropriate vision for the school community than the men. The difference lay more in the way the vision was determined. Men appeared more predisposed to transmit a vision from a position of hierarchical authority, women to engage in more collaborative processes.

There was also consistent support for the proposition that men perceive leadership in terms of maintaining authority, status and organizational control (Ferguson, 1984; Gray, 1989; Hudson & Jacot, 1991; Steinberg, 1993). They leaned more towards strong, directive approaches than women, and believed teachers and parents expect such leadership and comply with decisions made in this mode. These beliefs were allied with their tendency to view teachers as agents responsible for fulfilling the policy mandates of authorities, whether from an institutional or systemic level. A logical consequence was their preference for solid, structural boundaries for accountability and reporting within schools. They were also more oriented towards consistent policy and practice. Such tendencies were consistent with their stronger tendency to identify with the image of "line manager". Some would view these findings as evidence of a bureaucratic mindset and the polar opposite of the alleged relational modes of women. Men were also more inclined to see themselves as "initiators" and identify with metaphors of stability such as "a voice of authority" and "a rock in stormy waters". These could be typecast as the traditional masculine qualities which permeate leadership discourse (Blackmore, 1999; Gronn, 1995).

These findings were qualified when school size and sector were taken into account. The perception that teachers want "strong leadership from the top" increased according to school size. In the smallest schools, the proportions who agreed with such a statement ranged from 72% to 75%. In schools with more than 400 pupils, the range was from 82% to 87%. The proportion of women who agreed with the statement increased steadily in schools above 300 students, but then declined sharply in those with more than 800. The proportions of men in agreement were lower than women in medium sized schools but much higher in those with more than 800 pupils. This suggests that school size has different impacts on men and women.

It suggests that women are more likely to believe that staff want directive leadership if they are located in medium sized schools. The comments of one from a metropolitan secondary school illustrate such a perception:

> I think that staff would tend to say...leave major decisions to the top... The way that I operate is, to talk quite openly about what's happening what's been decided and to give detailed briefings about rationales for this ...and I think by and large it's accepted. In a lot of ways I'm quite autocratic and I think the size of the school makes this even more crucial.

Conversely, men from the largest schools were the most likely to believe that staff expected strong, directive leadership. Those in small primary schools were the least inclined to share their view.

Principals' perceptions of staff inevitably influence the way they work with them. Although male leaders consistently indicated a stronger preference for structures and control, gender was a less significant influence upon their relationships with staff than other factors. Secondary leaders were much more committed to the need for "clear lines of authority and accountability" than those from primary sites (92% compared to 86%). This was again linked to a linear progression in proportions of support from 67% in small schools to 90% in those with 600 to 800 students, and 97% amongst leaders with more than 1000 enrolments. This clearly suggests that increases in school size result in an exponential growth of support for bureaucratic structures. The trend was more noticeable amongst men than women.

ITEM: THIS SCHOOL IS A PLACE WHERE TEACHERS WANT STRONG
LEADERSHIP FROM THE TOP

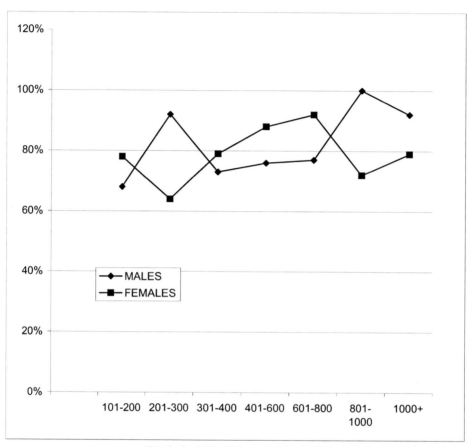

(Statistical Significance .02, 24df Female Principals Only)

*Figure 6. Proportions of Overall Agreement by School Size
and Principal Gender.*

Sector again tended to interact with and modify patterns according to gender as
a solitary variable. Support for clear lines of authority and accountability was
highest in the Government sector (92%) and lowest amongst Catholic leaders
(86%). Differences were more pronounced among male principals. The values and
culture of Independent schools appear to have amplified the tendency of men to
support structural approaches to leadership whereas Catholic school culture
appears to have modified it. Independent males were much more likely to agree
with the need for such structures than their Catholic counterparts (97% compared
to 81%).

ITEM: THIS SCHOOL IS A PLACE WHERE STAFF ARE PROVIDED WITH
CLEAR LINES OF AUTHORITY AND ACCOUNTABILITY

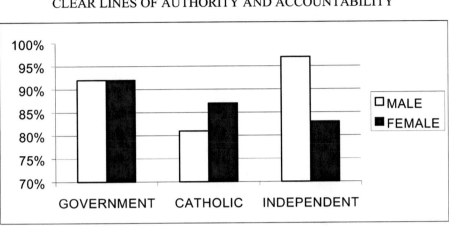

(Statistical Significance .02, 6df)

*Figure 7. Proportions of Principals in Overall Agreement by Principal Gender
and Sector.*

The unanimity between men and women from Government schools also stands in stark contrast to the gender gaps in the other sectors. It is testimony to the power public accountability exerts over such leaders. However, it is also evident that the focus of control differs between Government and Independent schools. In the former, it is driven by the need to implement public policies. In the latter, it seems to be more a matter of traditions of strong masculine control at particular sites, most notably boys' schools within the sector.

The size of the organization appears to be a more powerful influence upon a principal's beliefs about staff management than his or her gender. The tendency for both genders at the secondary level to favour "clear lines of authority and accountability" suggests that it is organizational complexity rather than gender, which fosters such attitudes. In this respect, secondary schools conform to Bredo's concept of "instrumental rationality". The collective ethic of the primary leaders is more aligned with his concept of "organic structures" (Bredo, 1999, pp. 256-261) and lends some credence to Gray's portrayal of primary schools as "feminine realms". However, the findings also suggest that the juxtaposition of bureaucratic and organic forms of leadership in previous discourse overlooks complex aspects of schools as organizations. It appears that larger schools need more structured forms of leadership than the "collective mode" which emerges naturally in small primary sites.

Working with Parents

If the findings about working with teachers tend to qualify claims that women are more relational and inclusive than men, those related to working with parents and community tend to refute them. Women were less responsive in this area than men, who were more willing to consult parents and to engage them as participants in the school community. Indeed, there is strong evidence to suggest that the alleged receptiveness of female leaders may not extend beyond the schoolyard.

School sector appeared to be a stronger influence on beliefs about parent involvement than principal gender; there were radical differences between leaders from Government and non-government schools.

ITEM: IN THIS SCHOOL PARENTS ARE REGULARLY
CONSULTED BY THE PRINCIPAL

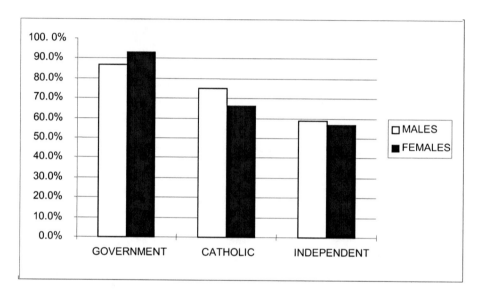

(Statistical Significance .01 6df.)

Figure 8. Proportions of Overall Agreement by
School Sector and Principal Gender.

It would also appear that sector contributed to wider differences amongst women than men Government school leaders were markedly more committed to parent consultation than those from Catholic and Independent sectors (90% compared to 70% and 58%). The contrast can be explained by a tradition of active parent involvement in Government school councils, which was initiated in the 1970s and re-enforced in the 1990s (Blackmore, 1999; Caldwell & Haywood, 1998). It was the only sector where higher proportions of women supported parent consultation, and it therefore appears that sectorial culture re-enforced their relational predispositions. However, in the other two sectors, it would appear that sectorial traditions over-rode such impulses.

In the Catholic sector it would appear that the more collaborative ideology of the men, which was identified in their relationships with staff, also extended to their views about parents. Women from the Independent sector were the least likely to consult parents. Interview responses confirmed the statistical pattern and indicated considerable antipathy towards extensive parent involvement. One principal asserted that "the idea of a parent-controlled school is absurd and that's what some of them are looking for. They've only got self-interest at heart." Another insisted:

> Often what parents want is precisely what we don't.... there are many parents who want the entire school to change to accommodate their child.

A third added that while "the wants of parents are taken into consideration", they are not the determining influence, and cited conflict over the introduction of notebook computers into Year 9 as an instance where parent opinion was overruled.

The warmth of these comments from women in Independent schools suggests that they may experience more conflict with parents than those from other settings. It is likely that the market economy model which prevails in this sector may prompt some parents to become demanding clients. However, it is also possible that the women principals have adopted some of the attitudes of earlier women who conducted dame schools in Victoria as private realms where outside interference was not tolerated. The histories recall colourful incidents when female leaders asserted their authority over those who dared to question it. Jeannie McCowan, Headmistress at Mentone from 1937 to 1955, was a famous matriarch who "tended to have firm ideas on many matters and put them into effect without reference to anyone." (Burren, 1984, p. 101). It would appear that the women leaders of such schools have inherited an exclusive culture which sets them apart from women in Government sites. A similar history has also produced indifference amongst the leaders of boys' schools. In contrast, the explicit emphasis upon parent engagement by authorities in Government schools means that principals in that sector are more committed to it, even if it is a mandate rather than a personal preference.

CONCLUSIONS

This study provides empirical support for many previous claims that there are significant differences in the perceptions and beliefs of male and female principals. However, it also qualifies previous discourse by establishing that leader gender is not a solitary or unilateral influence. The beliefs of principals are strongly shaped by the institutional contexts in which they work. Factors such as level and size of school, sectorial traditions and student gender contribute to organizational cultures, which both reinforce and undermine gender differences. On some issues, they draw men and women towards consensus, on others they generate divisions within each gender. We are forced to conclude that principal perceptions and beliefs are shaped by multiple and interactive forces at the institutional level, and that their gender socialization is only one such force.

Criticisms of essentialist accounts of leadership are justified (Blackmore, 1999; Connell, 1995; Grogan, 2000; Reynolds, 1995). They constitute a broad-brush approach to theory development; the imposition of questionable generalizations and frameworks upon the subject of inquiry that inevitably distort reality. When cameo studies are undertaken, there is a genuine danger that observations are adapted to preconceived ideas about male and female differences, rather than lead to careful re-examination of the theory. Such theory fragments in the face of complex organizational mosaics.

Reliance upon gender typecasts has also produced caricatures of male and female leaders. While there is considerable evidence to indicate that male leaders lean more towards authoritative and managerial forms of leadership, there has been a negligent silence about their ability to be nurturant and collaborative in settings such as primary schools and sites which have a rich heritage of pastoral care. The collegial style of women leaders with staff has been rightfully praised for its ability to generate collaborative cultures. Regardless, there has been an unhelpful silence about the tendency of women leaders in some sites to exclude parents from meaningful participation in decision-making. The stereotypes also ignore the history of stern, matriarchal regimes in specific schools where women leaders have replicated the most exclusive practices of patriarchs. Gender polarities are also frequently overstated, and ignore the possibility that male and female leaders may share common belief platforms under the influence of factors such as level of schooling or sectorial values. In such instances, organizational cultures actively modify potential gender divides.

It is therefore clearly time to replace outmoded concepts of leadership and gender with more sophisticated frameworks which comprehend the full complexity of the landscape. Such theory will acknowledge that leader gender is an important and frequently overlooked dimension of administration; however, it will also acknowledge that gender is only one variable in a matrix of interacting forces. The concept of organizational culture as composed of multiple strands, which interact to produce a fluid and evolving construct, is a useful one. It interacts with leader gender in a variety of ways; some of which reinforce differences between men and women while others draw them towards consensus. The very diversity of schools and the cultural forces which operate within them, means that there are multiple forms of male and leadership and contemporary theory needs to be based upon this premise.

NOTES

[1] In 1993, men held over 50% of primary principalships and 80% of secondary headships in England and Wales (Department of Education, 1993). In the US, it has been estimated that 34% of principalships were held by women in 1993 (Montenegro, 1993). In New Zealand men occupied 73% of primary and 81% of secondary principalships in 1995 (Pringle & Timperly, 1995). Proportions of women in the principalship are even lower in continental Europe. In the Netherlands they only occupied 12% of primary and 4% of secondary positions (Shakeshaft, 1994). In Sweden, despite a decade of affirmative action policies, they were still less than a third in both school types by 1993 (McMaster & Randall, 1995). Greece, France and Ireland record higher proportions of women in primary principalships (41% to 47%) but markedly lower proportions in the role in secondary schools (Shakeshaft, 1994).

[2] This may reflect the fact that large numbers of women from religious orders were principals in this sector in the past; however, the proportions have been in sharp decline since the 1970s.

[3] Women from Government secondary schools provided a particularly low response rate. Several had been replaced by men in the interval between the construction of the Curriculum Corporation

database and the administration of the questionnaire twelve months later. Investigation indicated that many of them were on sick leave, and that men were acting in their place.
⁴ A small number of Catholic secondary schools are members of the Associated Grammar Schools which constitute the most privileged schools in Victoria. There were five such schools in the sample.

REFERENCES

Acker, S. (1989). *Teachers, gender and careers*. New York: Falmer Press.

Adler S., Laney, J., & Packer, M. (1993). *Managing women: Feminism and power in educational management*. Buckingham, UK: Open University Press.

Antonucci, T. (1980) The need for female role models in education. In S.K. Biklen & M.B. Brannigan (Eds.), *Women and educational leadership* (pp. 185-192). Lexington: Lexington Books.

Austin, A.G. (1977). *Australian education 1788-1900: Church, state and public education in colonial Australia*. Carlton: Pitman.

Australian Bureau of Statistics (1993). *Census of population 1991*. Canberra: ABS.

Australian Bureau of Statistics (1998). *Census of population and housing: Selected family and labour force characteristics*. Canberra: ABS.

Barcan, A. (1980). *A history of Australian education*. Melbourne: Oxford University Press.

Bass, B.M. (1970). *Bass and Stodgill's handbook of leadership, first edition*. New York: Free Press.

Bass, B.M. (1990). *Bass and Stodgill's handbook of leadership, third edition*. New York: Free Press.

Biddulph, S. (1994), *Manhood: An action plan for changing men's lives*. Sydney: Finch Publishing.

Blackmore, J. (1993). In the shadow of men: The historical construction of educational administration as a masculinist enterprise. In J. Blackmore & J. Kenway (Eds.), *Gender matters in educational administration and policy: A feminist introduction* (pp. 27-47). London: The Falmer Press.

Blackmore, J. (1995). *A taste for the feminine in educational leadership*. School of Education, Deakin University: Unpublished paper.

Blackmore, J. (1999). *Troubling women: Feminism, leadership and educational change*. Buckingham, UK: Open University Press.

Bredo, E. (1999). Ethical implications of organization theory. *Leading & Managing, 4*(4), 256-274.

Burren, P.B. (1984). *Mentone: The place for a school*. South Yarra: Hyland House.

Caldwell, B. J., & Haywood, D.K. (1998). *The future of schools: Lessons from the reform of public education*. London: Falmer Press.

Coleman, J.S., & Hoffer, T. (1987). *Public and private high schools: The impact of communities*. New York: Basic Books.

Coleman, M. (1998). The management style of female headteachers. *Educational Management and Administration, 24*(2), 163-174.

Connell, R.W. (1987). *Gender and power*. Cambridge: Polity Press.

Connell, R.W. (1995). *Masculinities*. St. Leonards: Allen & Unwin.

Court, M.R. (1998). Women challenging managerialism: Devolution dilemmas in the establishment of co-principalships in primary schools in Aotearoa/New Zealand. *School Leadership & Management, 18*(1), 19-35.

Craib, I. (1987). Masculinity and male dominance. *Sociological Review, 34*, 721-743.

Curriculum Corporation (1996). *Victorian schools database*. Carlton: Curriculum Corporation.

Darley, J., & Lomax, P. (1995, April). *The continuing role of women as primary school headteachers in the transformed British School System*. Paper presented at the annual meeting of the American Educational Research Association, San Francisco.

Department for Education. (1993). *Full-time teachers in maintained nursery, primary and secondary schools in England and Wales*. London: Analytical Services Branch.

Edgar, D. (1997), *Men, mateship, marriage: Exploring macho myths and the way forward*. Sydney: Harper Collins.

Evans, M .A., Murray H., & Evans, J. (1995), *Optima semper: The history of Frankston High School, 1924-1994*. Burwood: Brown, Prior, Anderson.

Evers, C.W., & Lakomski, G. (1996a). Postpositivist conceptions of science in educational administration: An introduction. *Educational Administration Quarterly, 32*(3), 341-343.

Evers, C.W., & Lakomski, G. (1996b). Science in educational administration: An introduction. *Educational Administration Quarterly, 32*(3), 379-402.

Evetts, J. (1994) *Becoming a secondary head teacher*. London, Cassell.

Fennell, A. (1999). Power in the principalship four women's experiences. *Journal of Educational Administration, 37*(1), 23-49.

Ferguson, K.E. (1984). *The feminist case against bureaucracy.* Philadelphia, PA: Temple University Press.

Fiedler, F.E. (1967). *A theory of leadership effectiveness.* New York: McGraw-Hill.

Fitzpatrick, K. (1975). *PLC Melbourne: The first century.* Burwood: PLC.

Fiedler, F.E. (1967). *A theory of leadership effectiveness.* New York: McGraw-Hill.

Fogarty, R. f.m.s, (1957). *Catholic education In Australia, 1806-1950: Volumes 1 & 2.* London: Melbourne University Press.

Ford, P. (1997) Gender difference in leadership style: Does it make a difference? In C. Connors, & T. d'Arbon (Eds.), *Change, challenge and creative leadership: International perspectives on research and practice* (pp. 224-235). Hawthorn: ACEA.

Gamble, L. (1982). *St. Bede's College and its Mc Cristal origins.* Burwood: Brown, Prior, Anderson.

Gardiner, L. (1977). *Tintern School and Anglican girl's education 1877-1977.* East Ringwood: Tintern CEGGS.

Gilligan, C. (1982). *In A different voice: Psychological theory and women's development.* Cambridge, MA: Harvard University Press.

Gray, H.L. (1989). Gender considerations in school management: Masculine and feminine leadership styles. In C. Riches & C. Morgan (Eds.), *Human resource management in education* (pp. 110-123). Buckingham, Open University Press.

Greenfield, T. (1975). Theory about organization: A new perspective and its implications for schools. In M. Hughes (Ed.), *Administering education: International challenge* (pp. 71-99). London: Athlone Press.

Grogan, M. (2000). Laying the groundwork for a reconception of the superintendency from feminist postmodern perspectives. *Educational Administration Quarterly, 36*(1), 117-142.

Gronn, P. (1995). Greatness re-visited: The current obsession with transformational leadership. *Leading & Managing, 1*(1), 1-11.

Hall, V. (1996). *Dancing on the ceiling.* London: Paul Chapman.

Hansen, I.V. (1986). *By their deeds: A centenary history of Camberwell Grammar School, 1886-1996.* Camberwell: Camberwell Grammar School.

Hearn, J. (1993). *Men in the public eye: The construction and deconstruction of public men and public patriarchies.* London: Routledge.

Helgeson, S. (1991). *The female advantage: Women's ways of leadership.* Garden City: Doubleday.

Hersey, P., & Blanchard, K. (1982). *Management of organizational behaviour: Utilizing human resources.* Englewood Cliffs, NJ: Prentice-Hall.

Hurty, K.S. (1995). Women principals: Leading with power. In D.M. Dunlap & P.A. Schmuck (Eds.), *Women leading in education* (pp. 380-406). Albany, NY: SUNY Press.

Johnson, N.A., & Holdaway, E.A. (1991). Perceptions of effectiveness and the satisfaction of principals in elementary schools. *Journal of Educational Administration, 29*(1), 51-70

Kanter, R.M. (1977, 1993). *Men and women of the corporation.* New York: Basic Books

Kruger, M.L. (1996). Gender issues in school headship: Quality versus power? *European Journal of Education, 31*(4), 447-461.

Kvale, S. (1996). *InterViews: An introduction to qualitative research interviewing.* London: Sage Publications.

Limerick, B. (1995). Accommodated careers: Gendered career paths in education. In B. Limerick & B. Lingard (Eds.), *Gender and changing educational management: Second yearbook of the Australian Council for Educational Administration* (pp. 68-78). Rydalmere: Hodder Education.

Limerick, B., & Anderson, C. (1999). Female administrators and school-based management. *Educational Management and Administration, 27*(4), 401-414.

McMaster, M., & Randall, S. (1995). Issues in changing the gendered culture of educational organizations. In B. Limerick & B. Lingard (Eds.), *Gender and changing educational management: Second yearbook of the Australian Council for Educational Administration*(pp. 7-66). Rydalmere: Hodder Education.

Marshall, J. (1982). *Women managers: Travellers in a male world.* Chichester: John Wiley & Sons.

Montenegro, X. (1993). *Women and minorities in school administration.* Arlington, VA: American Association of School Administrators.

Noddings, N. (1984). *Caring: A feminine approach to ethics and moral education.* Berkeley, CA: University of California Press.

Ozga, J. (1993). *Women in educational management.* Buckingham, UK: Open University Press.

Pascal, C., & Ribbins, P. (1998). *Regarding heads: Primary lives and careers.* In C. Pascal & P. Ribbins (Eds.), *Understanding primary headteachers* (pp. 1-30). London: Cassell.

Parsons, T., & Bales, R.F. (1956). *Family socialization and interaction process.* London: Routledge/Kegan Paul.

Pringle, J., & Timperley, (1995). Gender and educational management in New Zealand: Co-option, subversion, or withdrawal? In B. Limerick & B. Lingard (Eds.), *Gender and changing educational management: Second yearbook of the Australian Council for Educational Administration* (pp. 162-173). Rydalmere: Hodder Education.

Reynolds, C. (1995). In the right place at the right time: Rules of control and woman's place in Ontario Schools, 1940-1980. *Canadian Journal of Education, 20*(2), 129-145.

Ribbins, P. (1996). Producing portraits of educational leaders in context: Cultural relativism and methodological absolutism. *Commonwealth Council for Educational Administration and Management Paper, Malaysia,* 1-16.

Ribbins, P. (1999). On redefining educational management and leadership. *Educational Management and Administration, 27*(3), 227-238.

Rusch, E.A., & Marshall, C. (1995, April). *Gender filters at work in administrative culture.* Paper presented at the annual meeting of the American Educational Research Association, San Francisco.

Russell, R.A. (1995, April). *Beyond survival: Women leaders as agents of change.* Paper presented at the annual meeting of the American Educational Research Association, San Francisco.

Seidler, V.J. (1994). *Unreasonable men: Masculinity and social theory.* London: Routledge.

Shakeshaft, C. (1987). *Women in educational administration.* Newbury Park, CA: Sage Publications.

Shakeshaft, C. (1989). The gender gap in research in educational administration. *Educational Administration Quarterly, 25*(4), 324-337.

Shakeshaft, C. (1994). Women in educational administration: United States. In T. Husen & T. Postlethwaite (Eds.), *The international encyclopedia of education* (pp. 6727-6731). London: Pergamon Press.

Shum, L.C., & Cheng, Y.C. (1997). Perceptions of women principal's leadership and teachers' work attitudes. *Journal of Educational Administration, 35*(2), 165-184.

Steinberg, W. (1993). *Masculinity: Identity, conflict and transformation.* Boston: Shambhala.

Tacey, D. (1997). *Remaking men: The revolution in masculinity.* Ringwood: Viking-Penguin.

Teese, R. (2000). *Academic success and social power: Examinations and inequality.* Carlton: Melbourne University Press.

Theobald, M. (1978). *Rhyton remembers 1878-1978.* Melbourne: The Hawthorn Press.

Theobald, M. (1996). *Knowing women: Origins of women's education in nineteenth century Australia.* Hong Kong: Cambridge University Press.

Twycross, D. (1994). *School Leadership: Comparative perceptions and experiences of men and women principals.* Murdoch University: M.Ed. (Hons.) Thesis.

Vlahogiannis, N.L. (1989). *Prinny Hill: The state schools of Princess Hill, 1889-1989.* Melbourne: The Princess Hill Schools.

Wajcman, J. (1998). *Managing like a man: Women and men in corporate management.* Sydney: Allen & Unwin.

Weiler, K.A. (1988). *Women teaching for change: Gender, class and power.* South Halley, MA: Bergin & Harvey.

Weiner, G. (1994). *Feminism and education.* Milton Keynes, UK: Open University Press.

Zainu'ddin, A.G.T. (1982). *They dreamt of a school: A centenary history of Methodist Ladies' College Kew 1882-1982.* Melbourne: Hyland House.

OLOF JOHANSSON

SCHOOL LEADERSHIP AS A DEMOCRATIC ARENA

Abstract. This chapter explores the nature of school leadership work in the Swedish context using the metaphor of arenas as a structuring framework. This facilitates a consideration of questions, such as: What is the relationship between the school governance actions taken by principals and the political goals of the local community government? What is the appropriate relationship between the principal's role as a leader and his/her role as the manager? The chapter also explores the challenges that school leaders experience as outcomes of the influence of several arenas external to the immediate school environment.

According to the findings of a recently conducted study (Skolverket, 2001), over eighty percent of Swedish parents that were surveyed reported that they are, in general, very satisfied with their children's school and pleased with the work of the teachers in support of their children's learning. However, as supportive as these parents appear to be of the local school, a majority of the same parents are very critical of all other schools and are much inclined to take issue with the   school system in their municipality. How are we to explain such contradictory opinions? Why is it that parents appear to value only the school their own children attend as a good learning environment? These views on schools seem to be inconsistent and even irrational statements, until one considers how the opinions of parents about schools might be rooted in a lack of knowledge about the schools upon which they pass judgment. Their judgments may be those of others, garnered from third party sources such as media reports or talk among friends and work associates.

This conflicted public opinion situation illustrates the complexity of a school principal's work. One implication is that a principal wishing to be viewed as a successful administrator must do more than manage his or her own immediate school community. They must also attend to the perceptions held by members of the outside community about their school; in effect, they must be conscious of and cultivate their influence in a multi-arena environment. The parental perception situation cited above illustrates two important arenas of which a principal must be conscious - one internal to the school, the other external to the school. Both of these arenas can be further divided into subset arenas (Berg, 1995). Identifying and reflecting on the nature of these arenas can contribute substantially to our understandings of the work of principals.

Most principals with whom I have interacted in a workshop setting, during seminars or while conducting interviews for research, are inclined to see their work as relating to a single arena – the school. They tend to describe this arena as a very complex one, yet when led to consider the existence and relevance of other arenas in a workshop setting, they have little difficulty identifying other arenas and the linkages between them.   One common pattern in their conceptualizations of these arenas is their perceptions about the core groups associated with the school. Two core groups - staff and students - are most often closely associated to the principal's role. The next most important arenas in their view are what I term the policy arenas. These include local and national curriculum and a functional arena,

P.T. Begley and O. Johansson (eds.), The Ethical Dimensions of School Leadership, 201–219.
© 2003 *Kluwer Academic Publishers. Printed in the Netherlands.*

pedagogical leadership. Among the arenas that principals do not consider central to

Even parents are identified as an arena situated away from the core arenas of concern. The political arena in particular is often placed well outside the sphere of the principal's responsibility.

These perceptions of the arenas that principals consider most relevant to their roles reveals much about how they view their work. It is clear that they often have strong opinions about what is important to their role and, at times, it is surprising to see what they leave behind or dismiss as being of low value or of no relevance. In a workshop or seminar setting, it can be interesting to engage principals in a discussion about their work patterns using the metaphor of arenas as a structure. They begin to examine the relationships and linkages among the various role functions and stakeholder groups they identify as arenas - moving the arenas around and considering what would happen if, for example, the arena of curriculum was placed between the principal and the staff and the students. A much more sophisticated level of discussion begins to take place when these dynamics are introduced. They begin to consider other kinds of relationships with key stakeholder groups, within their school community and external to it.

This chapter explores the nature of school leadership work in the Swedish context using the metaphor of arenas as a structuring framework. This facilitates a consideration of questions, such as: What is the relationship between the school governance actions taken by principals and the political goals of the local community government? What is the appropriate relationship between the principal's role as a leader and his/her role as the manager? The chapter also explores the challenges that school leaders experience as outcomes of the influence of several arenas external to the immediate school environment.

LOCAL GOVERNANCE OF SCHOOLS WITHIN A POLITICAL ARENA

A study conducted in Sweden and the United States by Johansson and Bredeson (1999) found that the capacity of local government agencies (the policy community) to govern professional educators and schools (the learning community) by decree is a myth. Governing by decree is ineffective in that policies are often badly constructed, uninformed by professional educator expertise, and such policies seldom get properly implemented. The most effective policies - that is, the ones that influence the values of educational leaders and the educational process - are those created within the educational community and subsequently transferred to the policy community for entrenchment as policy. However, the execution of a policy development process in this manner implies and requires a great deal of democratic leadership activity on the part of the school leader at the school level. These are activities that are aimed at having the school community identify, embrace and defend the same values as the greater political community the school purportedly serves.

If one were to focus strictly on the content of decisions made by a local community government (the educational policy community in Sweden), it would appear that most decisions do not directly focus on values; however, policy decisions relating to education do tend to be value-laden, which makes educational reform initiatives so difficult to implement. For example, democratic process is a key value associated with most political decision processes in Sweden and other democratic societies. Democracy is an ethical ideal to which most people would explicitly subscribe, and it is easy to imagine the school policy community (municipal government in Sweden, school district office in the USA and Canada) and the learning community of the school would share this valuing of democratic process and democratic culture; however, there is much empirical evidence that demonstrates that this is not the case in schools. Schools are not necessarily very democratic places. The traditions of authority grounded in professional expertise, the summative standards and transactional processes associated with educational achievement, and even the historical patterns of school governance do not necessarily lend themselves to democratic processes. So, the reality of educational policy-making, as it most often occurs, is as illustrated in Figure 1. The political community (local community government or school district office) makes a policy decision. Then the decision is passed on to the school learning community for implementation. If the school-based learning community has a different set of values and culture (e.g., notions of democratic processes appropriate to schools), it may view the original policy through a different set of lenses. These lenses change the substance and perhaps even the intent of the original policy (Begley & Johansson, 1998). Figure 1 represents this transformation of the policy in terms of a shift from white to gray. What is clearly a 'white' policy from the perspective of the policy community translates to varying shades of 'gray' when filtered through the professional/educational context of the school community. The values of the learning community culture literally colour the policy and it becomes implemented as 'gray', not 'white' as originally intended by the policy community (Johansson & Bredeson,1999).

Certain kinds of decisions by the policy community are less likely to be implemented in the intended way by the school community. These are decisions that challenge the existing values and norms of the school learning community and its culture (Johansson & Kallós, 1994) as well as policy decisions that are very political in nature. New policies emanating from the policy community can, of course, also vary in consistency with each other (i.e., varying shades of 'white') because they may be outcomes of political compromises. Principals are many times confronted with this situation --policies passed on by the local government which reflect conflicting or inconsistent value orientations. Another category of situation which can be equally problematic for principals occurs when a political majority in the local governance structure has been able to make an ideology-based decision which principals know will not be accepted by the majority of the school-based learning community. These two types of decisions can be seen as extremes on a continuum. A middle category of problematic policy decision that can be imagined is an ideologically sound decision that is in conflict with the prevailing culture of the community, not just the school-based learning community.

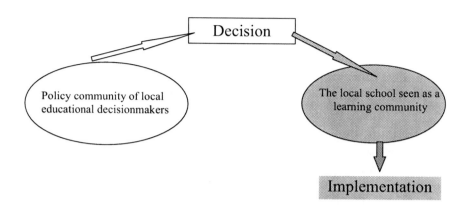

Figure 1. Value Orchestration by the Policy Community for the Learning Community.

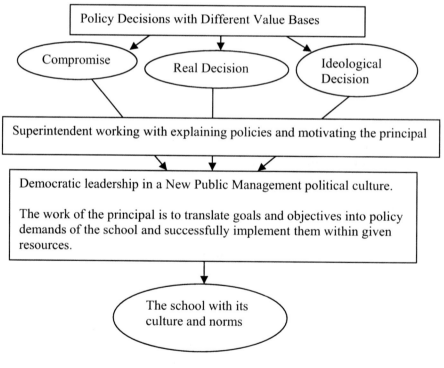

Figure 2. The Principal in the Policy Stream.

To be a leader in a public sector activity like a school is in some respects very different from being a leader in a private sector company (Ekholm, 1994). In public schools, the role of the principal is to implement the goals and objectives set by the political community that are value-based. This involves explaining policy and motivating staff to act in accordance with political decisions, implementing policies, handling resources (both fiscal and personnel) carefully, developing and expanding activities within given political value constraints, and maintaining good morale among students and parents. Doing all this would be much easier if the political decisions the principal is supposed to implement were all clear and concise and accepted by everyone in the political community. When people speak of policy, they usually imagine them as clearly articulated and accepted by all members of the policy community. However, this is seldom the case.

Figure 2 illustrates three types of decisions made by the policy community: compromises, real decisions and ideological decisions. 'Compromises' are decisions that have no real value character because the intent of the decision has been blurred by all the changes that have been made to the policy in order to obtain majority support for the decision. A 'real decision' occurs when a majority of the members of the political community, even if they represent different parties or interests, agree on the decision and want to see the policy decision implemented and fulfilled (Gustafsson, 1983). Finally, an 'ideological decision' is a decision made by members of the policy community that share a similar understanding on an ideological aspect of education. These various forms of decision by the policy community place different demands on the principal operating within a decentralized system of educational governance. In a centralized system based on governing by-laws, the principal can always turn to the state for help or authoritative backing and support; however, in a decentralized system, he or she must often act alone and achieve a double mandate - acting in ways consistent with the national school laws, as well as implementing local policies within given resources. (Hagström, 1990; Johansson, Moos, & Möller, 2000).

Principals often encounter situations where politicians have different interpretations about the content of the decisions they have made. What sometimes makes the situation even more problematic is that politicians too often believe that once they have made a policy decision, it has been instantly implemented. Under these circumstances, it can be difficult to keep everyone - politicians, members of the community, the media, parents, students and staff - happy. In the Swedish context, what principals must do is work towards achieving the goals of both the national and local curriculum; that is, be a democratic leader locally and, at the same time, work as a manager/leader in a New Public Management culture (Hughes, 1998; Ekholm, 1989). They have to translate goals and objectives coming from both curricular authorities into specific policy action for the school. They then must successfully implement these policy demands within given resources and in a school environment that has its own set of potentially competing special interest groups and stakeholders. Formal policies become specific policy demands once the principal decides he or she wants to implement the decision in the school with accuracy and fidelity to the original intents of the policy makers (Nygren, 2000).

Parents are a very particular category of local stakeholder group associated with the learning community of a school. Their interests are primarily focussed on their own children's well-being and academic training. Accommodating parental needs and concerns has always been a part of the principal's workday; however, in recent times, we see more parents organizing together in formal and informal groups to represent and achieve their special interests. Teachers and principals increasingly must acknowledge these parental collectives - what amounts to a parent-school arena. For example, in Ontario, Canada, parent councils are now formally recognized and mandated school governance bodies. They amount to local school boards with advisory authorities. Research (e.g., Parker, 1998) suggests that the success of those advisory counsels is often predetermined. If a school has a tradition of active, collective parental involvement in the school, teachers and principals in the school are more likely to value the parents interaction and see this new legislation as a tool for improving schools. But if there is an implicit understanding among the teachers and the principal, in effect a silent pact, that parents should not participate in school-based change processes, then this prevailing school culture can dominate or neutralize every external pressure for change. This occurs in a variety of ways, including delaying processes launched by the educational professionals, educators showing no interest in collective roles for parents or deliberately placing obstacles in the path of the policy implementation process, or by posturing ethical or other arguments in opposition to the proposed change (Parker, 1998).

For the foreseeable future, it is predictable that more and more interest groups, especially outside agencies with a range of interest in educational affairs, will want to play a role in the local educational governance process (Svedberg, 2000). This trend is difficult to block in a democratic society where participation is an entrenched right for all citizens. As a consequence, school principals increasingly require sophistication, in terms of professional skills and knowledge, to communicate and manage these stakeholder groups. Principals need to be aware of a range of educationally relevant arenas of interest groups. They must also represent the educational profession and be familiar with the language and expertise of the professional education sphere. It is inevitable that stakeholders will, from time to time, disagree about what is desirable in policies, procedures and outcomes. Finally, there can also be an important difference between the values articulated by a group and the values to which the group is actually committed (Begley, 1998). Principals must be able to recognize these situations and understand the actual level of motivation reflected by individuals and groups. This amounts to considerable pressure on the school principal to make sound decisions - decisions which are professionally justifiable, consistent with policy in its various forms, and also politically astute.

The pressures and complexities associated with administrative decision-making are illustrated in Figure 3. A successful principal in Sweden or other democratic states must balance two broad categories of influence. They need to understand the importance of the community or school district's political decisions relating to the school and the national goals for the school. They must also be able to act as democratic leaders of a professional staff. This means acknowledging the expertise of teachers as professionals, but also motivating them to understand and achieve the political goals of the community for the school (Berg, 1990). In practice, principals make choices. They choose to recognize and understand the importance of some goals and objectives, just as they ignore or reject others. Those accepted goals and objectives become policy goal demands for the principal (Nygren, 2000). When a Swedish principal can manage to balance both sources of policy demands (local community government and national government) as well as the concerns of the local school community, he or she satisfies both politicians and the staff, and an ideal situation is achieved. If neither the staff nor the politicians are satisfied with the performance of the school leader, then the principal is a disaster in his/her role.

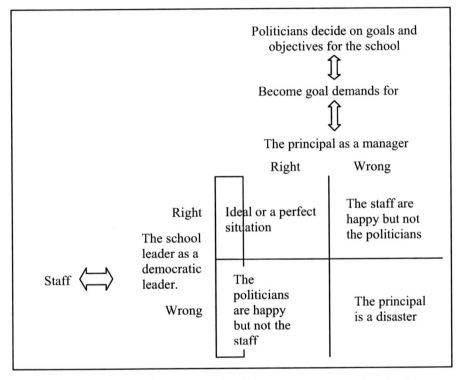

Figure 3. Relationship Between the Roles of Manager and Leader for a School Leader.

Interviews with school leaders in Sweden reveal that superintendents and principals often articulate the need for better ways to make good quality decisions. They aspire to work in a way that allows both politicians and professional staff to be satisfied with outcomes, but find this objective very difficult to achieve. The main reason for this failure to achieve consensus is the variety of opinions/values held by stakeholders about what is in the best interests of children and the school. They also report that it is difficult at times to distinguish between personal, professional, organizational and social values in these situations. For school leaders, it is very important to use educational arguments that are grounded in the value system of good democratic education. They must know which values are appropriate to a situation and justifiable by educational leaders (Begley &

Johansson, 2001). School leaders are agents of society accountable to an established system of educational governance, professionals, and members of the community served by the educational system, and accordingly must understand how to use values in their decision-making (Begley, 1998).

According to much administrative theory (e.g., Simon, 1965), the basis for administrative decision-making is, or ought to be, objectivity and rationality; however, our research suggests that administrative decisions very often can be better characterized as 'ritual rationality'. Ritual rationality occurs when the decision-maker veils the real intention or obscures unintentional effects of the decision by highlighting values acceptable to the stakeholders. This frequently occurs in relation to social demands for fiscal restraint and it is important for leaders to recognize when this is happening. Analyzing decision processes from a values perspective facilitates these insights (Begley, 2000; Johansson, 2001a).

All the situations discussed thus far share a common implication - successful implementation of policy by principals in the professional context of schools can only be achieved through insightful and open communication. Such communications must also be grounded in sound educational arguments for the proposed policy. The suggestion that principals and leaders of schools should argue points from their own field of expertise - education - might seem to be obvious advice and a natural approach, but in practice, this is not always what happens. Begley and Johansson have shown that principals, both in Canada and Sweden, when they are confronted with critical decision-making situations involving value conflicts tend to justify their actions using other kinds of criteria. In one study, the kinds of arguments used to address critical decisions occurred in a ratio of six managerial arguments for every three leadership arguments, and only one educational argument (Johansson, 2000b). A reverse order would probably be a more appropriate and successful professional strategy.

SUCCESSFUL DEMOCRATIC SCHOOL LEADERSHIP

A prerequisite to successful democratic school leadership is the capacity to combine two roles, that of manager and leader. Successful leaders of schools challenge co-workers' assumptions about learning and teaching. Leadership in a learning organization means to lead one's fellow workers' learning as well as to create a deeper understanding of the task on the part of all those active within the school and its stakeholders (Lakomski, 1998; Scherp, 1998; Strandberg, 2000). Leaders must also give priority to their own learning. The principal or head teacher, as well as their teacher co-workers, must together take active responsibility for their own learning in order to develop the school into a learning environment (Wahlberg, 2000). In a learning organization, co-workers have considerable freedom and responsibility for their own work within the shared parameters of understanding about the organizational objectives. In a Swedish school context, the leader's work is focused on one aim - all students should achieve the goals laid down in the national and local curriculum, i.e., a successful school (Lärande ledare, 2001).

School leadership must be based on understanding the task and embracing the values of the national curriculum. The leader comprehends the breadth of his/her duties and has a well-grounded knowledge and a deep understanding of these tasks. He/she pursues a clear and active leadership. Leading and developing a school based on a democratic foundation means that the leader must identify with, as well as be carrier and defender of, the values incorporated in the curriculum. He/she must ensure that the perspective and dimensions associated with these values clearly permeate his/her work and the school's activities (Törnsén, 2000).

The leader clearly expresses and communicates his/her visions, goals and results for which he/she is responsible. The leader links them to the national steering documents, the municipal school plan and the local schools working plan. The leader initiates and maintains discussion and dialogue on the school's goals and work, both between him/herself and co-workers as well as among the co-workers themselves (Ärlestig, 2000). The leader and his/her co-workers embrace shared goals and visions as guiding principles for the work in the school. The leader's and his/her co-workers' most important task is to guarantee the quality of the activities and help his/her staff create a good and appreciated learning environment for the children (Duke, 1998).

Leading the learning process means to plan, create and encourage constant testing of how the duties and visions can be realised. A significant task for the leader is to challenge his/her colleagues' assumptions about learning and teaching. It is important for the development of the school that all those working together in the school take responsibility for the quality of the school's activities, communicate with each other and reflect together on the school's work and the amount of freedom available with regard to how this is carried out (Törnsén, 2000). The leader expresses clearly his/her high expectations and strong belief in his/her colleagues' abilities and their commitment to their duties and learning. Part of the school's work includes following up, evaluating and documenting results as a basis for further reassessment, learning and change (Johansson, 2001b). The leader's and his/her colleagues' knowledge, based on experience, is tested against new knowledge. Competence development in the learning organisation comprises, amongst other things, learning through work that takes as its starting point the possibilities and difficulties that the leader and his/her colleagues meet in their efforts to realise the school's visions. It is important that the leader and his/her colleagues can reflect on their practice and develop a learning and reflective approach to their profession[1] (Geijer, 2000).

This line of argument highlights the extent to which leadership by the principal is important to the creation of successful democratic schools. Once again, however, the reality in schools does not always match the ideal. During many research seminars with principals in Sweden and abroad, I have conducted group work focussing on the notion of successful schools. I have asked principals to discuss the idea in small groups and than write down what they think characterizes a successful school. The answers are always the same. Their replies typically include references to a good working climate, good learning opportunities for the students, and happy parents; however, they very seldom identify a good principal and a dedicated and engaged teaching staff as characteristic of a successful school. It seems so strange that they do not recognise their own importance to the success of their schools. We know from studies and personal observations that the so-called successful schools always have a good principal and a dedicated and engaged teaching staff. To be properly supportive to teachers, the principal must understand his/her own importance to the success of others in the school (Bredeson, 1998). In most cases, teachers understand their own importance to the success of the children in their classes. When people observe the performance of a successful class of school children, they typically say "That group of children has a good teacher that has helped the children achieve success". The same should be true for principals. Their most important task is to help their staff to be successful. A school leader can never be successful without good and dedicated teachers and staff. The principal creates success through a communications process focussed on fostering a common vision, encouraging learning, and understanding the purpose of school.

ARENAS OF SCHOOL LEADERSHIP

Both as a leader and as a manager, the principal works within several arenas inside and outside of the school which combine and operate interdependently of each other. Within different arenas, a principal plays different roles. As manager, the principal is a local government official and as such is expected to enforce and uphold all rules and policies. In some cases principals can be charged for misconduct when rules or laws are not upheld. This arena can be view as the *law arena*. The principal is also responsible for implementation of both national and local goals and objectives for the school. The managerial part of this is to be a guarantor for high quality and effective work. This arena can be called the *policy arena*. Closely allied to these two arenas is a third arena with managerial implications, the *political arena*. When working in the political arena, the principal represents the school as an administrative unit in relation to local politicians. Most of these political arena activities are in relation to the school board. The role of the principal is to be a messenger, a defender and a discussant of local political decisions. Political goals and objectives become goal demands for the principal. One other manager role can be identified, this one relating to theories of new public management. This role involves ensuring that school operations and activities are as effective as possible in relation to the goals and objectives of the school within given economic resources. This arena can be called the *effectiveness arena*. A role that sometimes is in conflict with the effectiveness arena is the principal's role as an ombudsman. Principals have the responsibility to ensure that students, parents and other stakeholders are treated in appropriate ways, an arena that can be called the *service arena*.

All the arenas identified to this point focus on the managerial aspects of the principal's role; however, leadership qualities are also needed. Several additional arenas can be identified with a reversed emphasis - that is, leadership skills more than managerial skills are needed for success. The first arena in this leadership oriented category is the *professional arena* in which the principal must show that his/her knowledge in the field is substantial and trustworthy from the perspective of all staff and the other stakeholders. These leadership roles align well with what is termed transformational leadership in the literature. In application this means that the principal takes the goal demands associated with his/her management role in the political arena and works hard with his or her staff to interpret and implement the requirements by creating a common vision and understanding of the purposes of schooling (Leithwood, 1998). One other leadership role related to this professional arena is the instructional leadership role. Working within this arena means that the principal focuses on three specific things: improving and leading the reform of teaching, improving and leading the development of teacher professionalism, and promoting teachers' reflection on national and local curriculum and the goals of the school. The focus here is on improving the quality of school activities involving pupils in order to create the possibility of exceeding minimum levels of performance (Leithwood, Jantzi, & Steinbach, 1999).

One other arena emphasizing leadership activity on the part of the principal is the *democratic arena*. In any country, the school plays a critical part in the upbringing of new citizens. In democratic states, an important part of that function is learning about democracy. The Swedish curriculum integrates many discussions along this line of thought. Indeed, democracy forms the foundation of the national school system. The School Act stipulates that all school activity should be carried out in accordance with fundamental democratic values and that each and every person working in the school should encourage respect for each person as an intrinsic value, and for the environment we all share. The school has responsibility for the critical task of imparting, instilling and forming in pupils those fundamental values on which our society is based (Lpo 94, p. 6).

As well as being open to a variety of ideas and encouraging their expression, the Swedish school should also emphasize the importance of forming personal points of view and provide pupils the opportunities for doing this. Education should be objective and reflect a range of different approaches so that parents will be able to send their children to school in confidence that they will not be prejudiced in favor of a particular view. All who work in the school should uphold these fundamental values as stated in the School Act and should disassociate themselves from anything that conflicts with these values (Lpo 94, p. 7). It is not in itself sufficient that education imparts knowledge of fundamental democratic values. Education must reflect democratic methods and prepare pupils for active participation in civic life. By participating in planning and evaluation of their daily education, and exercising choices over courses, subjects, themes and activities, pupils will develop their ability to exercise influence and take responsibility (Lpo 94, p. 8). The school should also stimulate each pupil towards self-development and personal growth. It should focus not only on intellectual but also practical, sensual and aesthetic aspects. Pupils should have the opportunity to experience the expression of knowledge in different ways. They should also be encouraged to try out and develop different modes of expression.

The role of the principal within this democratic arena is to be a democratic leader (Johansson, Moos, & Möller, 2000). In the literature, this role is sometimes described as moral leadership. It is also 'authentic leadership' which implies a genuine kind of leadership - a hopeful, open-ended, visionary and creative response to social circumstances, as opposed to the more short-sighted, precedent-focused and context-constrained practices typical of management (Begley & Johansson, 2001). This is a values-informed leadership, a sophisticated, knowledge-based, and skillful approach to leadership. It is also a form of leadership that acknowledges and accommodates in an integrative way the legitimate needs of individuals, groups, organizations, communities and cultures -

not just the organizational perspectives that are the usual preoccupation of much of the leadership literature. Finally, authentic leadership is in its form both shared and distributed. That form of democratic leadership must not prevent the leader from, at some time, making limits clear by referring to laws and policies or other regulating documents in order to protect the purpose of school. The qualities of the authentic leadership style can therefore be seen as a pre-requisite for a successful democratic leader.

RESEARCH FINDINGS ON SPECIFIC ARENAS OF LEADERSHIP

This section of the chapter considers some empirical data that has been analyzed using the arenas theory just introduced. The data sets used are from the three Scandinavian studies[2] that used the same questionnaire. The arenas that will be analyzed are; the political arena, the teacher union arena, the implementation arena and the loyalty arena. The principals were asked to respond to a series of statements. The responses they selected are a valuation of the statement. In that way, their answers provide an insight into the relative value coherence among the principals from each country that participated.

The Political Arena

The first arena that will be considered is the political arena. Principals were asked for their opinion of the primary focus of interest among local politicians in their school board. Two statements were used to solicit data on this point. One statement indicates that politicians are only interested in economic matters as they relate to schools. The other statement indicates that local politicians are not interested in how goals and objectives are implemented through pedagogical activities. A four-response scale was employed with answers spanning a range from disagree totally to agree totally. The values not included in the four tables represent response rates that were too low to warrant considering as valid.

According to the data, most principals believe that local politicians are only interested in financial matters. The consistency between countries is greater between Norway and Sweden than with Denmark. Denmark shows the same pattern but another distribution. Almost one third of the Danish principals do not think this is the case. The corresponding figures for the other countries are less than 20 per cent.

Table 1. The School Leaders' Views on Local Political Representatives.

		Disagree Totally			Agree Totally
Politicians are only	D	4%	24%	34%	37%
interested in school	N	3%	14%	36%	48%
finance and budget	S	1%	16%	39%	44%
Politicians are not	D	9%	29%	48%	15%
interested in teaching	N	13%	35%	40%	11%
and pedagogic matters	S	13%	36%	45%	13%

Note: D=Denmark, N=Norway and S=Sweden. Row per cent.

The responses to the second question reveal a more interesting pattern, and this pattern is almost identical for all three countries. There is a spread of answers over all possible categories, consequently indicating that the principals have no collective opinion on this question. They evaluate what the politicians do in very different ways. This is interesting because the same principals reflected rather high levels of consistency on the first statement. The question that becomes obvious is, why is the co-variation between the two statements so low? The almost random distribution of answers on the second question raises other questions. For example, what kind of thoughts do these school leaders have about the political arena that their responses would be so very negative and united in opinion on one statement, but so scattered in opinion on a related statement. One possible interpretation is that much of the political debate has been focussed on financial cutbacks, and that politicians have been identfied by professional educators as those responsible for this situation - whereas there has not been an equivalently broad debate among educators in relation to the politicians motives and interest in the pedagogics of schools.

The Teacher Union Arena

The teacher union arena can be viewed as a special case of the political arena. The main difference between the two is that the teacher trade unions campaign for the rights of teachers while the local politicians focus on what is good for everyone in the school, but especially the children. The questions posed in the questionnaire are about the latest trade union agreements for the schools. The basic content in the agreements has been the same for all Scandinavian countries, thereby permitting a degree of reliability in the responses across the sample. The first statement to which principals responded concerned an agreement on more team teaching. The second statement related to whether the new agreement has led to more union consciousness among the teachers. A third statement asks if the trade agreement has led to higher goal fulfillment.

Table 2 shows that principals from Norway, in general, feel more positive towards the latest trade agreement, but the overall pattern is the same in all three countries. Both in Denmark and Sweden, one-third of the principals do not think that the trade agreement has led to more teachers working in teams. The corresponding figure for Norway is 19 per cent. The next statement about higher union consciousness among the teachers reveals a very divided group of principals in both Denmark and Sweden. Once again, however, the Norwegian group expresses a more positive view. The final question, which asks if the trade agreement led to higher goal fulfillment, is viewed more positively in Norway and Sweden than in Denmark. Only 20 per cent don't think goal fulfillment was improved in the first two countries while the figure for Denmark is 40 per cent.

Table 2. The School Leaders' Views on the Last Teacher Union Agreements
for the School.

		Disagree Totally			Agree Totally
The agreements have led	D	7%	24%	34%	31%
to more co-operation in	N	5%	14%	50%	32%
teacher teams	S	7%	23%	59%	11%
The agreement have led	D	11%	30%	47%	12%
to higher union under-	N	6%	23%	48%	23%
standing among teachers	S	11%	36%	45%	8%
The agreement have led	D	11%	29%	49%	11%
to higher goal fulfill-	N	6%	18%	54%	22%
ment	S	5%	18%	53%	24%

Note: D=Denmark, N=Norway and S=Sweden. Row per cent.

For the questions reflected in this table, there is a rather high agreement among countries but, at the same time, a rather high level of disagreement within countries. The response patterns once again raise questions about the amount of discussion taking place within principal groups concerning important school matters. For instance, the responses from Swedish principals on the first two questions give a very scattered picture and clearly show that there is no real unity among the principals on these questions. Several explanations can be offered for this pattern, but one obvious conclusion is that these questions are not discussed at great length among the principals at their meetings. The opinions they hold are therefore more personal than the outcome of professional discussion.

The Implementation Arena

When operating within the implementation arena, the principal can be concerned with many different aspects of life in school. For the purposes of this chapter, attention is focused on principals' work associated with the implementation of the trade agreement referenced in the preceding section. Three questions from the questionnaire are considered in the display presented in Table 3. The first one is regarding the role played by colleagues in the implementation process. The second question addresses the relative importance to the process of accurate information from the central office. The final question concerns the principal's communications with the staff about the implementation of the school improvement process.

For all three questions, the same general picture emerges as relevant to all three Scandinavian countries. The school leaders agree that all aspects are of importance for a successful implementation process. The greatest variations in response occur between principals in Denmark and the two other countries regarding their contacts with colleagues. Almost 90 per cent in Denmark say that these contacts are very important. Corresponding figures in Norway and Sweden are a bit lower, but still very high. Finally, Norwegian principals view communications about school improvement with the staff as more important than do principals in the two other countries.

Table 3. The School Leaders' View on the Implementation Process.

		Disagree Totally			Agree Totally
Contacts with colleagues	D	3%	10%	39%	48%
on other schools are vital	N	8%	25%	42%	25%
for our implementation	S	5%	18%	53%	24%
Information from the	D	10%	19%	38%	34%
central office is vital	N	21%	29%	29%	21%
for our implementation	S	8%	17%	40%	35%
School improvement	D	3%	8%	43%	46%
talks with my staff are	N	1%	5%	34%	60%
vital for the process	S	4%	14%	49%	33%

Note: D=Denmark, N=Norway and S=Sweden. Row per cent.

Also, the response patterns for two of the questions reveal large differences within countries in the way principals evaluate the statements. The greatest variations in response can be observed in how important principals view the information from the central office. These results can probably be explained in the same way as in the preceding section - that is, not a lot of dialogue or reflection among principals on the matter. However, a related but different explanation may be that a majority of the principals are lonely, operating in isolation from each other in their schools. When they meet colleagues at small or big meetings, they talk about practical day-to-day matters (i.e., looking for the best practices) but they very seldom meet to evaluate and study leadership processes in a detailed way.

The Arena of Loyalty

The last arena to be considered is perhaps one of the most difficult for principals to handle because school leadership must be based on a clear understanding of the tasks associated with schooling as well as the values of national and local curricula and goals. The leader must comprehend the breadth of his/her duties and have a well-grounded knowledge and a deep understanding of these tasks. He or she must manifest a clear and active leadership. Leading and developing a school grounded on a democratic foundation means that the leader must identify with, and be a carrier of, the values incorporated in the curriculum. As well, a principal must ensure that the perspective and dimensions associated with these values clearly permeate his or her work and the school's activities. All this implies that there could be conflicts of loyalty. The questionnaire used three statements to highlight three potential sources of loyalty conflicts. One related to conflict between school district policies and the principal's relations with the staff. A second related to a potential loyalty conflict occurring between the principal's need to express critical views and his/her loyalty to the school district when the school conditions are not good. The third inquired about a situation when the demand for organizational loyalty prevents the principal from being the leader he/she wants to be.

Table 4. Experienced Loyalty Conflicts for School Leaders.

		Disagree Totally			Agree Totally
There is often a conflict	D	24%	33%	34%	9%
of loyalty between me,	N	14%	32%	40%	14%
the teachers and the city	S	15%	24%	53%	8%
There is often a conflict	D	25%	27%	31%	17%
between me and my need	N	15%	29%	38%	18%
to express critic and the	S	15%	32%	43%	10%
City.					
The demand for loyalty	D	29%	35%	30%	9%
with local politics stops	N	17%	29%	35%	19%
me from being the leader	S	32%	35%	26%	7%
I want to be!					

Note: D=Denmark, N=Norway and S=Sweden. Row per cent.

As Table 4 demonstrates, almost no differences between countries are apparent in the data display. There is also almost a totally random distribution of answers within the countries. One explanation for these scattered patterns of response is that loyalty questions are seldom discussed in public, but nevertheless recognized as problematic by many principals. That suggests once again that the data is more representative of personal opinions than of collective professional statements. Another potential explanation is that matters involving values tend to be discussed on a very superficial level, leading to a culture of consensus and operational harmony but not to deeper understanding of relations and purposes for schooling.

CONCLUSION: ADOPTING AN ARENAS PERSPECTIVE ON SCHOOL LEADERSHIP

This chapter demonstrates the practical utility and conceptual insights that accrue from applying an arenas perspective to the school leadership role. Conceptualizing school leadership practices in this way provides a simple metaphor for conveying the dynamics, complexities and interactive relationships associated with the multiple functions of the school leadership role. It also reveals the relationships among groups of stakeholders that compete for attention and scarce resources within the educational enterprise. The sources of educational values as well as value conflicts among those arenas become apparent. Finally, the notion of leadership arenas has proven to be an effective workshop strategy for encouraging school administrators to analyze and reflect upon their practices.

When the notions of managerial and leadership arenas is incorporated as part of a research methodology, it becomes apparent that principals hold a range of opinions in relation to the various arenas. For some arenas, principals appear to share strong united professional opinion, whereas in relation to other arenas a common pattern of response is not detectable. In support of a future study, it would be interesting to use the notion of arenas as a starting point for analyzing and understanding the formation of professional attitudes - that is, the formation of a shared professional opinion. It would be interesting to trace the external as well as the internal influences on the formation of professional attitudes within the variety of arenas associated with schools.

NOTES

[1] The above section is based on the Swedish Government Office for Education, Memorandum 2000-11-08; *Leadership of the school of today and tomorrow means to challenge co-workers' assumptions about learning and teaching* (author's translation and editing. The author was a member of the Government's Expert Group on the Role of the Swedish School-Leader).

[2] In Denmark (Moos, 2001), in Norway (Møller & Paulsen, 2001), and in Sweden (Johansson, 2002) questionnaires were distributed to a representative sample of school leaders in each country. In Denmark to all school leaders (2001), in Norway (2000-2001) and Sweden (2001) to members of the national unions. The return rate for questionnaires was 70 per cent or more in each country, giving us a robust basis for statistical analysis.

REFERENCES

Ärlestig, H. (2000). Lärares lärande måste bli en del av livet självt – om rektors betydelse för lärares lärande och skolutveckling. Ingår i L. Lundberg (red.), *Görandets lov – Lov att göra – om den nya tidens rektor*. Skrifter från Centrum för skolledarutveckling 2000:1, Umeå universitet.

Begley, P.T. (1998). The nature, form and function of values in school administration. Ingår i O. Johansson & L. Lindberg (red.), *Exploring new horizons in school leadership: Conference proceedings, March 25-27, 1998*. Skrifter från Centrum för Skolledarutveckling 1998:4, Umeå universitet.

Begley, P.T. (2000). Cultural isomorphs of educational administration: Reflections on the Western-centric approaches to values and leadership. Special issue of *Asia Pacific Journal of Education, 20*(2), 23-33.

Begley, P.T., & Johansson, O. (1998). The values of school administration: Preferences, ethics and conflicts - a research report. Ingår i O. Johansson & L. Lundberg (red.), *Rektor en språngbräda för utveckling – om rektor i skärningspunkten mellan erfarenheter och utmaningar*. Skrifter från Centrum för skolledarutveckling, 1998:2, Umeå universitet.

Begley, P.T., & Johansson, O. (2001, January). *Leadership for democratic schools*. Paper delivered at the fourteenth annual International Congress for School Effectiveness and Improvement, Toronto.

Berg, G. (1990). *Skolledning och professionellt skolledarskap. Perspektiv på skolledares uppgifter och funktioner*. Pedagogisk forskning i Uppsala, 92, Pedagogiska institutionen, Uppsala universitet.

Berg, G. (1995). *Skolkultur- nyckeln till skolans utveckling. En bok för skolutvecklare om skolans styrning*. Göteborg: Förlagshuset Gothia.

Bredeson, P.V. (1998). Paradox and possibility: Professional development and organizational learning in education. Ingår i O. Johansson & L. Lindberg (Eds.), *Exploring New Horizons in School Leadership – conference proceedings, March 25-27, 1998*. Skrifter från Centrum för Skolledarutveckling 1998:4, Umeå universitet.

Duke, D.L. (1998). School leadership and the hard work of helping individual students to learn. Ingår i O. Johansson & L. Lindberg (Eds.), *Exploring new horizons in school leadership: Conference proceedings, March 25-27, 1998*. Skrifter från Centrum för Skolledarutveckling 1998:4, Umeå universitet.

Ekholm, M. (1989). Skolledarskap, forskning och några svenska funderingar. Ingår i T. Tiller (red.), *Ledelse i en skole i utvikling*. Oslo: Tano.

Ekholm, M. (1994). Skolledarskap och styrning i en decentraliserande tid. Ingår i A. Hård Af Segerstad (red.), *Skola med styrfart – En antologi om styrning och ledning av skolans verksamhet*. Rektorsutbildningen: Uppsala universitet.

Ekvall, G. (red.) (1996). *Navigatör och inspiratör: Om chefer, ledarskap och förändring*. Lund: Studentlitteratur.

Ellmin, R., & Levén, S. (1994). *Ur tid är ledningen: Nära ledarskap 3*. Stockholm.

Falk, T., & Sandström, B. (1995). *Rektors upplevelse av ett nationellt och kommunalt uppdrag: En balansakt på slak lina*. En arbetsrapport inom Skolverkets projekt 'Samverkan mellan statlig rektorsutbildning och kommunal ledarutbildning', Stockholm.

Geijer, L. (2000). Att göra tillsammans istället för att ge upp: En retrospektiv betraktelse. Ingår i L. Lundberg (red.), *Görandets lov – Lov att göra – om den nya tidens rektor*. Skrifter från Centrum för skolledarutveckling 2000:1, Umeå universitet.

Gustafsson, G. (1983). Symbolic and pseudo policies as responses to diffusion of power in policy. *Science, 15*, 269-87.

Hagström, B. (1990). *Chef i offentlig verksamhet – forskning kring offentligt ledarskap*. Lund: Studentlitteratur.

Hughes, O.E. (1998). *Public management and administration, second edition.*. Houndsmills: Macmillan.

Johansson, O. (1994). Om rektorsrollen vid målstyrning av skolan. Ingår i A. Hård Af Segerstad (red.), *Skola med styrfart – En antologi om styrning och ledning av skolans verksamhet*. Rektorsutbildningen, Uppsala universitet.

Johansson, O. (2000). Om rektors demokratiska, lärande och kommunikativa ledarskap. Ingår i L. Lundberg (red.), *Görandets lov – Lov att göra – om den nya tidens rektor*. Skrifter från Centrum för skolledarutveckling 2000:1, Umeå universitet.

Johansson, O. (2001). School Leadership Training in Sweden. Perspectives for tomorrow *Journal of Inservice Education, 27*(2), 185-202.

Johansson, O. (2001). Swedish school leadership in transition: In search of a democratic, learning and communicative leadership. *Pedagogy, Culture, & Society, 9*(3), 387-406.

Johansson, O. (2002). *Demokratiska, lärande och kommunikativa skolledare: En empirisk prövning med utgångspunkt i skolledares vardag*. Skrifter från Centrum för skolledarutveckling 2002:1, Umeå universitet.

Johansson, O., Moos, L., & Møller, J. (2000). Visjon om en demokratisk reflekterende ledelse. Noen sentrale perspektiver i en forståelse av nordisk skoleledelse. In L. Moos, S. Carney, O. Johansson, & J. Mehlbye (red.), *Skoleledelse i Norden: En kortlægning af skoleledernes arbejdsvilkår, rammebetingelser og opgaver. En rapport till Nordisk Ministerråd, Nord 2000:14, Köpenhamn*.

Johansson, O., & Bredeson, P. (1999). Value orchestration by the policy community for the learning community: Reality and myth. In P. Begley (Ed.), *Values and Educational Leadership* (pp. 51-72). Albany, NY: SUNY Press.

Johansson, O., & Kallos, D. (1994). Om rektorsrollen vid målstyrning av skolan", ingår i Hård Af Segerstad, Anita (red.), *Skola med styrfart – En antologi om styrning och ledning av skolans verksamhet*. Rektorsutbildningen, Uppsala universitet.

Johansson, O., & Lundberg, L. (2002). Changed leadership roles – or school leadership by goals and objectives. In A. Lidström & C. Hudson (Eds.), *Local educational policy: Comparing Sweden and England* (pp. 179-204). Houndsmitts: McMillan.

Lakomski, G. (1998). Leadership, Distributed Cognition And The Learning Organization. Ingår i O. Johansson & L. Lindberg (red.), *Exploring new horizons in school leadership: Conference proceedings, March 25-27, 1998*. Skrifter från Centrum för Skolledarutveckling 1998:4, Umeå universitet.

Lärande ledare (2001). *Report from the Swedish Government Office for Education*.

Leithwood, K. (1998). Organizational Learning and Transformational Leadership. Ingår i O. Johansson & L. Lindberg (red.), *Exploring new horizons in school leadership: Conference proceedings, March 25-27, 1998*. Skrifter från Centrum för Skolledarutveckling 1998:4, Umeå universitet.

Leithwood, K., Jantzi, D., & Steinbach, R. (1999). *Changing leadership for changing times*. Buckingham, UK: Open University Press.

Lidström, A. (1996). Skolledaren, handlingsutrymmet och effektiviteten. Ingår i O. Johansson & D. Kallós (red.), *Tänk utveckling! En antologi om skolans kvalitet och effektivitet – vad kan ledaren göra?* Rektorsutbildningens skriftserie nr 3, Umeå universitet.

Lpo 94. *Läroplaner för det obligatoriska skolväsendet och de frivilliga skolformerna*, Utbildningsdepartementet 1994.

Møller, J., & Paulsen, M. (2001). *Skoleledares arbetsforhold I Grunnskolen: Ved ingangen til ett nytt tusenår*. Universitetet I Oslo: ILS.

Moos, L. (2001) *Folkskoleledernes arbetsförhold*. Danmarks Pedagogiska universitet.

Nygren, A.M. (2000). Rektors görande utifrån målkrav. Ingår i Lundberg, Leif (red.), *Görandets lov – Lov att göra – om den nya tidens rektor*. Skrifter från Centrum för skolledarutveckling 2000:1, Umeå universitet.

Parker, K. (1998). *School councils and classroom change*. Ontario Institute for Studies in Education/University of Toronto: Doctoral thesis.

Scherp, H. (1998). *Utmanande eller utmanat ledarskap*. Göteborg studies in educational sciences 120, Göteborg: Acta Universitatis Gothenburgensis.

Simon, H. (1965). *Administrative behaviour, second edition*. New York: Free Press.

Skolverket (2001). Barnomsorg, Skola, Vuxenutbildning – Skolverkets lägesbedömning 2001, Dnr 2001:803, Skolverket, Stockholm.

Strandberg, L. (2000). Göra nytt och tänka nytt – förnyelsearbete ur ett Vygotskyperspektiv. Ingår i L. Lundberg (red.), *Görandets lov – Lov att göra – om den nya tidens rektor*. Skrifter från Centrum för skolledarutveckling 2000:1, Umeå universitet.

Svedberg, L. (2000). *Rektorsrollen: Om skolledarskapets gestaltning*. Stockholm: HLS Förlag.

Törnsén, M. (2000). Ledarskap i skolan – det möjligas konst! Individuell erfarenhet och internationell forskning. Ingår i L. Lundberg (red.), *Görandets lov – Lov att göra – om den nya tidens rektor*. Skrifter från Centrum för skolledarutveckling 2000:1, Umeå universitet.

Wahlberg, K. (2000). 'Jag upptäcker hela tiden att jag lär mig när jag arbetar...' – ett skolkort om en lärande skola i en lärande miljö. Ingår i L. Lundberg (red.), *Görandets lov – Lov att göra – om den nya tidens rektor*. Skrifter från Centrum för skolledarutveckling 2000:1, Umeå universitet.

CHRISTOPHER HODGKINSON

CONCLUSION: TOMORROW, AND TOMORROW, AND TOMORROW: A POST-POSTMODERN PURVIEW[1]

Abstract. This chapter critically surveys the cultural and educational context of the period 1960 - 2020 and seeks to analyze the implications for educational leadership. Sources range from early contributions of Donald Willower to the latest prognostications of experts in Cambridge and the USA. Both general and special conclusions are drawn and a new test, the A3M3, is introduced as part of the presentation.

> Tomorrow, and tomorrow, and tomorrow,
> Creeps in this petty pace from day to day,
> To the last syllable of recorded time;
> And all our yesterdays have lighted fools
> The way to dusty death (Macbeth)

These words of Shakespeare seem to imply a deep despair or cynicism about the possibility of benevolent change in human affairs. They are surely the very antithesis of American optimism and progressivism. For organizations they bespeak drudgery, wage slavery, Dilbertian anomie, pathological compartmentalization, ennui. They deplore meaninglessness. But they refer not to some sort of Nietzschean eternal recurrence of the same but simply to the line of time each one of us inhabits, a line which never wavers and always runs from past through present to future.

As one ages (and there's an absolute for you) one automatically has more past and less future. More behind, less in front. Less hope, more regret. And so the very natural tendency is to approach the future, as McLuhan once put it, looking in the rearview mirror. I shall try to struggle against this tendency. To that end the bulk of this paper will deal with what is to come, with what might be and the lesser part with the past, with what might have been or seemed to be. But what of that past? It cannot be ignored.

The Way It Might Have Been

One of the aims of this chapter is to heighten our sensitivity about the cultural impress that is always determining, subliminally and subconsciously, our value orientations and judgments. We are always creatures of our times and the times themselves are a flood of events that are always somehow out of focus. In short my topic is what used to be called history but that word has fallen into contention[2] and today is being displaced by exotica such as cultural anthropology, sociobiology, evolutionary psychology. and bio-genetics. Yet history or temporality conceived as the intellectual linkages between past, present, and future

221

P.T. Begley and O. Johansson (eds.), The Ethical Dimensions of School Leadership, 221–231.
© 2003 *Kluwer Academic Publishers. Printed in the Netherlands.*

is the very province and substance of administration. Certainly it is the meat of leadership[3] in that administration is the management of the future and its achievements become the legacy of the past. The conference for which this chapter was originally prepared hardly came about without past planning and a complex cascade of policy and managerial decisions, each of which was present in its own instance. Administration is also karma-in-action for the past comes back to haunt it. As an eminent management consultant recently put it, somewhat facetiously, 'The leader knows the future and has agreed to share it with the company instead of using this awesome power to make a fortune gambling.'[4] But to comprehend or understand the future - the way things *might* be, it is logically necessary to understand the past - the way things were or, at least, *seemed* to be. As for the interim between these two things - the so-called present - let's leave this for the moment; I'll come back to it.

Shortly before my lamented and esteemed colleague Donald J. Willower sadly left us to join what he would call the Great Majority he gave me a now-treasured possession. This was an inscribed book he had edited, together with Jack Culbertson, back in 1964 (Willower & Culbertson, 1964). It is a chorus of voices from the past and serves to remind us, as Nietzsche put it, that 'The living are only a species of the dead, and a rare species at that.' Included in the contributors were such greats as Roald Campbell, Dan Griffiths, and Joseph Schwab. Also among them was a professor of medicine, George Miller. The book taken as a whole presents a vision of what educational leadership was seen to be and what the preparation of educational leaders might have been at the beginning of my survey period (c. 1960 - c. 2020). These clearly were the days of a new dawn. A heady sense of the importance and virtue of our professoriate existed. The Midwest Administration Centre at the University of Chicago was the centre of the world. Nevertheless, the general tenor and gist, if not the explicit agenda of the work, was to establish the intellectual credibility and respectability of a new discipline, grounding itself if not in science and theory *per se* then certainly in the social sciences and even in philosophy. Its place in the academy was formidably asserted. There was a distinct flavour of elitism and the development of the professorship in educational administration was favourably compared to its equivalent in medicine. Schwab, a 'mathematical geneticist by training and a philosopher by choice'(Willower & Culbertson, 1964, p. 48) , felt it reasonable to commend to administrators 'a sophisticated and cynical grasp of about a dozen separate and distinct bodies of theory' (1964, p. vii). And even though the young Don Willower's contribution was more down to earth, it too stressed the ideal and the philosophical components of our art. The field was to appeal to 'the imaginative, inventive individual who wants to work in a profession which seeks to contribute to human progress and growth' (1964, p. 150). He had already enunciated the theme he was to pursue throughout his career: a pragmatic reconciliation of theory and practice but with a marked stress on reflection and reflective methods concomitant with a commitment to educational ideals. Dewey *revividus*. All in all it was an inspiring manifesto, both dignifying educational administration and projecting for it a future where, as once perhaps in the past, men of action were also men of contemplation, of wisdom, of passion and honour.

Did all this what-might-have-been come about? You be the judge. Well, perhaps the timing was a little, out.

Recall the 1960s. Remember San Francisco where, then, one wore a flower in one's hair. I was at Berkeley at the time. Momentarily it was the epicentre of a new revolution: the counter-culture. Wonderful as it all was in its beginnings things soon soured. In the end they even had to create concentration camps in California to hold some of the more exuberant dissidents. And the challenge to authority had slogans like 'Burn, baby, burn'. Mao buttons were *de rigueur*, Minutemen and Black Panthers were lionized as were communes, long hair, and free casual sex. It was the time of Sharon Tate and the Manson gang. Vietnam. Drugs. Sex. Dionysus. (we'll return to him later.)

In the end order was restored. But by then Thom Greenfield had fired the epistemological shot that was heard around the world of educational administration. The authority of science itself was now challenged. Reality was a social construct. Organizations were moral entities, or should be. Camps formed and camp followers lined up. In Canada Royal Commission followed Royal Commission, each more eager than the rest to overturn the traditional order. Change was equated with progress. Permissive lib-chic became the orthodoxy of the day. (It still is, only now crystallized into a non-permissive political correctitude. The University of Alberta extended its influence, via educational administration, to Australia while the newly formed Ontario Institute for Studies in Education became a world-class centre for our subject. This too still is. Heady times. Great debates: Greenfield-Griffiths, Greenfield-Hills, Greenfield-Willower. Back then only 6% of the population in Canada had a university degree. Now 90% of school superintendents have a master's and 10% the doctorate.

The Elusive Present

Between past and future lies a mystery. The present. Now. 'Now' in logic is a very fuzzy term. Taken as the moment it doesn't exist, in the same sort of way as it doesn't make sense to talk of instantaneous velocity in the differential calculus. But the calculus works and our sense of time seems real enough. Yet subjective experience and inner attention are always a mixed-up blodge of the past (memory) and the future (hopes, fears, and expectations). Unless you want to go the Zen route and aspire to be like the samurai who can pick a mosquito out of the air with his chopsticks, 'now' would not be precisely meaningful. I fancy, however that most educators inhabit a permanent state of bell-ringing anticipation: blissful if it signifies the end of a class or a lecture, and the contrary otherwise.

Collectively the same holds true. 'Today's news wraps tomorrow's fish', 'You can't step into the same river twice'. Postmodernism, the label for our now, is a-historical and chimerical. Fuzzy logic writ large.

So 'now' does not mean right now. It means rather a blurry spread of contemporary events stretching back a bit and forwards a bit. In administration it may be fairer to say that it stretches back a lot and forward a lot for we stumble into the future hobbled by plans and commitments made in the past and our forward reach exceeds our grasp. As for the present as often as not there's no 'there' there. For our purposes then it is sufficient to simply regard the now as the last decade or so together with the shadow it extends into the future. This historical sound-bite (*sub specie aeternitatis*) is increasingly recognized and classified as postmodern and postmodernism is something we must look at more closely. This NOW is, however, *radically* different from its predecessors. The following items are indicative of this difference: the pill (perhaps the most revolutionary technical advance since the wheel), the chip, the micro-chip, the PC, the global village, day-trading, cloning, genetic engineering, social engineering, E-commerce, E-everything, Mars orbiter, jumbo-jets, Concorde, neutron bombs, cell-phones, websites, quantum physics, astrophysics, astroturf ...

All this and much more comprise the technological infrastructure of our present culture. All in the 'now'. Technology has always been around but previous infra structural changes like the Industrial Revolution occurred over much larger sweeps of time. The present curve of change (and its learning curve) is, in comparison, exponential. All such changes affect the social superstructure or culture because they change context: the *mise-en-scène*. But there is a complication. Culture is dependent on science and technology but it is also autonomous. It's not simply a matter of correlative dependency and interaction. The explanation for this is a logical difference between value and fact. Science speaks on facts but is silent on values. The humanities speak (or used to speak) on values but have to accept whatever facts are placed before them. The gulf between these two realms of discourse is radical. To try to get values from facts is to commit the naturalistic fallacy --- a fallacy that has never been refuted. You can't get an 'ought' from an 'is'. But you have to take the is's into account. As Third Reich scientist Werner von Braun used to say, 'I send the rockets up - Who cares where they come down?' Worrying about where or when they should come down is not science, it's administration.

For example, will the final mapping of the genome change human nature? No, but it will give us more power perhaps, and certainly it will add to the information overload that we have already. Great changes occur; the scientific sands are shifting underfoot. But the really interesting thing is that human nature changes very little. Crucifixion is out of fashion at the moment but a Roman soldier returning to earth today, after due wonderment at the technical changes about him and a sigh of despair at the state of the Colosseum, would soon feel at home. Genocides and holocausts, man-made events, are still around. On the other hand there has been no nuclear war (yet) and no world war since Hiroshima. (And no army used gas in World War II.) This emphasis on human nature is important because to be an educator is by definition to be a humanist, maybe even a classicist. Certainly there are two Greek gods we should get to know. Their names are Apollo and Dionysus. Apollo is blond and beautiful, impeccable, he is the god of the sun, of light, of reason. A worthy representative of science but also a bit of a fascist. Dionysus is dirty, dishevelled, wild, the god of orgies and sensuous destructive abandon; the god of all things irrational, against all order, for all chaos, all indulgence, a sort of über-hippie. These two gods represent a dialectic ever-present in human nature and human history. Very crudely put the post-Enlightenment period of modernism could be called Apollonian and the philosophical confusion that followed on Nietzsche's lament of God's death in the late Victorian era with its consequent cataclysm in 1914 - postmodernism in other words - can be called Dionysian.

This dialectic occurs at many levels in human nature. It is exemplified in our times as a psychological contest between reason and passion; desire for order and rebellion against restraint; the triumph of science and the naturalistic fallacy concomitant with the malaise of moral relativism and the malaise of totalitarian political correctness. You can apply this analysis to education for yourself and all of you have been exposed and are being exposed to the stress and tension which these two immortal archetypes, these two gods, create in our cultural fabric. Listen for a moment to Nietzsche commenting on the death of God:

> ... Are we not plunging continually? Backward, sideward, forward, in all directions? Is there any up or down left? Are we not straying as through an infinite nothing? Do we not feel the breath of empty space? Has it not become colder? Is not night continually closing in on us? ... God is dead. God remains dead. And we have killed him ...

Not too bad a description of the postmodern condition. But postmodernism is not merely relativistic about value it is also nihilistic about truth. Our Roman soldier could well ask Pontius Pilate's famous question with even more justification. What is truth? What is the truth about truth? (Anderson, 1995). That there is no truth. There are only Nietzschean 'perspectives' or 'interpretations'; only Lyotard's 'incredulity towards meta narratives'; only Derrida's 'il n'y a pas de hors-texte" - there's only a text, and its only meaning is that provided by its reader.

This then is the structure of NOW. On the one hand hyper-rational bureaucratic legalistic complex organizations (school systems, multinationals, governments), on the other hand increasingly stressed individuals and small groups divested of, but searching for, meaning and value in an endless variety of ways from hedonistic materialistic consumerism to profound and authentic spiritual search and striving.

The Way it is becoming. What comes after postmodernism? Such a question invokes the great imponderable - the future - which, while it extends to infinity really only concerns us within the range of our immediate mortality. Soon we too will be part of the Great Majority. And, as always, there is a dialectic of opinion: the sun of Ecclesiastes under which there is nothing new and the river of Heraclitus into which one cannot step twice. *Plus ça change, plus c'est la même chose ...* and yet the new forever being born. With this dialectical tension in mind let us look fleetingly at the short term ahead. To help us do this I have resorted to alma mater Cambridge. From those hallowed cloisters emerges a picture of post-postmodernity based on Cantabridgian expertise. This in very digested and kaleidoscopic form I now present for your consideration.[5] But first a Persian thought, even a Caribbean one? ...

> Ah, fill the cup - what use is to repeat
> How time is slipping underneath our feet
> Unborn 'Tomorrow', and dead 'Yesterday',
> Why fret about them if 'Today' be sweet!

Population. By 2050 two-thirds as much more protoplasm than we have today: 10 billion bodies. But food production efficiency outpaces population growth. Risks to the environment, however. 'Better governance, better institutions, better markets, better schools' will be necessary. But desire for progeny may decline.

Climate. Nothing really bad until at least 2050. Need to get rid of present type of cars, however. Scientific opinion is split. Hotter? Colder? We don't know.

Water. Massive pipeline shifts, Canada to U.S. Also, dams don't exist forever, they're aging. Water will soon be metered like electricity. The poor already have a water crisis. A problem of equity rather than engineering.

Energy. Plenty of it but again the environmental problem. Correlated to living standards as one might expect. New cars needed. 'Globality and 24-hour, hyperactive, inter-connected, e-mail fuelled, sleep-deprived' new millennium is upon us.

Superpowers. Present condition an historical first (if one excludes Rome). Other powers on the rise, e.g., China and a revitalized Russia. And ethnicity a problem. Presently Pax Americana.

Trouble Spots. China still long way behind U.S. The Middle East, of course. Africa and the heart of darkness. Bio-chemical weapons. Nuclear waste. Drugs. Human rights. Terrorism.

United Nations. Richest 20% have 86% of the world's wealth. Poorest 20% have 1%.. U.N. is aging now, too. Like the dams.

East and West. China's tough line on population control has been a great contribution to humanity. Europe? Conflicting theories: Britain wants 'community', France 'nations', Germany a 'state'. But all very exciting and Europe could become number one in 30-40 years time.

Money. Capitalism is 'the permanent equilibrium state of human society. Everything else was a sideshow.' 'The motivation to compete, to own and acquire wealth is a fundamental fact of human existence, just like the need to eat or have sex.' But the mixed economy form now well established and no more crises for at least 15 years.

Markets. Stock markets will be electronic and global. Big problem of regulation. Companies must grow or die. But double-entry bookkeeping will remain, as it has, since the 15th century.

Electronics. The symbol of the 1980s was the personal computer. The symbol of the 90s was the web. The next thing will be sensors. These will be low-cost, very high performance, and they'll be everywhere, 'from Macdonald's fries to insulin delivery for diabetics'. We will soon have entire PCs on a chip. But information technology will be supplanted by biotechnology. The genome and all that.

Internet. This could be a liberating force in the Third World. Can also be cultural dumbing-down (Hollywood and porn). It's an information toy but how long can interest be sustained?

Cars. Next big step the automated road: regulating vehicles in convoys. Sensors can make this a reality. 'You would just pay a toll, couple your car into an electronic convoy and sit back to enjoy the ride'. Adelaide already has automated bus routes.

Aircraft. Flight has lost its glamour. Passengers are bored and uncomfortable. The aim will be speed. Airlines will either have to get you there faster or make flying more enjoyable. Fuel and turbulence set technological limits and problems.

Space. Lots of other planets but life on them may have been millions of years in the past or will be millions of years in the future, our time. So don't bet on extra-terrestrials.

Families. System breaking down in the West. Women can't do it all: adopting a male agenda in life arguably only another form of submission. Smaller families and more childless families. Being a parent used to bring social status, it doesn't now.

Ethnicity. Very complex. Very postmodern. 'Identity' will depend more on one's set of values than where one comes from.

Crime. Up but more property crime than violent crime. Prison populations up.

Christianity. Technology cuts both ways. Contrast U.S. televangelism and the Pope. Ecclesiastical and liturgical contortions in response to postmodernity.

Islam. Growing West and East. Current modes (military and dynastic leadership) may shift towards democratic forms. Big problem remaining: fundamentalism.

English. World language for next half-century then shift to possibly Spanish. Chinese if they can solve the orthography problem. But English will fragment. Process well under way. English teachers jobs very secure. (Even in Quebec.)

Bodies. Twenty-five percent of the population will be over 60. But healthier. Cliché problem is to 'add life to years' rather than converse. Big educational implications.

Minds. Depression, dementia, stress, Alzheimer's. Boomers already trembling. Four- and five- generational living families. Grandparents may be too busy minding great-grandparents to look after grandchildren.

Reproduction. Divergence between developed and developing regions. In the former sex for pleasure and conception for the laboratory. More test-tube babies, sperm and egg-banks. Chinese interventional experiments need watching.

Funding Health. Seven percent of UK Gross Domestic Product presently goes to Health; 9% in Netherlands, 10% France and Germany. But outcomes very comparable. Probable shift from universal coverage to 'top-up' or 'opt-out' schemes; i.e., basics paid, user-pay for the rest. Even so higher taxes and rationing on the way. (Since health and education compete for the public purse one can safely predict more stresses and strains in both systems.)

This is by no means all. It is only a sampling of the multiple facets of postmodern life as examined by the Cambridge experts cited but it is surely a peek at the shape of things to come. That shape, through a glass darkly, may disappoint - or it may excite - but futurology is perforce a very modest business since the future itself is a combination of the causal and the casual: of past determining forces which have yet to run their course and the totally unforeseen. So prophets had better be modest. Nevertheless what is glaringly conspicuous by its absence from the above forecasts, what is missing from all this arcana of tribal peoples, telecoms, film, even Judaism; what is totally lacking in this glimpse at the coming century is the category of *philosophy.* And this from the academic home of Russell, Moore, and Wittgenstein. This from the institution that gave an honorary degree to Derrida! Not a peep, not a peek. To the end of history must now be appended the demise of philosophy. But before leaping to this conclusion let us look at the view from our side of the water.

The American View

As part of the same millennial frenzy that inspired the Cambridge authors, a special issue of *Time* magazine[6] was devoted to such questions as: Will we live on Mars?, travel in time? discover another universe? figure out the brain? get rid of cockroaches?, etc. Admittedly, the questions are scientific-technological, but they are carefully considered by the finest expertise in the respective fields, including many Nobelists. To make a short story even shorter the answers can be summarily summed as no time travel, no extra-terrestrial contact, no final 'theory of everything', no explanation of consciousness, no solution to the mind-body problem, no perpetual motion machinery, and no controlling the weather. Or cockroaches. And again no *philosophy* even though several commentators had inevitably to deal with issues such as mind, consciousness, and meaning. Granted the project was non-normative, rationalistic, and scientific-technological in the best tradition of the Enlightenment and the Age of Reason. And, come to think of it and if memory serves, *Time* has not devoted a special issue to philosophy for over thirty years. At which time it declared it dead, killed by the academicians. Even *Time* gets things right on occasion.

GENERAL CONCLUSION

The values of the short-term future are implicit if not explicit. It is likely to be an unholy Apollonian-Dionysian mix of rationalistic legalistic bureaucratic scientific technological pragmatics and a reactive postmodern relativistic hedonistic narcissistic materialistic nihilism. For education this might imply a skew towards the digital, the mathematical, the marketable, and the meritocratic. That is to say, not the mindless but the meaningless. And all the consequent Dionysian reactions of rage, resentment, ressentiment, and violence this might invoke. I hope these words are not prophetic and a product more of dimmer than of clearer sight. But I have long perceived with some empirical verification the cultural tendencies to valorexia and philosophobia: the twin diseases of loss of meaning and abhorrence of philosophy.

Of course we as educators must be concerned with literacy of all types, including the digital; of course we must attend to earning-learning of all the marketable kinds; but we must also restore our responsibility for general social decorum, even in postmodernity; we must hand down traditions and history even if they offend some multicultural persuasions; and we must have a concern with the larger purposes of being human. Failing this we are not educators but just another form of teaching machine: programmers, trainers, info-dispensers. Information may equate to knowledge but knowledge does not equate to understanding. None of this is to say we cannot joyfully embrace the future. *Amor fati* is always an option.[7] That the questions which this admittedly disjointed and tumultuous sweep of time and events are always: what changes and what stays the same? Mark Twain's remark is relevant, 'History does not repeat itself. But it sure rhymes.'

Simply put what changes is context, what doesn't change is human nature. But, as already mentioned, human nature just happens to be the essential raw material of education. More, it is also the essence of administration and leadership. (Think *character* instead of *characteristics*.) Moreover still, human nature and the human condition are the quintessential subject matter of real philosophy. John Dewey said, and our late colleague Don Willower endorsed this, that the whole of philosophy is the general theory of education. I would go further and assert that the whole of philosophy is also the general theory of administration.[8] True, philosophy in the academic sense is largely remote from practical affairs but *administrative* philosophy is a discipline the whole aim of which is to inform practicality. And this sort of philosophy is the birthright of everyone. To make my point please take the following A3M3 test:

1. Do you really know how to tell right from wrong?
2. Do you really know how to tell good from bad?
3. Can you tell a sound argument from a fallacious one?
4. Do you know enough about human nature?
5. Do you know enough about the human condition?
6. Do you really know yourself?
7. Are your answers to the above questions adequate for your role as leader or aspirant to leadership?

SPECIAL CONCLUSION

The test you have just been subjected to calls for some further words of comment. Contrary to what you might now modestly assume, it is possible to score a perfect seven. At the very least it is possible to *impute* or ascribe such a score since the test may be extroverted and attributed onto unwitting targets. Thus, all the great charismatic leaders for good or evil might score a 7: Jesus Christ, Gandhi, the Lord Buddha on one side and Josef Stalin, Adolf Hitler, and Pol Pot on the other. I myself have known leaders who, for me at least, fit the 7 bill nicely: my mentor Sir Geoffrey Vickers for one and a certain university president for another --- although both might well have been loath to acknowledge the ascription.

More importantly, the test implies an agenda for leadership preparation and research the component parts of which are already established and need only to be assembled. Essentially they suggest a shift in theory emphasis from epistemology to axiology[9] ; a short course in elementary logic and rhetoric[10] ; some exposure to the arts in the Greenfield tradition[11] and due consideration of pathology (see Greenfield & Ribbins, 1993).

As for research the work already done in the leadership initiative of these conferences is one example. Credit must be given in this respect to the labours of Professor Begley.[12] Analytical tools for value praxis already exist[13] and the ethnological studies of Peter Ribbins in the United Kingdom (Ribbins & Sayer, 1998) and Peter Gronn in Australia (Gronn, 1999) provide examples of how insight can be gained into the administrative form of life. This curricular emphasis should supplement and complement rather than displace the current studies in social science.

In the A3M3 quiz the crucial question, which cannot be formulated so as to yield a precise answer, is of course number 6. Philosophers and non-philosophers alike may argue cogently and validly that it is unanswerable in any objective sense, short of mystical illumination or transcendental revelation. Nevertheless it is always possible to arrive at a tentative *subjective* judgment, and the question should always be held before us for if it is not asked then it *is* answered --- in the negative. Not for nothing was the exhortation 'Know thyself' above the Temple of Apollo at Delphi in ancient Greece.

Finally, two lesser considerations: first, the test is subject to modification in that the rigid requirement for a dichotomous yes or no answer might be relaxed and, second, perhaps the test calls for a more innocuous and user-friendly title than the one temporarily assigned: Administrative Arrogance And Managerial Modesty Measure.[14] I am sure that neither the A nor the M attributes exceed the limits of propriety in the present audience, and that the circle of what might have been can be closed into what yet still might be.

NOTES

[1] This chapter is a revised and updated version of a paper originally presented at the Conference of the UCEA Centre for the Study of Values and Leadership, Bridgetown, Barbados. It has also been previously published as an article in a special issue (Vol. 4, No. 4, 297-307) of the International Journal of Leadership in Education (2001).

[2] A thesis made famous by Francis Fukuyama (1992).

[3] For the identity between leadership and administration see Christopher Hodgkinson (1978 / 1982, 1983, 1991, 1996).

[4] Scott Adams, 'The Dilbert Principle', as cited in James Wolcott (2000).

[5] Direct quotations are indicated by quotation marks, otherwise paraphrase and commentary. The headings are those used in the source CAM No.28 Michaelmas 1999 and the authorities are respectively: 'population' (economist Sheilagh Ogilvie), 'climate' (Judge Institute's Chris Hope), water (geographer Bill Adams), 'energy' (consultant Dan Yergin), 'superpowers' (Centre for International Studies' James Mayall), 'trouble spots' (Guardian Editor Ian Black), 'United Nations' (former U.N. Under-Secretary Dame Margaret Anstee), 'East and West' (M.C. to King of Nepal Chiran Thapu), 'money' (Chief Economist of *The Times* Anatole Kaletsky*)*, 'markets' (Judge Institute's Richard Barker), 'electronics' (Silicon Valley Institute director Paul Saffo), 'internet' *(Washington Post* Editor David Ignatius), 'cars' (Professor of Engineering David Newland), 'aircraft' (Rank Professor of Engineering Shbn Ffowes Williams), 'space' (Royal Astronomical Society's Jacqueline Mitten), 'families' (research psychologist Penelope Leach), 'ethnicity' (anthropologist, Sue Benson), 'crime' (Institute of Criminology's Andrew von Hirsch), 'Christianity' (Bishop of Rochester Michael Nazir-Ali), 'Islam' (scholar and author Akbar Ahmed), 'English' (Director Research Centre for English and Applied Linguistics Gillian Brown), 'bodies' (Professor of Clinical Gerontology Kay-Tee Khaw), 'minds' (Director Research Centre on Aging Felicia Huppert), 'reproduction' (Head of Department. of Biological Anthropology Nick Mascie-Taylor), and 'funding health' (Master of Sidney Sussex Sandra Dawson).

[6] *Time,* April 2000

[7] Nietzsche's solution. But this depends on the degree of freedom and reality of the will. Which calls for another paper beyond this one.

[8] The position expounded in Christopher Hodgkinson (1978/1982, 1983, 1991, 1996).

[9] Theoria, op.cit. note 4; and also Macmillan (2001).

[10] From experience I can recommend Robert Thouless (1974). The elements of argument do not change with the fashions of the times and this was first published in 1930.

[11] See publications in note 2, especially Hodgkinson (1996, pp. 187-211).

[12] Paul Begley, 'Praxis', Part II of a trilogy presented to BEMAS, U. of Manchester, 1999; Paul Begley (1999); P. Begley and P. Leonard (1999)

[13] As for note 2.

[14] For the robust distinction between administration and management see: Hodgkinson (1978/1982, p. 4; 1983, pp. 26-29; 1991, pp. 50-53; 1996, pp. 27-33; and Vickers (1979).

REFERENCES

Anderson, W.T. (1995). *The truth about the truth*. New York: Putnam.

Begley, P.T. (Ed.) (1999). *Values and educational leadership*. Albany, NY: SUNY Press.

Begley, P.T., & Leonard, P. (1999). *The values of educational administration*. London: Falmer Press.

Fukuyama, F. (1992). *The end of history and the last man*. New York: Free Press.

Greenfield, T.B., & Ribbins, P. (1993) *Greenfield on educational administration: Towards a humane science*. London, UK: Routledge.

Gronn, P. (1999). *The making of educational leaders*. London: Cassel.

Hodgkinson, C. (1978/1982). *Towards a philosophy of administration*. Oxford: Blackwell.

Hodgkinson, C. (1983). *The philosophy of leadership*. Oxford: Blackwell.

Hodgkinson, C. (1991). *Educational leadership: The moral art*. Albany: SUNY Press.

Hodgkinson, C. (1996). *Administrative Philosophy*. Oxford: Elsevier.

Macmillan, R.B. (2001). *Educational administration: The Greenfield legacy*. Toronto: Althouse Press.

Ribbins, P., & Sayer, J. (1998). *Management and leadership in education series*. London, UK: Cassell.

Thouless, R. (1974). *Straight and crooked thinking*. London: Pan.

Vickers, G. (1979). *Public administration*. 57(?), 229-230.

Wolcott, J. (2000). How to succeed without really breathing. *Vanity Fair, June*, 62.

Willower, D.J., & Culbertson, J. (1964) *The professorship in educational administration*. Pennsylvania State University: UCEA.

INDEX

STUDIES IN EDUCATIONAL LEADERSHIP

1. P.T. Begley and O. Johansson (eds.): *The Ethical Dimensions of School Leadership.* 2003   ISBN Hb 1-4020-1159-8; Pb 1-4020-1160-1
2. J. Ryan: *Leading Diverse Schools.* 2003
            ISBN Hb 1-4020-1243-8; Pb 1-4020-1253-5

KLUWER ACADEMIC PUBLISHERS – DORDRECHT / BOSTON / LONDON